CW00832208

The Streets of London

Dedicated to the memory of
Roy Porter (1946–2002),
a great historian and Londoner

The Streets of London

FROM THE GREAT FIRE TO THE GREAT STINK

Edited by
Tim Hitchcock and Heather Shore
Foreword by Roy Porter

RIVERS ORAM PRESS
LONDON SYDNEY AND CHICAGO

First published in 2003 by
Rivers Oram Press, an imprint of Rivers Oram Publishers Ltd
144 Hemingford Road, London N1 1DE

Distributed in the USA by
Independent Publishers' Group
814 North Franklin Street
Chicago, Ill 60610

Distributed in Australia and New Zealand by
UNIReps, University of New South Wales, NSW 2052

Set in Baskerville by NJ Design
and printed in Great Britain by T.J. International Ltd, Padstow, Cornwall

A catalogue record for this book is available from the British Library

ISBN 1 85489 130 8 (cloth)
ISBN 1 85489 131 6 (paperback)

Contents

List of Illustrations and Tables

List of Illustrations

List of Tables

Notes on Contributors

Rick Allen, a former review editor of *Victorian Studies*, is a principal lecturer in English and director of studies in humanities and arts at Anglia Polytechnic University in Cambridge. He is the author of *The Moving Pageant: A Literary Sourcebook on London Street-Life, 1700-1914*, as well as articles on Dickens, George Eliot, Gissing, urban writing, and fictional realism.

Brenda Assael is a cultural historian and a lecturer in modern British history at the University of Wales, Swansea. Her book on the Victorian circus is being published by the University Press of Virginia. Her piece on child acrobats appears in Martin Hewitt, ed., *An Age of Equipoise?: Reassessing Mid-Victorian Britain* (2000). She has also written short articles on theatre and performance for Kelly Boyd, ed., *The Encyclopedia of Historians and Historical Writing* (1999) and *The New Dictionary of National Biography* (forthcoming).

John Black gained his doctorate on the subject of illegitimacy and the urban poor in eighteenth- and early nineteenth-century London. He is currently working at the University of Sheffield helping to develop an electronic edition of the *Old Bailey Sessions Proceedings, 1674–1834*. With Tim Hitchcock he edited *The Chelsea Settlement and Bastardy Statements, 1733–66* (London Record Society, vol.33, 1999), and is a former Scouloudi Research Fellow.

Lisa Forman Cody is an assistant professor at Claremont McKenna College in Southern California. She has published several articles on gender and medicine in eighteenth-century Britain and France, and is completing a book entitled, *The Birth of a Nation: Childbirth, Medicine, and Identity in England,1660–1840*.

Anna Davin is a founding editor of *History Workshop Journal* and a research fellow at Middlesex University. Her book, *Growing Up Poor: Home, School and Street in London 1870–1914* was published by Rivers Oram Press, London, in 1996.

Tim Hitchcock is professor of Eighteenth-Century History at the University of Hertfordshire. He has published widely on the history of eighteenth-century social policy, religious millenarianism, urban history and sexuality. His most recent books include *English Sexualities, 1700–1800* (Basingstoke, 1997), with Michèle Cohen, *English Masculinities, 1660-1800* (1999), and with John Black, *Chelsea Settlement and Bastardy Examinations, 1733–1766* (London Record Society, vol.33, 1999). He is currently working on a monograph on how to beg on the streets of eighteenth-century London.

Mark Jenner is a lecturer in the history department of the University of York. He has published extensively on the social history of early modern medicine and on sixteenth- and seventeenth-century London. He recently edited (with Paul Griffiths) *Londinopolis: Essays in the Cultural and Social History of Early Modern London* (Manchester University Press, 2000), and is currently completing books on ideas of cleanliness and dirt in early modern England and on the history of London water supply.

Lawrence E. Klein is a lecturer in history at the University of Cambridge. He is the author of *Shaftesbury and the Culture of Politeness* (1994) and articles on eighteenth-century culture and discourse. He has also edited Shaftesbury's *Characteristics* (2000) and co-edited (with Anthony LaVopa) *Enthusiasm and Enlightenment in Europe, 1650-1850* (1998). His current work concerns changes in cultural institutions and ideas in later seventeenth- and early eighteenth-century England.

John Marriott teaches history in the department of cultural studies, University of East London. His research interests are in the relationship between metropolis and empire, and as part of that project has recently edited two six-volume collections of primary materials *The Metropolitan Poor: Semi-factual Accounts, 1795–1910*, and *Unknown London: Early Modernist Visions of the Metropolis, 1815–45*, both of which are published by Pickering and Chatto. He is currently working on a monograph exploring homologies between representations of the London poor and colonial subjects in the long nineteenth century.

Deirdre Palk has recently completed her doctoral thesis, 'Gender, Crime and Discretion in the English Criminal Justice System, 1780s to 1830s', at the University of Leicester, and is continuing her research in the areas of gender, crime and the criminal justice system, and in the lives of the urban poor. She previously completed her masters degree in women's history at Royal Holloway College, University of London, and currently works as a management consultant.

Robert B. Shoemaker, reader in history at the University of Sheffield, is currently writing a book about changing forms of street conflict in eighteenth-century London, entitled *The Rise and Fall of the London Mob*. He is also, with Tim Hitchcock, director of Old Bailey Online, a project which will make the entirety of the printed *Old Bailey Proceedings* available and searchable on the internet.

Heather Shore is a lecturer in history at the University of Portsmouth. She is the author of a recent monograph, *Artful Dodgers: Youth and Crime in Early Nineteenth-Century London* (Royal Historical Society, 1999), and co-editor with Pamela Cox of, *Becoming Delinquent: European Youth 1660-1960* (Ashgate, 2002). She has published on various elements of criminality in the eighteenth and nineteenth centuries, and is currently researching the history of organised and professional crime in London, for her next monograph, *Underworlds: Professional and Organised Crime in London from 1700* (to be published by London Books).

Cynthia Wall is associate professor of English at the University of Virginia. She is the author of *The Literary and Cultural Spaces of Restoration London* (Cambridge UP, 1998), the editor of the Bedford Cultural Edition of Pope's *The Rape of the Lock* (1998), and co-editor (with J. Paul Hunter) of the *Bedford Anthology of Eighteenth-Century Literatures in English* (forthcoming). She has published on Defoe, Pope, Lady Mary Wortley Montagu, the English auction house, the gendering of architecture, film adaptations, and narrative detail, and is currently working on the history of spatial description in eighteenth-century narrative and poetry.

List of Abbreviations

BL	British Library
CJ	*Commons Journals*
CLRO	Corporation of London Records Office
CSPD	*Calendar of State Papers Domestic*
GL	Guildhall Library
LMA	London Metropolitan Archives
OBSP	*Old Bailey Sessions Proceedings*
PP	*Parliamentary Papers*
PRO	Public Records Office
SCPM	*Select Committee on the Police of the Metropolis*, 1817, VII
WAC	City of Westminster Archives Centre

Foreword
Roy Porter

Hell Upon Earth (1729), an early Georgian squib, depicted London as a:

> great, wicked, unweildy [*sic*] overgrown Town, one continued
> hurry of Vice and Pleasure; where nothing dwells but Absurdities,
> Abuses, Accidents, Accusations, Admirations, Adventures,
> Adversities, Advertisements, Adulteries, Affidavits, Affectations,
> Affirmations, Afflictions, Affronts, Aggravations, Agitations,
> Agonies, Airs, Alarms, Ailments, Allurements, Alterations,
> Ambitions, Amours, Amphitheatres, Anathemas, Animosities,
> Anxieties, Appointments, Apprehensions, Assemblies, Assessments,
> Assurances, Assignations, Attainders, Audacities, Aversions, &c'.

The list continued. It perfectly epitomizes the great paradoxes of the preindustrial capital as explored by the authors of this innovative, richly
researched and eye-opening book. It was viewed as a city caught in a whirl
of bizarre, baffling, bewildering scenes, a hotch-potch of weird and shock-
ing happenings. And yet, as the alphabetization makes clear, metropolitan spectators and writers were simultaneously shouldering the burden of
surveying, documenting and docketing it, compiling its inventories. And
this enterprise of ordering disorder, elucidating the obscure, if *prima facie*
self-defeating, is the task the editors have, in their turn, a couple of centuries
later, set this book's contributors.

In a sequence of chapters ranging from early Georgian attempts to give
order to street addresses and to administer rival hackney carriages, through
to the policing of the parks in the late Victorian era, this book addresses

the ways in which polite and propertied— but also prim and prurient—
Londoners handled the problems of living amongst the great unwashed in
that monster city, that Great Wen which was in the process of becoming
easily the largest conurbation the world had ever witnessed.

It is not surprising that the endeavours charted in the following pages
display a double face. We may be revolted by the zeal (and impunity) with
which mercenary magistrates and their adjutants slung women caught out-
of-doors after dark into their pestiferous lock-ups on suspicion of being
street-walkers or thieves; in one case recorded here they were simply left to
die. But would we ourselves actually want to live in a *Beggar's Opera* world
of fences and cut-purses, with their omnipresent urban pickers and steal-
ers? After all, it slightly takes one aback to find that shoplifters were routinely,
it seems, lifting not just spoons and handkerchiefs but *seventeen-yards long*
hanks of cloth, concealed under their cloaks. Academic readers might
equally be caught in two minds in the *furore* which surrounded Charles
Babbage. That crotchety inventor of the mechanical calculator wanted
organ grinders banned from the streets: was he a dreadful killjoy, or just
someone, all too familiarly like us, trying to get a little peace and quiet at
home in which to work?

What is clear from these essays is that, in the generations from the
Restoration, London grew narcissistic, preoccupied with navel-gazing, witness
the *Spectator* (which used as an epigraph Horace's *ex fumo lucem dare*—bringing light out of darkness), Samuel Johnson's love/hate affair with London
and Hogarth's urban odysseys. From the Georgian age, the metropolis
became remarkably self-referential. Londoners relished and demanded art
and novels, journalism and theatre about themselves and their world. They
lapped up Ned Ward's *The London Spy* and John Gay's *The Beggar's Opera*, they
relished the familiar and local writings of Daniel Defoe and Henry Fielding,
and they loved George Lillo's tragedy, *The London Merchant, or the History of
George Barnwell*, produced at Drury Lane in 1731, which broke new dramatic
ground because it made apprentices and harlots into tragic figures. The
metropolis, as Raymond Williams once stressed, was a new moral arena: 'As
London grew, dramatically, in the eighteenth century, it was being intensely
observed, as a new kind of landscape, a new kind of society'. That is the
London, bursting with disorderly activity but trying to make sense of itself,
which is the subject of this engrossing book.

Introduction

Tim Hitchcock and Heather Shore

On a clear morning in late July 1827, Francis Place sat at his window at number 16 Charing Cross, looking out over the street. His heart was filled with wonder at the scene that played itself out below:[1]

> The people in the street were variously garlanded; workmen—market people with baskets of fruits and flowers on their heads, or on their donkeys, or in their small carts, numbers of them with vegetables, newsmen and boys running about to sell their papers to the coach passengers at least a dozen of which leave the Golden Cross or pass it about 7 o'clock, gave a *coup d'oeil* which cannot be witnessed in any other country in the whole world, and perhaps at no other place in the world than at Charing Cross.

For Francis Place the streets of London were in themselves a miracle of colour and interest. From his first floor window, which protruded over the street allowing him to look in both directions, he counted the horses and carts and people that passed below. A large proportion of his extensive archive and autobiography is dedicated to recording the sights and sounds of these public spaces of late eighteenth and early nineteenth century London. But he was by no means alone in his fascination. From Pepys's obsession with the response of pedestrians to his new personal coach in the 1660s, to the works of John Dunton and Ned Ward, to Addison and Steele, to Gay, and on to Boswell, and later Dickens, and the social mappings of Booth and Mayhew, there is a constant strain of fascination for the public life of the metropolis, for the life that existed between the buildings. This volume re-examines those streets, and explores how Londoners' navigated and thought about their thoroughfares; how they used them for fights and sex, for public speaking, and as a blank sheet for their graffiti. It explores how the streets themselves became the site of conflict, how different groups, divided by class and gender, understood the same spaces in different ways, and how the authorities attempted to police these most unruly of places. It looks at both how Londoners imagined their city, and how the confines and limits created by real streets effected the behaviour of individual Londoners. It is a *vade mecum* to the most complex set of public spaces the world had ever seen, during the period in which these streets most comprehensively sustained the interest of both Londoners and visitors, and in which they had their greatest impact on the individuals who inhabited them.

The streets of London before the Great Fire of 1666 had been sites of profound ritual meaning. That long, broad artery of Cheapside and Poultry to the east, and Ludgate to the west tied the great cathedral of St Paul's into a network of routes through which the great and the good of early modern London processed; laying claim to the authority of church and state, while at the same time bringing the parishes and communities of the capital within a unified intellectual order. The small lanes and alleys leading from St Paul's and its associated streets, out to the suburban parishes, and down to the river, linked these central symbolic spaces to each corner of the whole, while until at least the sixteenth century, the Cathedral's 489-foot spire dominated the horizon. The nature and meaning of this landscape changed irrevocably in 1666. In what seemed to many contemporaries a profoundly symbolic event, the great Cathedral burned. John Evelyn described how, 'the stones of St Paul's flew like grenados, the melting lead running down the streets in a stream, and the very pavements glowing with fiery redness'.[2] In the process, the old city literally melted into the earth, creating a newly blank geography which slowly but deeply invaded the imagination of Londoners. Over the course of the next two centuries Londoners rebuilt and built again their city, supplying new meanings for the new spaces they created, and mapping new hopes and old fears onto the strangely organic shapes that emerged from the disorderly process of boom and bust, of the highly regulated, and unregulated building speculation that provided the fabric of London. What they created in the centuries after the Fire was (like its early modern predecessor) a pedestrian's London, tied together by the river Thames. But unlike its predecessor, this London was newly and increasingly divided by neighbourhoods defined by social divisions of class and fashion, while the boundaries of economic specialisation, so important in pre-Fire London, were radically redrawn. This new post-Fire London was both shockingly democratic, and uncompromisingly aristocratic. And generation after generation of immigrants and Londoners sought in this new world, to create divisions, to establish clubs, to define neighbourhoods, to both break down and build up new communities glued together by both geography and *mentalité*.

The streets of this new London were not simply, or even primarily, a means to navigate from one place to another. They were a stage upon which people acted. The street was central to the narratives of urban life individuals created to explain their environment and themselves. Elite commentators, city planners, social investigators, the flaneurs all had their own version of the way in which the London streets were experienced. As a result, one theme which runs through the essays in this volume is the imagined city—the city created in the minds of an elite group of men and women who observed and described, rather than participated in, the life of the streets.

After the Great Fire cleansed the old, medieval city with its clustered and archaic street arrangements, Londoners needed new guide books and new metaphors to help explain the meaning of the patterns of both architecture and behaviour that emerged. Even the cartographers, postmen, booksellers and merchants, the urban professionals whose job it was to know the streets, had trouble grasping where a particular address was located and what that 'address' meant. In the late seventeenth century both literary and non-literary writers endeavoured to chart the streets and thoroughfares, lanes and alleys that had been rebuilt after the Fire—creating an imagined, but comprehensible pattern to explain what, by this time, had grown beyond individual comprehension. In the process their works came to define this newly unfamiliar London. Guidebooks and maps produced in the late seventeenth and early eighteenth century disingenuously claimed a full and complete knowledge of the city. But what they defined was only a partial and limited vision of the reality. In 1722, for instance, in his *Remarks on London* William Stow claimed to have charted, 'where every Street, Lane, Court, Alley, Yard, Green, Close, Square, or any other Place, by what Name soever call'd, is situated'.[3] Yet neither Stow, nor his contemporaries could do more than provide a schematic outline of the complex totality. These writers were mere cultural magpies, collecting the bits and shards of a recognisable city, and attempting to mould them into a guide for professional and polite society; guides to the still new and raw post-fire buildings, and the ever expanding suburbs to the west.

The streets these commentators imagined took a wide variety of forms. In the eighteenth century, for instance, observers like Steele and Addison re-invented some of London's streets as a 'polite town'. For them, the streets became sites of gentility, learning, politeness. Writing in the *Spectator* in 1725, Steele described how he, 'lay one night last week at Richmond; and being restless, not out of dissatisfaction, but a certain busy inclination one sometimes has, I arose at four in the morning, and took boat for London, with a resolution to rove by boat and coach for the next four and twenty hours, till the many different objects I must needs meet with should tire my imagination, and give me an inclination to a repose more profound than I was at that time capable of '.[4] In his imagination, Steele invented the 'town', and in doing so created a new urban paradigm. The 'polite town' had specific boundaries and sites, and it was in the Strand, the Mall, St James, Covent Garden and the Haymarket where the polite found their version of the metropolis.

Others looked for and found another city. Throughout the eighteenth and nineteenth centuries the underbelly of the metropolis generated a dark mirror for the powder and wigs of the elite. While the poor were a visible figment of the London envisaged by the *Spectator* and its imitators, social commentators of the later eighteenth and early nineteenth centuries increasingly came to place the poor centre stage in their version of London's streets. In 1751 Henry Fielding imagined London as 'a vast Wood or Forest, in which a Thief may harbour with as great Security, as wild Beasts do in the Desarts of *Africa* or *Arabia*'.[5] The sense of unease and threat conveyed by Fielding was reproduced by many of his fellow commentators. Gradually they created a 'moral Baedaker' that charted poor, disorderly and criminal space in the back alleys and rookeries of the eighteenth and nineteenth centuries.

Reformers like the Fieldings, Jonas Hanway, and Patrick Colquhoun began the process of ordering and identifying these disorderly spaces. While nineteenth-century writers and commentators such as Charles Dickens, John Hollingshead, and James Greenwood took this point of departure and constructed from it a new vision of the streets which was soon dominated by this 'underworld'. In their mind's eye the gentleman no longer rubbed shoulders with the beggar, the respectable woman with the prostitute, or the pickpocket with his mark, as they did in the fictional urban voyages of Tom and Jerry in the 1810s.[6] By the second quarter of the nineteenth century street-life was increasingly synonymous with an 'underworld' defined by difference, and by fear of the 'other'. By the later nineteenth century, this nightmare vision had been superimposed on racial stereotypes. Within two years of the completion of Bazalgette's Embankment, Blanchard Jerrold and Gustave Doré's, *London, A Pilgrimage*, characterised London's streets as dangerously full of Lascar's, Jews, and the Chinese, wreathed in the symbols of their exotica.[7]

One story this volume tells is that of this constantly evolving literary and imagined city. But the streets of London also existed in real space, and played host to real events. And while the febrile stench of the literary and imagined 'underworld' could not always be sustained in reality, the poor, disorderly, and even the criminal were certainly a presence on the streets of London. Their lives were far more ordinary and mundane than that envisaged by their richer contemporaries. But, in this volume we can see normal people fighting, confronting authority, socialising and making love. We can see them as they stole and drank and gambled, preached and prophesied and argued.

Perhaps the most reliable guides to these material spaces of London were the Hackney coachmen. Unlike the cartographers, or the commentators of the polite town, unlike Steele and Addison and their contemporaries who could make do with a partial knowledge, London's coachmen were defined by their understanding of the metropolis. They provided the quintessential link between the fears and expectations of the élite, the imagined city, and the real lives and events that were played out on the streets. Hackney coaches and their drivers enabled individuals to move about the city without the need for maps, in relative privacy even in these public spaces, secure in the knowledge that they would be whisked past the less desirable streets and alleys. Yet because a part of a coachman's job was to protect their passengers from the streets, they themselves were necessarily a part of that street scenery. Known for their 'saucy, impudent Behaviour',[8] and like other professions or groups for whom the streets were their workplace, coachmen were forced to negotiate these spaces. Conflict and confrontation, with authority, with neighbours, with customers and clients, were the everyday lot of anyone willing or needing to use the streets. And just as the fears and fictions which drove rich Londoners to seek the protection of a coach changed over the course of our period, the reality of street life negotiated by their coachmen changed as well.

In the late seventeenth and early eighteenth centuries, while the agents of Societies for the Reformation of Manners sought to entrap homosexuals and prostitutes, control of the streets became a primary goal of both local government and the magistracy. But it was a goal that was always just out of reach. This was a period when many medieval parishes and practises lost their power in local government, and in which population growth (particularly after the mid-eighteenth century) began to transform the physical environment of the streets. As a result, the early eighteenth century saw an increasing urgency in the conflicts for control of these spaces. In a single incident such as the St Martin's round-house disaster of 1742 in which a number of street-walkers and beggars died as a result of the venality and corruption of local government officials, we can see a complex negotiation of power for the control of the streets. We can also see the web of gender and class relations that conditioned public and private space. Women for whom the street provided sustenance and trade were vulnerable to the tensions produced by the evolution of local government and policing practise. By the early nineteenth century, gender boundaries implicitly shaped the way in which men and women used the street. Male and female criminals operated in very different ways, for instance. Male pickpockets used daylight, crowds, and public space. Female pickpockets on the other hand, used the semi-private environment of public-houses, lodgings, brothels, dark alleyways, dead-end streets, and yards in which to conduct their operations. The female pickpocket was overwhelmingly a creature of the night. More significantly, she used the semi-private spaces which by the late eighteenth and early nineteenth centuries were increasingly a site for conflict, disorder and what elite perception read as immorality.

This same pattern of conflict and 'privatisation' can also be seen in the context of cases of defamation and violence. In the seventeenth century the public arena—the street itself—was the space in which local conflicts, arguments and challenges were fought and resolved. In the eighteenth century these conflicts gradually moved away from the public arena to more private spaces. Over the course of the eighteenth and early nineteenth centuries, as the physical environment of London rapidly evolved, new expectations about how one behaved on the street began to emerge. Insulting your neighbours and adversaries in the 'public streets' was no longer an accepted method of resolving conflicts; instead defamers and their targets increasingly argued in doorways, through windows, in taverns and shops; a foot each in the public and private. Likewise fights moved into inns, taverns, and coffee-houses, before then spilling out into the street. And while fights were still frequently acted out in the street, a degree of privacy was increasingly being introduced into the proceedings, with disputants often limiting their audience, and seeking to avoid publicity. In other words, just as the streets became more regulated, just as the Bow Street Runners and then the Metropolitan Police reached out and brought London into their dampening embrace, conflicts that would traditionally have been acted out in these public spaces, were moved indoors, into the shadowy spaces at the boundaries between the street and the domestic. What we see in the first half of our period is the primacy of the street as a collective public space. But as time goes on, the focus of forms of behaviour the authorities perceived as disorder gradually shifted off the pavement and indoors. By the nineteenth century public houses, low-lodging houses, brothels, bawdy-houses, and flash-houses had become the prime repositories for what were perceived as disorderly activities. And if the use of public space was being contested on the streets in the eighteenth century, by the nineteenth the contest for this control had moved to the boundaries between the public street and private house. This transition happened in part because of the changing nature of the street itself. The new domestic and street architectures of the Georgian period, with their railings, bollards and pavements, when combined with the bureaucratic and legal forces created to cope with disorder, effectively forced the inhabitants of the streets out of the thoroughfares. By the early decades of the nineteenth century, police, magistrates, reformers and social investigators had renamed the haunts of the criminal and disorderly poor as rookeries, alsatias, stews and dens, zones of immorality which were ironically seen as beyond the reach of authority.

It would be wrong, however, to see the contest for the streets as one played out predominantly between authority and disorder. What the newly formed police and social investigators read as disorder and vice was often only their jaundiced and myopic vision of the activities of 'ordinary' people. Drinking and gambling, courtship and the 'getting of a livelihood' were easily transposed by elite perception into activities tinged with criminality and disorder. This increasingly easy misreading is perhaps an indication of the growing distance between the lived experience of people on the streets, and the lives of those who attempted to control and regulate the spaces in their neighbourhoods—the distance, perhaps, between the Hackney coachman and his fare. Nevertheless, the sense of belonging to a neighbourhood, a local community, for many people conferred a sense of responsibility and the desire to maintain order within it. Inevitably this led to conflicts about how public space was used, who controlled public space, what sort of 'groups' had access to that space. Understandably, ordinary people, who historically used the street for work and play, were active participants in these conflicts, and acted both on the side of greater regulation, and on that of greater freedom.

By the mid-nineteenth century public spaces had become both subject to a new kind of politics, and regulated by a new sensibility. The parks and green spaces of the capital, for instance, contributed to and supported a new popular politics (both religious and secular). What a century earlier had been an unfocussed, if visceral, conflict, would by 1850 be played out in the arena of public discourse. The ballad singers and noisy beggars of eighteenth-century London were replaced by the stump preachers and radical speechifiers, in spaces that somehow sit between the ordered park of utopian imagination, and village common of an older English tradition. While in the neighbourhoods, on the residential streets of an ever expanding metropolitan behemoth, the tenuous control wrested from the poor, encouraged a petty bourgeois sensibility, in which the orderly street became an extension (however disputed) of an orderly domestic world.

By the end of our period, the streets of London had been transformed. In the imagination of urban flaneurs, such as Sala and Munby, and social investigators such as Mayhew, the streets became possessed of an almost romantic quality. And while the hustle and bustle, the highs and lows of street-life were at the core of their observations, they seem increasingly anachronistic even as their writings become more detailed. In the third quarter of the nineteenth century, with the carving up of London for the railways, with the dramatic expansion of the suburbs beyond the distance one could easily walk in an hour or so, with the radical separation of the old City from its life-giving river by the building of the Victoria Embankment, the spaces, the life, the vibrancy of the streets of London were relegated to smaller and increasingly embattled quarters. But, in the two hundred years before these radical disjunctures the street had been a site in which authority, control, gender, and class were contested. They had witnessed both an ideological transformation that created a series of new mental maps to the metropolis, while at the same time they had seen the creation of new material conditions that shaped the way individuals could and did behave. They had been the sites where community had been first created, and then redefined; and where a great world city was made.

1. 'At Shakespear's-Head, Over-Against Catharine-Street in the Strand'

Forms of Address in London Streets

Cynthia Wall

In 1722, William Stow, author of *Remarks on London*, pointed out just one of the many little inconveniences of keeping track of the city streets in the eighteenth century.[1]

> Some People are so ignorant, especially in the Country, as to think *London*, *Westminster*, and *Southwark*, is all *London*, because contiguous to one another, which is a grand Mistake; for if you should send a Letter to a Friend in *King-street*, which is in *Westminster*, but write at the bottom of the Superscription, *London*; how should the Postman know, whether you mean *King-street* by *Guildhall*, *King-street* on *Great Tower-hill*, *King-street* in *Spittle Fields*, *King-street* in *Prince's street* near *St Anne's* Church, *King-street* near *Golden Square*, *King-street* in *Dean-street* by *Soho-square*, *King-street* in *Covent-garden*, *King-street* by *Hay's Court* near *Newport Market*, *King-street* in *Upper Moor-fields*, *King-street* by *Old-street Square*, *King-street* by *Bloomsbury Square*, *King-street* by *St. James's Square*, *King-street* near the *Six Dials* [sic], or *King-street* in the *Mint*?

This is without question a goodly number of King Streets. Besides the postman's bewilderment at his choices, any contemporary Londoner would also recognize how richly homonymous the name 'King Street' could be: virtually every instance of the same name implied socially, commercially, and visually different worlds. During the seventeenth and eighteenth centuries, when London underwent some of its most dramatic and profound physical as well as demographic changes—from the Great Fire of 1666, which destroyed four-fifths of the medieval centre, through its rebuilding in the

Restoration and the galloping expansion of the fashionable west—the experience of navigating (not to mention inhabiting) London changed enor-
mously. Even those whose profession it was to know the streets—cartographers,
coachmen, postmen, booksellers, merchants, and criminals—had trouble
grasping where a particular address was located and what that 'address'
implied. Literary as well as cultural representations of the forms of address—
of ways of identifying and fixing location, both topographical and social—
reveal not only a certain excitement about the *possibilities* of the new urban
spaces, but also anxieties about its incomprehensibility and unreliability.

Eighteenth-century textual representations of London share a paradox-
ical rhetorical pattern: both literary and non-literary works tend to announce
with great confidence their mastery of the city, while at the same time
confessing an uneasy defeat. Urban guide books busily assert their unique
comprehensiveness and then defensively explain why they are not comprehensive; urban characters seem to know the streets by heart and yet constantly
lose their way. Buildings were not numbered until the 1770s (after the proclamation against signboards in 1762) and it was not until very late in the eighteenth century that those numbers were used regularly as *forms of address*.
For the most part, 'forms of address' were almost implicit, written into the
inherited (though not fixed) lore of local significance. This chapter will
analyse a series of texts—cultural and literary—concerned with the problems of getting lost and getting found. By setting Boswell's *London Journal*
(1762–63), Frances Burney's novels *Evelina* (1778) and *Cecilia* (1780), and
Burney's own diary in the context of guidebooks, advertisements, and booksellers' imprints, I want to highlight the spatiality of textual correspondences
in Edward Soja's sense of 'the concrete expression of a combination of
instances, an "historical ensemble" of interacting material elements and
influences.'[2] Both kinds of texts may help produce a new sense of cultural
space—appropriating the meaning of place, determining the position of
self, and purchasing a hold on the fluctuating meanings of London—but
they also seem to *reproduce* lingering spatial anxiety long after the 'real'
London was fully rebuilt, repeopled, and institutionally better-organised.

Cultural navigation

Although the King Street dilemma was not exactly new—writers long
before the Fire complained vociferously about the close impenetrability of

1. 'A Map or Grovndplot of the Citty of London ... since the last sad accident of
fire', by John Leake, engraved by Wenceslaus Hollar (1666)

London's streets—the most sustained textual representations of street names and the problems of 'address' appear after the Great Fire of 1666, when four-fifths of the medieval City disappeared within a few days.[3] Wenceslaus Hollar's image of London burned [illustration 1] notes starkly: 'The blanke space signifeing [sic] the burnt part & where the houses are exprest, those places yet standing.'[4] That visible white space is what gets literary as well as cultural attention during the next fifty or sixty years. The Fire and rebuilding generated a kind of urban chaos where little was familiar, much was confusing, and many could get lost.

The rush of maps, newspapers, and guidebooks after the Fire points to this gaping need for reassurance.[5] Here I would like to summarize their over-lapping rhetorics as a context for another suggestive development in topo-graphical specificity: title-pages. Maps boasted visual comprehensiveness:[6]

> *A Large New and Exact MAP, with a true Description of the City of* London, *and its Ruines, as it now stands faithfully surveyed….A distinction of the* Wards *formerly well known, now marked in this MAP with prickt Lines….The names of the Streets, Lanes, and Alleys, Wharfs, and Passages. As also the Places where the Churches were. And the several Halls of the Worshipfull* Companies, *where they formerly stood…As also the manner of the re-building of the said* City; *and the number of* Churches *to be re-built with other Things, well* worthy to be known both of Natives and Foreigners.

The guidebooks promise textual comprehensiveness: William Stow's *Remarks* claims in its title page and again in its preface to show 'where every Street, Lane, Court, Alley, Yard, Green, Close, Square, or any other Place, by what Name soever call'd, is situated.'[7] All these maps and guides, in some form or another, describe themselves as works '*very necessary*…[f]or Travellers, Quartermasters, Gatherers of Breefs, Strangers, Carriers, and Messengers with Letters, and all others that know the name of the place, but can neither tell where it is, nor how to go unto it.'[8] And the newspapers tell one where to go:

> The Shop-keepers that were formerly in the *Royal Exchange* in *Cornhil*, are now removed to *Gresham-Colledge*, Where they have built themselves Shops, both above and below Stairs, and carry on their ancient and respective trades. (*London Gazette*, no. 113, 13–17 December 1666)

These are to certifie, That the Kentish *and* Sussex Post-Office, *formerly kept at the* Rand-House in Love-lane, *is now removed to the House of Mr.* John Dyne, *in the Passage to and from* Tower-Hil, *near the Pump in Crutchet-Fryers. The Porter will further inform you.* (*London Gazette,* no. 93, 4–8 October 1666)

The various texts consistently emphasise mastering the unknown—addressed to those for whom one would presume London to be best known.

These topographical concerns find an intriguing parallel in publishers' imprints: title-pages of virtually every kind of book follow the same *directional* patterns. The 'Large New and Exact Map' mentioned above, for example, was 'to be sold by Nat. Brook *Stationer, at the* Angel *in the second Yard going into the* Exchange *from* Bishops-gate-street in Gresham Colledge.' The imprint of *A Book of the Names of all Parishes, Market Towns, Villages, Hamblets and Smallest Places, in England and Wales* (1677) is 'Printed by *S. S.* for *John Garret,* at his Shop as you go up the Stairs of the *Royal Exchange* in *Cornhil*'. One Jones offers as a title page: 'Jones of Hatton-Garden, two doors from the sign of the *New-Hole* in the *Wall,* his book of cures' (1674).

This emphasis on topographical direction in title-pages is a fairly distinct but oddly undiscussed phenomenon in printing history. Title-pages themselves evolved comparatively late: they were almost unknown before the printed book, and A. F. Johnson argues that early printers 'frequently said nothing as to place of printing, probably with the deliberate intention of concealing the fact that the book was produced by mechanical means. The title-page as we know it, giving the title, author's name and an imprint, being in fact, a kind of advertisement of the book, was not well established until some years after 1500.'[9] Once established, we see an important difference between English and continental practice in this regard. English printers always favoured detailed topographical information in their imprints that other European printers did not include. For example, as Theodore Low De Vinne illustrates, in England 'the device [a graphic printer's symbol above or below the colophon] most liked was that which conveyed to the reader a pun on the printer's name or a suggestion or pictorial description of his sign, or *of the house or the street in which he worked.* On the Continent geometrical designs or angular additions to the cross were customary. Heraldic emblems were preferred in Germany.'[10] This peculiarity increasingly marked the English booksellers' and printers' imprints in seventeenth- and eighteenth-century title pages. European imprints generally, and the earlier English imprints (fifteenth to early sixteenth century), simply noted name and place:

LONDON,
PRINTED BY ROBERT YOUNG.
M. DC. XXXIV.

*****

A ROTTERDAM,
Chez REINIER LEERS,
M DCCI.
*Avec Privilege de Nosseigneurs les Etats
de Hollande & de West-Frise.*

*****

FLORENTIÆ, MDCCV.
Typis REGÆ CELESTUDINIS.
Superiorum Permissu.

*****

Increasingly, English printers—unlike their European counterparts—added topographical specificity to their imprints:

London, Printed by *W.D.* for *T.D.* at the *Ship* in St. *Mary Axe,*
and *T.L.* at the *Golden Lyon* near the *Meal-Market* in
Southwark Stationer, 1675.

*****

London,
Printed by *R. Holt,* for *Obadiah Blagrave,*
at the *Bear* and *Star,* over against the little
North Door in St. *Paul's Church-
Yard.* 1687.

*****

LONDON:
Printed for J. and R. Tonson, at *Shakespear's-
Head,* over-against *Catharine-street* in the *Strand.*
MCCDXL. [sic]

Although there are numerous instances of such specificity in the early seventeenth century (corresponding, I would suggest, with the marked increase in urban congestion, traffic, and trans-city travel),[11] the bulk of such imprints seems to cluster around the mid-seventeenth- to the mid-eighteenth-century, while imprints in Europe continued with basic name, basic place (i.e. city). By the end of the eighteenth century—when buildings were finally numbered and one might argue that the rebuilding and the new building were more or less culturally absorbed—English imprints adopted numbered addresses and/or lost their excess topographical baggage:

LONDON:
Printed for Harrison and Co. No. 18, Pater-noster Row.
M DCC LXXXI.
*****
LONDON:
Printed for J. Dodsley, in Pall-Mall.
M.DCC.LXXXII.
*****
LONDON.
Printed for John Fielding Nº 23, Pater Noster Row, John Debrett
opposite
Burlington House, Picadilly [sic], and John Sewell Nº 32 Cornhill.
[1783]

Thus printing practices in England seem historically tied to spatial culture. Increasingly specific topographical directions in the imprint correspond fairly exactly to increasing urban anxieties about size, comprehensibility, locatability, and spatial meaning. More than in Continental countries, books, like people, identified themselves by their address.[12]

This argument is admittedly somewhat speculative. As De Vinne notes: 'It has been understood from the beginning of book-making that titles are not easily brought under fixed rules; that their words differ in quantity and their lines must differ in treatment; and that the title-page is the creature of arbitrary fashions which change capriciously.'[13] The seventeenth-century printer and globe-maker Joseph Moxon explains in *Mechanick Exercises* (*LONDON. / Printed for Joseph Moxon* on the West- / side of *Fleet-ditch*, at the

Sign of / *Atlas*. 1683), 'the mode of ordering Titles varies; as may be seen by comparing the *Title Pages* of every twenty years: Therefore a Lasting Rule cannot be given for the ordering them'.[14] An accurate tabulation of the hundreds of thousands of title-pages printed in these centuries is impracticable; however, various samples of different kinds of texts yield the same apparent patterns: English imprints of the seventeenth and early eighteenth centuries were far more topographically detailed than their European counterparts, precisely across the decades of the most cultur- ally and textually visible anxiety about urban navigation as witnessed by the vast new production of city maps, guidebooks, imprints, and urban fictions.[15] London had changed from a visual to a textual city. It supplanted its colourful signs that graphically denoted the availability of everything from dagger pies to coffins with verbal signs and numbered buildings. All this change meant that the city that had been to some extent navigable by sight now required knowledge of different kinds of codes. And clearly title-pages, like places, could be sites for sustained ordering, and like maps and guides, could reflect a growing cultural need for a sense of sorted, fixed, identifiable space.

But within all these textual efforts to make the navigation of cityspace secure, to make clear where things are, London manages to elude the attempts. In the case of the boastful topographies, the claim to compre- hensiveness at the very least implies and more often confesses a kind of defeat. Nathaniel Crouch (aka Robert Burton) claims in his *Historical Remarques and Observations of the Ancient and Present State of London* (1681) that 'it would too much inlarge this small Volume to give an Exact Account of the *City of Westminster*, and other parts which now seem swallowed up in *London*'.[16] William Stow accuses contemporary maps of 'not [describing] a fourth part of the Places contain'd in 'em: Moreover, was a Map 30 Foot long, and 20 deep to be projected, yet would it not comprehend the whole Town to an exact Scale of Feet.'[17] He notes: 'So large is the Extent of *London*, *Westminster*, and *Southwark*, with their Suburbs and Liberties, that no Coachman nor Porter knows every place in them; therefore this Book may also be a Guide for them, and prevent, as hath been too often done, their losing any more Portmanteaus, Trunks, Boxes, or Parcels.' And as late as 1732, when the rebuilding must have seemed an event of the rather distant past, the author of *New Remarks of London* declares: 'here are many

Alleys and Courts within the Bills of Mortality, which are not inserted in this Work; but then I must beg Leave to observe, that they never had any Names given them, or, at least, that they are so far lost, that the ancientest Inhabitants in or near those Places, never heard of any particular Names by which they are known and distinguish'd.'[18] It is this sense of the London unmapped by all these printed efforts to define and fix its boundaries—the essential failure of new technologies and new surveyings and new texts to 'know' the city—that perhaps underlies the sustained anxieties about forms of address and ways to get lost in the urban fiction later in the century.

Fictional navigation

The anxiety about losing oneself in London—either literally, in its bewildering King Streets, or socially, landing at the 'wrong' address—seems paradoxically to increase rather than diminish in the literature of the eighteenth century, just when, as Edward Copeland argues, the city was fixing its institutional hold on itself.[19] Despite—or perhaps in line with—the intense directionality of *practical* documents from maps to title-pages, urban fiction spends a great deal of time worrying about the social and conceptual possibilities of becoming *lost*, of ending up in the *wrong* place, or of never finding the *right* one. 'Directions' imply the possibility of losing one's way. In this section, I will offer a series of literary stories—fictional and autobiographical, male and female—that engage the perceived topographical enormities of London and its fraught forms of address. Though the selections I have chosen from Boswell, Burney, and Defoe represent different genres and express various gendered viewpoints, they share with the guidebooks, advertisements, and imprints a striking combination of comprehensive urban knowledge and an obvious anxiety about comprehending London.

In Frances Burney's novel *Evelina* (1778),[20] the heroine leaves her safe retreat at Berry Hill in the country, where she was under the gentle guardianship of the Reverend Mr Villars, to make her entrance into the world with friends in London. In volume one she is introduced to polite society and lives with her friends the Mirvans in Queen Anne Street, off Portland Place. Her trials are primarily those of minor social embarrassment—learning how to say no to fops, how not to burst into inappropriate giggles, how to make polite conversation with a handsome young lord. In volume two, however, she is taken possession of by Madame Duval, her

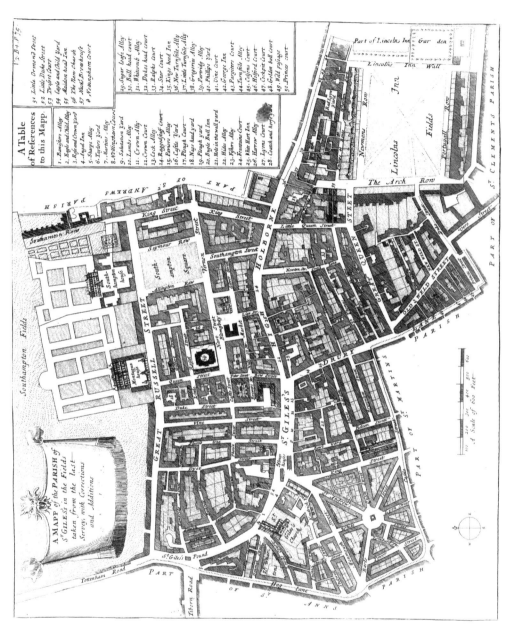

2. 'A Mapp of the Parish of St Giles's in the Fields', from John Strype, *Survey of the Cities of London, Westminster, and Southwark* (1720)

maternal grandmother (once an English barmaid who married well a second time in France), and by her boorish, upwardly mobile cousins, the Branghtons. As she writes dolefully to her confidante Maria Mirvan:[21]

> O Maria, London now seems no longer the same place where I lately enjoyed so much happiness; every thing is new and strange to me; even the town itself has not the same aspect: my situation so altered! my home so different! my companions so changed! But you well know my averseness to this journey.
>
> Indeed, to me, London now seems a desart; that gay and busy appearance it so lately wore, is now succeeded by a look of gloom, fatigue, and lassitude; the air seems stagnant, the heat is intense, the dust intolerable, and the inhabitants illiterate and under-bred. At least, such is the face of things in the part of town where I at present reside.

Part of the problem lies very directly, of course, in the obvious social descent in her physical address:[22]

> Mr. Branghton said our lodgings were in Holborn, that we might be near his house, and neighbourly. [He is a silversmith in Snow Hill.] …Our rooms are large, and not inconvenient; our landlord is an hosier. I am sure I have a thousand reasons to rejoice that I am so little known; for my present situation is, in every respect, very unenviable, and I would not, for the world, be seen by any acquaintance of Mrs. Mirvan…. My direction is at Mr. Dawkins's, a hosier in High Holborn. [illustration 2]

She is in another part of town—what has become another world. And the change in address, which at first seems simply to be a source of social mortification, comes to represent something much darker and more nebulous. Behavior corresponds to address. Pulled from the much more orderly topography of the West End, Evelina finds herself dragged into sexual as well as social darkness. At Vauxhall, Miss Branghton suggests that she, her sister Polly, and Evelina 'take a turn in the dark walks', where they are pounced on by 'a large party of gentlemen, apparently very riotous', who presume them to be prostitutes. One of the 'gentlemen' seizes Evelina:[23]

Terrified to death, I struggled with such vehemence to disengage myself from him, that I succeeded, in spite of his efforts to detain me; and immediately, and with a swiftness which fear only could have given me, I flew rather than ran up the walk, hoping to secure my safety by returning to the lights and company we had so foolishly left.

'Rescued' by Sir Clement Willoughby, an admirer from her former London life, she finds *his* manners depend quite literally on her whereabouts; here, he leads her down 'another of the dark alleys'[24] until she realizes and breaks away; later he follows her to Holborn, invites himself in, and treats her with the 'impertinent' social familiarity that preludes his sexual advances. The novel charts Evelina's progressive education in becoming more powerful than her address.

In her next novel, *Cecilia* (1780),[25] Burney explores not so much the social denotations of particular London addresses, but the larger implications of the incomprehensibility of London streets in aggregate. By the end of this novel, the heiress Cecilia Beverly, tormented by four selfish, obstructive guardians and her rather spineless, jealous lover, Delvile, finds herself psychologically dismembered, and Burney sends her running blindly through vague city streets, mapping her psychological distintegration:[26]

Mean while the frantic Cecilia escaped both pursuit and insult by the velocity of her own motion. She called aloud upon Delvile as she flew to the end of the street. No Delvile was there!—she turned the corner; yet saw nothing of him; she still went on, though unknowing whither, the distraction of her mind every instant growing greater, from the inflammation of fatigue, heat, and disappointment. She was spoken to repeatedly, she was even caught once or twice by her riding habit; but she forced herself along by her own vehement rapidity, not hearing what was said, not heeding what was thought. Delvile, bleeding by the arm of Belfield, was the image before her eyes, and took such full possession of her senses, that still, as she ran on, she fancied it in view. She scarce touched the ground; she scarce felt her own motion; she seemed as if enbued with supernatural speed, gliding from place to place, from street to street; with no consciousness of any plan, and following no other direction than that of darting forward where-ever there was most room, and turning back when she met with any obstruction; till quite spent and exhausted, she abruptly ran into a yet open shop, where, breathless and panting, she sunk upon the floor, and, with a look disconsolate and helpless, sat for some time without speaking.

This passage echoes in some extraordinary ways the prototypical flights of Defoe's urban characters, metaphorically in Crusoe after he sees the Footprint, more literally in Moll Flanders after her first theft:[27]

> I cross'd the Street indeed, and went down the first turning I came to, and I think it was a Street that went thro' into *Fenchurch-street*, from thence I cross'd and turn'd through so many ways and turnings that I could never tell which way it was, nor where I went, for I felt not the Ground I stept on, and the farther I was out of *Danger*, the faster I went, till tyr'd and out of Breath, I was forc'd to sit down on a little Bench at a Door, and then I began to recover, and found I was got into *Thames-street* near *Billingsgate*.

Moll's dizzying flight through nameless streets ultimately prefigures her descent into the criminal underworld; towards the end of the century, in a city much more professionally and institutionally settled in its urban networks, the same blank flight for Cecilia marks her descent into madness, as she takes refuge in a pawnshop all marks of coherent identity essentially 'pawned'.' The people of the house must *advertise* her—publish her 'direction' for the 'right' readers of her world:[28]

> MADNESS
> Whereas a crazy young lady, tall, fair complexioned, with blue eyes and light hair, ran into the Three Blue Balls, in—— street, on Thursday night, the 2d instant, and has been kept there since out of charity. She was dressed in a riding habit. Whoever she belongs to is desired to send after her immediately. She has been treated with the utmost care and tenderness. She talks much of some person by the name of Delvile.
> *N.B.* She had no money about her. May, 1780.

Cecilia and Evelina *find* themselves *lost* precisely because of *where* they are—because of what their address or their location implies. Evelina to some extent finds her proper address on her own; Cecilia must be 'claimed' (to whom—or where—does she 'belong'?) through the urban advertisement in order to be restored. In both late eighteenth-century novels, the implication seems to be that for a woman, at least—an upper-class woman at the very least—forms of address define identity, while topographical place defines vulnerability.

James Boswell, on the other hand, seems, like Moll Flanders, ultimately closer to mastering the city precisely by adapting himself to its darknesses. Coming to London for a year in 1762 as a young laird of twenty-two, he agrees with Addison's Mr Spectator and with Evelina in observing that 'one end of London is like a different country from the other in look and in manners.'[29] He takes lodgings in Downing Street, Westminster—'a genteel street, within a few steps of the Parade; near the House of Commons, and very healthful'—and finds, to his great if temporary satisfaction: 'I have begun to acquire a composed genteel character very different from a rattling uncultivated one which for some time past I have been fond of. I have discovered that we may be in some degree whatever character we choose.'[30] But he soon finds his own character is rather too much for him to refashion so easily—with or without a genteel address—and his personal anxieties about identity in the midst of this fashionable, powerful, and often dismissive world finds metaphoric representation in some of his urban descriptions. On 2 April 1763, for example, he makes a little visit to the Monument—that Wren memorial to the Great Fire—and finds that its tremendous height and potential power for visual command paradoxically shrivel him:[31] [illustration 3]

After dinner I sauntered in a pleasing humour to London Bridge, viewed the Thames's silver expanse and the springy bosom of the surrounding fields. I then went up to the top of the Monument. This is a most amazing building. It is a pillar two hundred feet high. In the inside, a turnpike stair runs up all the way. When I was about half way up, I grew frightened. I would have come down again, but thought I would despise myself for my timidity…. I mounted to the top and got upon the balcony. It was horrid to find myself so

The Monument

3. 'The Monument', from John Strype,
*Survey of the Cities of London, Westminster,
and Southwark* (1720)

monstrous a way up in the air, so far above London and all its spires. I durst not look around me. There is no real danger, as there is a strong rail both on the stair and balcony. But I shuddered, and as every heavy wagon passed down Gracechurch Street, dreaded that the shaking of the earth would make the tremendous pile tumble to the foundation.

Boswell's solution to this perspectival horror is to plunge back down into the topographical and sexual labyrinths of the city. For the next few weeks after his mortifying little sojourn up the phallic symbol, Boswell escalates his underworld adventures of urban conquest, essentially behaving Monumentally in his quest for control over dark urban space:[32]

At the bottom of the Haymarket I picked up a strong, jolly young damsel, and taking her under the arm I conducted her to Westminster Bridge, and then in armour complete did I engage her upon this noble edifice. The whim of doing it there with the Thames rolling below us amused me much.

And the next month (and after, and often) he reproduces his specific form of urban mastery:[33]

It was the King's birthnight, and I resolved to be a blackguard and to see all that was to be seen. I dressed myself in my second-mourning suit, in which I had been powdered many months, dirty buckskin

breeches and black stockings, a shirt of Lord Eglinton's which I had
worn two days, and little round hat with tarnished silver lace belonging to a disbanded officer of the Royal Volunteers. I had in my hand
an old oaken stick battered against the pavement. And was not I a
complete blackguard? I went to the Park, picked up a low brimstone,
called myself a barber and agreed with her for sixpence, went to the
bottom of the Park arm in arm, and dipped my machine in the
Canal and performed most manfully. I then went as far as St Paul's
Church-yard, roaring along, and then came to Ashley's Punch-house
and drank three threepenny bowls. In the Strand I picked up a little
profligate wretch and gave her sixpence....I came home about two
o'clock, much fatigued.

But not, urbanly or sexually speaking, daunted. Where Burney's characters are trapped, at least initially, by the dark spaces and darker implications of London streets, in deteriorating addresses and sinister locations,
Boswell 'conquers' the enormity of London in much the way the guidebooks, maps, and title-pages do: by articulating and appropriating all the
different forms of address of its streets. He feels himself in some ways pulled
back together rather than dismembered by his urban forays: 'My vanity
was somewhat gratified tonight,' he announces, 'that, notwithstanding of
my dress, I was always taken for a gentleman in disguise.'[34] Boswell,
through his various masculine enterprises in the city, secures his sexual and
social identity in the same spaces and by the same practices that threaten
Burney's female characters.

   But in a way Burney's own experiences in London might make a dainty,
well-washed parallel to Boswell's in that she, too, can slide carefully into
an address and 'form' it to herself. In August 1778, for example, she went
to London, in part to see her publisher Mr Lowndes to find out 'what sort
of answers he made to such curious inquirers' about the yet-unknown
author of *Evelina*. She and her stepmother buy a copy of the novel without declaring themselves and find that Mr Lowndes believes its author is
'a gentleman of the other end of the town' whose name will never be
known. Burney remarks: 'I grinned irresistibly, and was obliged to look out
at the shop-door till we came away.'[35] The exceptionally shy and retiring
Burney finds the same sort of relish in her assumed obscurity, in the power

of her own secret, in the *intactness* of her knowledge within these powerful urban spaces, as Boswell in his disguises, or Moll in hers. Burney and
Boswell imprint themselves on London.

William Stow's grammatically enigmatic remark—'There is no Place which
(to the best of my Knowledge) I have escap'd'[36]—in some ways supplies
an apt verbal image for the eighteenth-century experience of London. So
many things might be lost from a wrong direction, a wrong address: portmanteaus, property, self-knowledge, virtue, social respect, commercial business, sanity, life, a happy-ever-after. These literary excerpts, concerned
both with precise knowledge of London streets and with the threats and
possibilities of the 'mis-address', suggest that London, even in the second
half of the eighteenth century, still seemed topographically and socially
problematic, needing to be navigated and imaginatively *re* mapped—needing still, in fundamental phenomenological ways, to be *known*.
Topographical (and social and economic and psychological) success—for
historical as well as fictional inhabitants—seems to depend on carrying
maps in one's head, in which much was *assumed* about the meaning of a
specific location or 'direction.' Is one near or beyond, above or below, at
or over-against? 'Forms of address' become matters of respectability and
ruin, sanity and madness, life and death, because one cannot *escape* place.

2. The Polite Town

Shifting Possibilities of Urbanness, 1660–1715

Lawrence E. Klein

The year 1711 was an important date in the career of polite culture in England. It saw the end of the run of the *Tatler* and the commencement of the publication of the *Spectator*. It also saw the publication of what comes closest to a manifesto of eighteenth-century politeness, *Characteristicks of Men, Manners, Opinions, Times* by Anthony Ashley Cooper, the third earl of Shaftesbury (1671–1713). In addition, a lesser publication appeared in 1711 that was, in its way, just as good an indication of cultural developments. This was John Gay's *The Present State of Wit in a Letter to a Friend in the Country*.

In *The Present State of Wit*, Gay (1685–1732) writes as a gentleman in Town, signing the letter from Westminster. The addressee is a friend in the Country who, preoccupied by refurbishing an estate, is clearly a gentleman. Although absent from London, the friend expects to return to the metropolis and, to avoid being, as Gay reports, 'quite at a loss in Conversation among the *Beau Monde* next Winter', requests an account of 'the present state of Wit in Town'.[1]

Gay's account in the pamphlet of 'the present state of Wit' draws our attention to two aspects of the rise of polite culture. First, the 'wit' of the pamphlet's title, it turns out, is lodged in the periodical papers. Gay's response to his gentleman friend's request for an account of Town 'wit' is a survey of the periodicals of the previous decade from the standpoint of tasteful authority. Among other things, Gay stands in judgement of Daniel Defoe's *Review* ('contemptible') and ruthlessly condescends to the *British Apollo*, a periodical on which Gay himself had worked just a few years before.[2] But Defoe and the *British Apollo* notwithstanding, the pamphlet attests to the cultural authority that periodical literature assumed in the two decades after 1688. Periodicals were becoming polite, that is, an important source of gentlemanly cultural capital that readers, whether gentlemanly or not, could disburse in speech and action.[3] And, for Gay, there is no better instance of this new stature of the periodical than the *Tatler*, which appeared from 12 April 1709 to 2 January 1711, and was largely the responsibility of Richard Steele (1672–1729).

Second, in Gay's treatment the polite periodical press is physically and intellectually sited in London. As a result, Gay is able to link the politeness of the *Tatler* in particular to Steele's broader project of reinventing London itself, of vesting it with a new cultural dignity. According to Gay, Steele rescued 'Learning…out of the hands of Pedants and Fools…In the dress he gives it, 'tis a most welcome guest at Tea-tables and Assemblies, and is relish'd and caressed by the Merchants on the Change; accordingly, there is not a Lady at Court, nor a Banker in *Lumbard-Street*, who is not verily perswaded, that *Captain Steele* is the greatest Scholar, and best Casuist, of any man in *England*'.[4] Learning—which here is some humanistic amalgam of the literary and moral—is being taken away from 'Pedants and Fools' and newly located in the social and business world of contemporary London—a London conceived as a metropolis, embracing, in Gay's balanced clauses, both the Court end and the City end, both the feminized social world of the Town and the masculine business culture of the City.

Transferring the centre of learning and philosophy to this urban social world created new expectations for its inhabitants. It involved a condemnation of the many forms of moral laxity and intellectual dereliction, but it also created new responsibilities in the process and bestowed new dignity. One might say that, in order to please their readership and make it susceptible to their critical enterprise, Steele, Addison, and other writers of their ilk had to engage in a certain kind of polite flattery. One aspect of this flattery focused on the periodicals themselves, which were legitimated as vehicles for the conveyance of polite learning. However, another aspect of this flattery was spatial. It focused on London as a polite locale, a site inhabited by gentlemen and ladies, engaged in urbane and pleasurable sociability.

The influence of Steele's project to create London as a polite place is patent. Once established for London, polite urbanity was a model easily transferred to other towns and cities.[5] One thinks of the provincial lady who thought of Pontefract in the 1750s as a 'Capital of Politeness'.[6] Indeed, the diffusion of polite ideals and practices over Britain is so obvious that it is easy to take the phenomenon for granted. With good reason, scholars commonly point to the *Tatler* and the *Spectator* as obvious starting points for discussions of social and cultural ideals in the eighteenth century. In 1715, Dudley Ryder, born under the signs of Trade and Dissent and bound to become England's Attorney General, read *Tatlers* and observed in his diary: 'His [Steele's] characters of human life are extremely fine and judicious, his method of raillery very delicate and exact. Intend to read them often to improve my style and accustom myself to his way of thinking and telling a story and manner of observing upon the world and mankind'.[7] Half a century later, the journals of James Boswell attest to the continuing inspirational value of the Whig periodicals.[8]

What is less obvious is where these periodicals came from. Even if we attribute remarkable originality to the *Tatler* and *Spectator*, these publications nonetheless emerged from larger patterns in discourse and practice. Usually portrayed as the starting points for eighteenth-century culture, the periodicals were also an endpoint of an evolution, a dialectic between change in the character of London and change in the way that London could be discussed.

To appreciate the invention of a polite London, one must consider the kinds of urbanness previously available. In the early seventeenth century, there were a number of different ways to think about urban phenomena in England but politeness was not one of them. Steele's efforts need to be viewed against long-standing inhibitions to seeing London in this way.

The idea of a polite London in the early eighteenth century depended on a reconciliation of gentility and urbanness, which is precisely what the tripartite scheme of Court, Country, and City had militated against. This scheme had taken hold in the later sixteenth century and offered a neat set of environmental stereotypes, each with its stereotypical denizen: the courtier at Court, the gentleman in the Country, and the citizen in the City. In this scheme, the gentleman was not urban, and the urban could not be gentle.

However, as early as the 1620s, a new category, the Town, arose to supplement the categories of Court, Country and City. The Town appeared in response to the growing presence of gentlemen in London as a way of imagining the urban activities of the gentleman and formulating that side of urban life related to genteel leisure and its social and cultural possibilities.[9] Casting London as the Town involved more than simply adding another perspective to an established repertoire. In the course of the seventeenth century the tripartite model broke down and was replaced by a new and more integrated model and practice of élite culture, centred on the Town. This polite culture was capable of comprehending a wider section of society, from the middling sort upwards. It was an idiom capable of being appropriated in different ways to different extents by people with rather different experiences in the economic and social hierarchy.

The history of the Town as a whole from Charles I's reign to Anne's has yet to be written. It would have to cover both language and practice, both the ways people articulated the nature, traits, and meaning of the Town and the ways they organised themselves in institutions and practices within it. It would include a set of related developments which progressed unevenly within a long-term context of expansion and elaboration: the urban predilections of the gentry[10] and the cultural predilections of the better sort of non-landed;[11] the residential development of the West End and the evolution of places of public resort;[12] the history of shopping and the rise of the coffeehouses;[13] the very erratic history of the theatres and of many other cultural diversions.[14]

The history of the Town would have to trace at least two distinct long-term developments. First, it would have to delineate the shifting social demography of the Town. Though the Town was a gentle person's environment throughout, those who could claim gentility expanded in number. In its earliest manifestation in the 1630s, the Town was the urban outpost of the gentry: according to Martin Butler, it was a decisive symptom of 'the rise of the gentry'.[15] However, the Town grew to be populated by pseudo-gentry and indeed by those at the upper end of the middling sorts who managed to sustain a claim to gentility. By the time of the *Tatler*, the word 'gentleman' had entered on its notoriously obfuscatory eighteenth-century career.[16]

Second, the history of the Town would have to trace the changing nature of the Court—its personnel, its institutions, and its practices—in relation to those of the Town. In its earliest days, the Town may have had a degree of autonomy from the Court but it was fundamentally enmeshed in the life of the Court and courtiers. If anything, this relation may have intensified, in certain respects, after the restoration in 1660.[17] Again, however, by the time of the *Tatler*, the Town was thoroughly autonomous of the Court. Indeed, the Town had taken over the central space occupied previously in elite culture by the Court.[18]

The London represented by Steele in the *Tatler* was premised on the existence of those institutions and practices known as the Town, whose evolution and elaboration went back, as I have just noted, several generations. However, the precise representation of London found in the *Tatler* was of more recent origin. For the purposes of this essay, I follow John Gay, who associated the appearance of the polite Town with the rise of the periodicals.

During the 1660s, 1670s and 1680s, the appearance of periodicals was limited by licensing although lapses of regulation occasionally allowed brief spurts of growth. The publications of the Restoration decades were largely devoted to news and political comment. The most successful periodicals not concerned with these topics were devoted to science and useful knowledge: Henry Oldenburg's *Philosophical Transactions* (from 1665), Robert Hooke's *Philosophical Collections* (1679, 1681–82), and John Houghton's *Collection of Letters for the Improvement of Husbandry and Trade* (1681–84).[19] To the extent that these periodicals represented communities of gentlemanly amateurs engaged in conversation, they were progenitors of the polite periodicals that arose after 1688. London, however, was not an object of representation within their pages (although it was occasionally a subject of discussion).

If we are looking for representations of London in periodicals of the Restoration era, we have to turn to one of the more successful ventures of the period, associated with the name *Poor Robin* and attributed to William Winstanley (1628?–98). Here, a lively and disorderly London, traceable to Elizabethan pamphleteers, was alive and well. In a number of successive periodicals (including *Poor Robin's Intelligence*, 1676–1677; *Poor Robin's Memoirs*, 1677–78; *Poor Robin's Intelligence, Revived*, 1679–80), a representation of London was offered which centred on the streets, alleys, and courts of London, and the disorderly behaviour of their inhabitants. The *Poor Robin* periodicals were assembled, in imitation of contemporary newspapers, as a series of reports from different locations. In *Poor Robin* these were mostly London locations: Moorgate, Moorfields, Smithfield, Newgate, Whitefriars, Shoe Lane, Lombard Street, Aldersgate Street, Fleet Street. Its geographical compass was limited to the City and its oldest western extensions, Covent Garden and St Martin's. The Londoners represented were, on the one hand, merchants, shopkeepers, artisans, apprentices, and their wives and mistresses, and, on the other, rogues and bullies, prostitutes and thieving women. Fops and fashionable courtiers do occasionally appear as do members of the older professions: lawyers (mostly cheats) and medical men (mostly quacks) along with astrologers. There is also some coverage of the relations of gentlemen with ordinary people, especially prostitutes and tradesmen. But the gentleman is usually an outsider, a Country visitor or a slumming courtier. The favourite subjects of the *Poor Robin* series were crime, sex, and disorder. Its most frequent motifs were the abundance of credulity in the world and the effectiveness of deceit: the City was filled with tricksters, people outsmarting others and consistently getting away with it.

The representation of London in the *Tatler* was very different from the one in the *Poor Robin* series, but it is also clear that the rise of a polite vision of London did not simply supplant the scrappy and lusty version of the city. Not only did these kinds of characterization continue,[20] but they also evolved in response to the propagation of politeness. The satires on London that proliferated after 1688 from the pens of writers such as Edward Ward and Thomas Brown were partly derivative from the earlier traditions embodied in *Poor Robin*. At the same time, the satirists recognized and targetted exactly the sorts of polite pretensions that crystallized in the periodicals of Steele and Addison.

While *Poor Robin* was the progenitor of satirical texts that later savaged polite pretension, it was also an ancestor of the *Tatler* in that *Poor Robin* represented London with topographical and social specificity. Of course, *Poor Robin*'s London was very different from that of Isaac Bickerstaffe, Steele's persona in the *Tatler*, but their shared vision of a London made up of individual and well defined streets and coffee-houses, theatres and alleys ties them together in a three-legged perambulation of the capital. The nature of their connection, the journey from Poor Robin's London to that of Isaac Bickerstaffe, forms the subject of the rest of this essay.

After 1688, periodical journalism took a polite turn. What emerged was a new kind of periodical. First, these periodicals present themselves as of, for, and by gentlemen or ladies and frequently both gentlemen and ladies. Second, their contents mix *belles lettres*, moralism, and cultural reportage. Third, they use a range of stylistic devices to ingratiate their entertainingly didactic and improving ambitions with their genteel readers. Fourth, they embody sociability by creating the impression of a community of readers and writers and by asking for the active participation of readers in their broader project.[21] Significant examples of such polite journalism between 1688 and the publication of the *Tatler* include *The Gentleman's Journal* (1692–94), *The Diverting-Post* (1704–05, 1706), *The Muses Mercury* (1707), and *The British Apollo* (1708–11).

The earliest successful pioneer of this genre was Pierre (or Peter) Motteux (1660–1718), a Huguenot from Rouen who settled in London after the revocation of the Edict of Nantes (1685). Though he started out in trade, he gravitated toward the world of publishing and increasingly presented himself as a man of letters.[22] The full title of his periodical was *The Gentleman's Journal: Or The Monthly Miscellany. By Way of a Letter to a Gentleman in the Country*. Like Gay in *The Present State of Wit*, 'Motteux', the voice of the *Journal*, is presented as a gentleman, situated in London, providing infor- mation for a gentleman in the Country. The first letter begins: 'Sir, Indeed you impose too hard a task on me: Is it not enough that I send you what ever news or new things I meet with to divert you in your solitude, but you must oblige me to print my Letters?' Though much protest follows, 'Motteux' acquiesces: 'I grant that from *London*, the Heart of the Nation, all things circulating to the other parts, such news or new things as are sent me may be conveyed every where, being inserted in my Letter'.[23] Such claims for the centrality of London are not new, but the particularly polite and cultural orientation of Motteux's content is: the newest play by Thomas Southerne,[24] a new portrait of the Duchess of Grafton by Godfrey Kneller, [25] a new verse by John Dennis on the British naval victory over the French at LaHogue.[26] But 'Motteux' is often ahead of the news, able to deliver the word on what is to come: 'Mr *Congreve* will in some time give us another Play';[27] 'We are promised in a short time a Volume of Letters of Adventure, Love and Gallantry, by several Ladies'.[28]

In a way this anticipates the perambulations of Mr Bickerstaffe in the

Tatler. 'Motteux' represents himself as someone who moves in a topographically realistic urban setting. In the *Gentleman's Journal*, 'Motteux'
reports on St Cecilia's Day concerts at Stationers Hall, on concerts in
Charles Street and at York Buildings, on plays recently presented in the
several theatres.[29] He is a denizen of the Town, circulating among its
gentlemanly inhabitants. This is a *Gentleman's Journal*, after all, and the text
is studded with references to his gentlemanly acquaintance and readership. 'Motteux' presents himself as 'oblig'd to read, converse with the
Ingenious, see my Friends, and answer a world of Letters'.[30] On one occasion, he is in a bookshop and overhears comments about the *Gentleman's
Journal* itself.[31] On another, a person of quality honours him with a letter,
which he publishes.[32] On a third, he is 'in Company with several
Gentlemen' when one receives a missive from abroad, which again he
publishes.[33] He writes in summary: 'to be read by many Persons as eminent
by their Wit and Judgement as their Quality, and be told in above a thousand Letters that the undertaking pleased [is] to me a sure token of its kind
reception'.[34]

The practice (or at least the ambition) of this polite journalism was
summed up in 1704 by the *Diverting-Post*, which evoked a readership of
'Quality, Gentry, and others, who delight in the publick Diversions of the
Town'. For this readership, the *Diverting-Post* promised to convey 'What
Forreigner of either Sex is arriv'd Famous for Vocal, or Instrumental
Musick; when, and where will be an Entertainment, and the Names of the
Artists who Perform in it: What New Plays are on the Stocks, and the
Names of the Authors; what Persons of Honour are lately Married, and
an account of their fortunes; all new songs, Copies of Verses, Prologues,
or Epilogues which have not been printed, will be here Incerted [sic]'.[35]

But the Town, as it appears in the *Gentleman's Journal*, is more than a set
of sites or persons: it is a function and enjoys a kind of agency. The Town
is, in the first instance, a public that passes judgement, and 'Motteux'
inscribes these judgements in his periodical. Noting the premiere of
Thomas Southerne's *The Wives Excuse* in 1692, 'Motteux' mentions
Southerne's earlier triumph, *Sir Anthony Love*, 'which you and all the Town
have lik'd so well .... And tho' the Town hath not been so kind to this last,
as to the former, I do not doubt but you will own that it will bear a reading'.[36] Among the objects of the Town's judgment is the periodical itself.

'Motteux' notes the Town's acceptance of his own project: 'the Town begins to be reconciled to the *Novelty* [of the *Gentleman's Journal*], and to entertain some favourable thoughts of the Design'.[37] The periodical, of course, had to comply with the Town's appetites and tastes; but the relationship of the periodical to the Town was not merely servile. It was more complicated than that. While polite periodicals sometimes represented themselves as compliant servants of the Town, they also assumed other relations with the Town as well: sometimes as the Town's agent and representative; sometimes as the Town's elite and vanguard; and, when periodicals asked for contributions from readers, as the Town's partner. Moreover, it has to be remembered that the Town was just as much a fictive device as the voices of the periodicals. By depicting themselves as in a relationship of some sort with the Town (whether subservient, collaborative or *avant garde*), the periodicals were largely responsible for creating this entity called the Town.

Beginning in 1709, the *Tatler* extended the polite journalism of the preceding two decades with a more elaborate construction of a gentlemanly London in which the metropolis was represented, socially, topographically, and culturally, from a polite standpoint. Steele did not invent the Town as the mode for thinking about a gentleman's London. Yet, against the previous options for thinking about the character of urban life, his stood forth as a novel version of urban possibility. Thus, his enterprise in fictive journalism created a new and major paradigm of the urban.[38]

The novelty of the *Tatler* rested in the specific sort of London that it assumed, a London made manifest to the reader by the strong narrative elements structuring the *Tatler* essays. Though the heart of the *Tatler* was a set of moral, social, and critical pronouncements, the body was the world inhabited by the fictive character of Isaac Bickerstaffe. In other words, the framework for the moral and social prescriptions of the *Tatler* was a narration in which Bickerstaffe was the principal character. Bickerstaffe's reflections either stemmed from or led to narrative events. In some numbers, narrative led to reflection: for instance, 'having received Notice, That the famous Actor Mr. *Betterton* was to be interred this Evening in the Cloysters near *Westminster-Abbey*, I was resolved to walk thither, and see the last Office done'.[39] Meditations on the theatre as liberal entertainment for a free people followed. In other numbers reflections led to narrative. For instance, in one episode, Bickerstaffe made observations on fortune and Seneca, which he carried into the world: 'Full of these thoughts, I left my lodgings, and took a walk to the Court end of the Town'.[40] In this way, the moralizing and criticizing process was always situated in a narrative setting.

As a consequence, the moralism itself was situated with respect to specific places and to specific personnel. The moral was always illustrated, and the illustration was given a contemporary social setting. For instance, *Tatler* 186 concerned, among other things, modesty as an ingredient in reputation. Bickerstaffe's reflections led to a story: 'Walking the other Day in a neighbouring Inn of Court, I saw a more happy and more graceful Orator than I ever before had heard'. The orator turns out to be a young gentleman talking to himself whom Bickerstaffe then uses to illustrate a point about self-obsession and self-advertisement in the modern city.[41]

Steele took advantage of urban diversity to represent a mixed social environment. Bickerstaffe referred to the milk-maid in his neighbourhood, to the watchman on the lane, to the ruined upholsterer obsessed with news and politics, to the overly proud cobbler on Ludgate Hill.[42] Yet the references to tradesmen and mere citizens were far fewer than those to gentlemen. Bickerstaffe was an observer of an elite and metropolitan social world. In his own words, he was interested in 'the polite or busy Part of Mankind';[43] and, while these two terms appear to refer to two separate populations, they also refer to the double character of one population.

In other words, gentility lost its crisp boundaries in the *Tatler*. To be sure, the gentleman of the *Tatler* was not necessarily a member of the gentry. Steele explicitly advanced a definition of gentility founded in behaviour rather than in pedigree or land ownership. 'The Appellation of Gentleman is never to be affixed to a Man's Circumstances, but to his Behaviour in them', he wrote in *Tatler* 207. 'The Courtier, the Trader, and the Scholar, should all have an equal Pretension to the Denomination of a Gentleman.'[44] This helps to explain the social porousness between City and Town, at least at the upper reaches of the City, represented in the *Tatler*. Steele described a City potentate as residing 'for some Years in the Cities of *London* and *Westminster*, with the Air of his Imperial quality, but the Equipage and Appointment only of a private Gentleman'. This individual was immersed in the mercantile and financial activities of the City. 'But Wealth and Wisdom are Possessions too solemn not to give Weariness to active Minds…: This Emperor therefore, with great Regularity, every Day at Five in the Afternoon, leaves his Money-Changers, his Publicans, and little Hoarders of Wealth, to their low Pursuits, and ascends his Chariot to drive to *Will*'s; where the Tast is refin'd, and a Relish giv'n to Men's Possessions, by a polite Skill in gratifying their Passions and Appetites.'[45]

At the same time, the *Tatler* privileged gentility of a more traditional sort as embodied in the figure of Bickerstaffe himself. The medium of the *Tatler*'s insights was always Gentleman Bickerstaffe. His personal estate was said to have been modest; his household was small. On the other hand, he was of ancient and distinguished descent and, though his wide net of family affiliations appears to have covered a wide range of levels in landed society, some of his family connections were quite substantial indeed. His education was gentlemanly: he attended Merchant Taylors' and university and was a cadet in the Civil War on the royalist side.[46] Bickerstaffe functioned in the *Tatler* as the heir of a stock of English virtue and wisdom, amassed in the traditional English environment of the landed elite, though, in his re-articulation of this moral viewpoint, he drew on a wide stock of ancient and modern literary and philosophical material. His chief aim, however, was to bring this amalgam to bear on an urban environment.

Although the *Tatler* focussed its attention on London, its London was a gentleman's. Bickerstaffe himself lived in Sheer (or Shire) Lane, just within Temple Bar, in the oldest part of the West End. The street ran up from Fleet Street to Little Lincoln's Inn Fields (to the southwest of the Inn Fields proper). And while it would not have been a particularly prestigious address, this part of London remained sufficiently socially mixed, even later in the eighteenth century, that a respectable gentleman might have lived here. Had Bickerstaffe survived into the mid-century, he would have been only minutes away from Samuel Johnson's various residences off Fleet Street.[47]

Toward the latter end of the periodical's life, Bickerstaffe tended to address the reader more frequently from his own apartment, but earlier the practice was different. He announced from the first his intention to:[48]

divide our relation of the passages which occur in action or discourse throughout this Town as well as elsewhere, under such dates of places

as may prepare you for the matter you are to expect in the following manner. All accounts of gallantry, pleasure, and entertainment,
shall be under the article of White's Chocolate-house; poetry, under
that of Will's Coffee-house; Learning, under the title of Grecian;
foreign and domestic news, you will have from Saint James's Coffee-
house, and what else I have to offer on any other subject shall be dated
from my own apartment.

The coffeehouses were key locales in Bickerstaffe's environment. The obvious topographical fact about them is that they all lay to the west of Sheer
Lane. The Grecian would have been nearest, a short walk to the west along
the Strand (it was located in Devereux Court, in the Strand); Will's was a
bit farther, in Covent Garden (on Russell Street); the remaining two were
on St James's Street itself, in the fashionable district adjoining the Palace.[49]
The three sites (Sheer Lane, Russell Street, and St James's Street) form a
triangle, with a very long base and a shallow peak, covering a good deal of
the new West End. The *Tatler*'s London had its basis in the life of the West
End, where Bickerstaffe's most frequent resorts were located.

Bickerstaffe was not, however, bound by these limits: as only made
sense in early modern London, he was a walker in the city, an avid pedestrian. He frequently strolled along Fleet Street in one direction or the other,
as far as Westminster or, in the other direction, to the City proper. For
instance, he was to be seen passing through Cheapside, observing crowds
at the Bank, who became fodder for a reflection on fortune.[50] But more
often he was in the West End: in the Haymarket, on the Mall, at various
spots within St James's Park.

This topography was the setting in which the *Tatler* created its particular cultural world. This was a world, first and foremost, of visits.[51] The
narrative kernel of the majority of the *Tatler*'s numbers were visits, visits
to Bickerstaffe or visits by him to others. In visits, clothing, deportment,
and manners were on display. More important, every visit was an opportunity for conversation. Thus, the visit displayed people's social abilities,
intellectual interests, cultural tastes, and moral values. Bickerstaffe cease-
lessly observed and digested the scene of social commerce in his self-
appointed role of censor—the man who sorts the population into
categories and watches over them for violations of proprieties.[52]

Aside from making and receiving visits, Bickerstaffe sat in coffeehouses, taverns and other places of public accommodation and attended the theatres and opera of the West End.[53] Moreover, the streets of London themselves—the connective tissue which made this world move—always offered a site for observation and reflection. Bickerstaffe's famous lucubrations (studies at night by the light of a lamp) were in constant counterpoint with his perambulations. Solitude was in dynamic opposition with sociability.

It is noteworthy that the Court was peripheral to the social world assumed in the *Tatler*. Though consciousness of the Court was not entirely absent, this world was independent of its social milieu. The evidence here is negative: there are barely any references to the royal court. What one can observe is the emergence of a polite world, distinct from the Court, a social world based on leisure and situated in the metropolis. Bickerstaffe was a moralist, and he was, thus, not aiming to describe London social life, but his writings presupposed the existence of a new kind of London society with its own topographical and social landscape. The world presupposed in the *Tatler* was an elite social world located in London. Its population was composed of people whose ancestors might have identified themselves strongly with Court, Country, or City but who themselves were citizens of the polite Town.

3. Circulation and Disorder
London Streets and Hackney Coaches, c. 1640–c. 1740
Mark Jenner

> All is tumult and hurry…People, who keep their own equipages, drive through the streets at fullspeed…The hackneycoachmen make their horses smoke, and the pavement shakes under them.[1]

The coach traffic of which Matt Bramble complained was one of the most distinctive features of eighteenth-century London street life, and served as a common signifier of metropolitan existence. This chapter will use the coach, and, in particular, that early form of commercial public transport, the hackney coach, as a heuristic vehicle with which to explore the articulation, experience and contestation of metropolitan public space in the long eighteenth century.

Coaches attracted comment and carried particular symbolic significance because they were one of the capital's novelties. As eighteenth-century histories and guide-books explained, they only became an important form of élite self-presentation and a common mode of intra-urban passenger transport during the seventeenth century.[2] In the early 1620s John Taylor, the Water Poet, attacked the coach as '*an impudent…sawcie Intruder*'. The development of improved forms of carriage attracted the interest of Restoration virtuosi such as Robert Hooke and Christopher Wren who in 1676 walked round St James's Park discoursing 'about chariots'.[3] Their designs (like Hooke's proposals outlining ways in which humans could fly) do not appear to have been widely adopted, but by the late seventeenth century the coach had, as Susan Whyman has demonstrated, become a central feature of polite sociability within the capital.[4] Coaches thronged the streets of eighteenth-century London, and in the 1750s it contained some 4000 of England's 9,000 four-wheeled carriages.[5] Coach traffic even sustained criminal specialisms. In June 1718, for instance, Charles Hudson was indicted at the Old Bailey for 'stealing 2 scarlet Coach Seats'. Witnesses alleged that 'as the Coach was going slowly into little *Ormond-yard*', Hudson and an accomplice 'were seen about the Coach...,[and] that the other Person threw out the Seats' to Hudson who ran off with them. Hudson denied the charge, but the famous thief-taker, Jonathan Wild, told the jurors that Hudson was, 'the greatest stealer of Coach seats in *England*'.

Hudson may or may not have been national champion in the felonious acquisition of carriage seats, but similar offences noted in the *Old Bailey Sessions Papers* of the 1710s and 1720s[7] bear witness to the centrality of coaches in London life. By this date they also featured prominently in metropolitan funerals, with mourning coaches being hired for the interment of members of the middling sort.[8] Yet a private carriage was the preserve of the really rich or truly profligate. Many of the capital's more affluent residents could not afford to run a coach and horses, but periodically desired to use one when transporting a heavy package,[9] when the distance was too great, the weather too wet, or they were too drunk to walk.[10] Women of the middling and upper sort, in particular, often preferred to travel by coach rather than walk for too long amidst the unruly and demotic culture of the street. Above all, the many visitors to London, often living in cramped rented accommodation, created a market for carriages which could be rented by the journey or the day.

The number of such hackney coaches, (their name derives from the old meaning of hackney—a horse for hire) grew steadily in response to this demand and London's rising population. In 1637 Sir Edmund Verney reckoned 200 sufficient for its needs; an ordinance of 1654 set a maximum of 300 coaches;[11] a statutory maximum of 400 was established in 1662, which was raised to 700 in 1694, to 800 in 1715 and 1000 in 1771.[12]

As such statutory maxima indicate, the state sought to regulate London commercial public transport.[13] The most drastic response was Charles I's 1636 proclamation that no hired coaches be allowed in London or Westminster except for journeys of more than three miles out of the capital.[14] Cromwell and the Council of State similarly sought to control the 'increase and...irregularity' of London coaches, and in 1654 their ordinance named thirteen 'Master Hackney-coach-men' who were to establish a 'Company' of hackney coachmen governed by rules set down by the City aldermen.[15] Shortly after the Restoration, Parliament enacted that there should be 400 hackney coaches in the capital; the people operating these vehicles were placed under the authority of royal commissioners and were to pay £5 a year for their licence to ply for hire.[16] This legislation lapsed in 1679, initiating a somewhat chaotic period in which both City and Crown struggled to establish a system of regulation.[17]

A statutory system of licensing and regulation by royal commission was reestablished under William and Mary and lasted without significant change until 1831. Licenses might be better described as franchises. They were sold for cash and lasted for the duration of the statute, provided the licensee paid his or her annual rent. Like other private property, they were inherited, leased and sold.[18] Four or five salaried commissioners, assisted by clerks, messengers and a secretary, collected the annual payments. Every licensed coach had to display its license number on painted tin plates hung on the vehicle. This facilitated the regulatory work of the commissioners, for they also heard complaints about unlicensed drivers and levied fines for infractions of their by-laws. However, with only two streetmen at their disposal they could hardly exercise a draconian policy of policing, and the energy with which they collected license money varied considerably.[19]

This bald narrative does not explain why this particular aspect of London street life should have excited so much regulatory energy. The most obvious explanation is financial—coachmen paid for their licenses. Hackney coach licensing was considered as a way to clear the City's debts in the 1680s; when control by commission was reestablished in 1694 it raised money for the war with France—each licensed hackney coachman had to pay a £50 entry fine for their license (totalling £35,000).[20] In the 1790s licenses were raising around £24,000 a year for the Treasury.[21]

Yet the hackney coachmen's role as source of government revenue is not sufficient to explain the additional twenty proposals for their regulation introduced into Parliament between 1660 and 1740.[22] Rather, these marked some of the ways in which the conflicting uses of London public space were being renegotiated. For the increase in wheeled traffic and the élite's adoption of the coach helped to generate a new emphasis on the need to ensure the smooth circulation of traffic, people and goods *through* urban space.

Metaphors of circulation pervaded discussions of the proper functioning of trade in Augustan political arithmetic,[23] while later seventeenth-century City orders for environmental regulation shifted their concern from preventing stench and noxious airs to a preoccupation with ensuring 'conveniency of passage' and preventing any obstruction in the streets.[24]

The physical layout of the City's main thoroughfares after the Fire expressed this new priority. Streets were equipped with pavements—sidewalks in the North American sense—and traffic was separated from pedestrians, and pedestrians protected from traffic by posts placed along their edge.[25] The main streets of Restoration and Augustan London consequently became novel arenas of spectacle and the mutual gaze of coach passenger and pedestrian, particularly as coaches developed glass windows rather than tin plates with holes punched in them to let in the air.[26] As Pepys commented in December 1668, just after he had bought a coach, it was a 'mighty pleasure to go alone with my...wife in a coach of our own to a play; and makes us appear mighty great, I think, in the world'.[27]

This argument clearly resembles that of Lewis Mumford. Nearly forty years ago he argued that the Baroque city of display was constructed in a linear fashion and had street plans in which 'the movement of wheeled vehicles played a critical part'.[28] With the development of wide avenues, he wrote, 'the dissociation of the upper and the lower classes achieves form in the city itself. The rich drive; the poor walk. The rich roll along the axis of the grand avenue; the poor are off-centre, in the gutter; and eventually a special strip is provided for the ordinary pedestrian, the sidewalk.'[29]

Mumford's highly schematic picture discusses design not social practice. He does not explore, as Michel De Certeau does, how far spatial practices might re-inhabit and subversively re-construct urban form. In a critique of Foucault, De Certeau has argued that the walking of city streets is one of the many 'procedures that, far from being...eliminated by panoptic administration, have reinforced themselves in a proliferating illegitimacy...and combined...to the point of constituting everyday regulations and surreptitious creativities that are merely concealed by the frantic...discourses of observational organization.'[30]

An examination of eighteenth-century London suggests, moreover, that what one might (in the spirit of De Certeau) term the 'equestrian spatial practices' of the hackney coachman were profoundly disruptive of the order of the streets. Far from being pliable servants of civility, the 'Insolence, Abuses, and Exactions' of hackney coachdrivers caused frequent complaint. The Cornhill wardmote inquest complained repeatedly in the 1690s of the 'abusive language profane Swearing and rudeness' of hackney coachmen standing by the Exchange. In 1719 Clement Leworth, Beadle of the Poultry, told the House of Commons how he was unable to prevent stops in the street because of 'the Unruliness of the Hackney Coachmen', who whipped him and ran their horses directly at him. When constables tried to arrest John Prickett in January 1692 because his coach was obstructing the highway in St Stephen Coleman Street, he struck them with a bayonet and declared 'that the L[or]d Mayor should kiss his A—'.[31] The coachmen's reputation for truculence was further enhanced as they were incorporated into Augustan reworkings of Roman satire. Thus Sir John Oldham's 'Imitation of the Third Satire of Juvenal' tells of how Londoners' sleep is disturbed by 'the Brawls of Coach-men, when they meet/ and stop in turnings of a narrow Street.' In a passage indebted to the same lines of Juvenal, Gay describes how as the evening closes in by St Clement Danes's Church,

> Now Oaths grow loud, with Coaches Coaches jar,
> And the smart Blow provokes the sturdy War;
> From the high Box they whirl the Thong around,
> And with the twining Lash their Shins resound.[32]

Such riotously combative behaviour is best understood, not as an expression of generalized resistance as De Certeau's model would have it, but as part of what the anthropologist and social theorist Pierre Bourdieu might have termed the coachmen's hexis, the bodily regime by and in which they pursued their livelihoods. For, because they had to make as many journeys as possible in order to build up their income, hackney coach drivers needed assertive, even aggressive, physical skills in order to move their horses and their carriage effectively through crowded city streets. It is not surprising, therefore, that coachmen were notorious for the ferocious way in which they flogged their horses,[34] and that many contemporaries noted that hackney coach drivers, like carmen and draymen, often failed to move according to the deferential choreography that was supposed to govern London traffic. A persistent theme in the regulation of hackney coaches was that they should give way to persons of quality, and gentlemen's coaches, and there were equally persistent complaints that they did not do so.[35] Shortly after the Restoration the Lord Mayor found subversive implications in the persistent failure of hackney coachmen, draymen and carters to do so, complaining that their conduct exemplified how 'the unruly and meaner sort of people, haveing under ye late usurped powers, [had] been encouraged and borne up in their unduetifulnesse and contempt of their Superiour, especially ye Nobility & Gentry'.[36]

Yet disruptions to the journeys of the polite could not always be put down to the deliberate insubordination of hackney coachmen. There were many complaints, particularly in the later seventeenth century, that the sheer number of hackney coaches was making it impossible to pass through the streets and was even threatening the trade of the capital. In 1679 Juries of Nuisances in Westminster and the Duchy of Lancaster Liberty off the Strand complained that the numbers of hackney coaches 'were insufferable Grievances'; in 1683 the common council of the City declared that their numbers had 'become so many, that the Streets and Common Passages...are...so filled...That the...Inhabitants of this City, and the People repairing thereunto, are greatly hindered in their Affairs,...the Passages of Carts...necessary for the conveying of Goods greatly obstructed, and the Trade of this City...much prejudiced'. In 1687 the Grand Jury of Middlesex and 'a great number of Shopkeepers' petitioned King's Bench against the nuisance caused by the excessive number of hackney coaches.[37] In 1720 the House of Lords complained to Westminster JPs that there was 'such an interruption by Hackney Coaches, Carts and Drays' in Old Palace Yard, Westminster, that peers were 'frequently hindred from comeing to the Parliament house'.[38]

One possible solution to this problem was Charles II's proclamation of October 1660, which commanded that those hiring out hackney coaches were not to ply for trade on the streets. They had rather to remain in their stables and yards until someone came to hire them. This order collapsed through the coachmen's resistance and the willingness of many Londoners to take full advantage of their illegal services. As Pepys noted on 7 November: 'notwithstanding this was the first day that the King's proclamacion against Hackny Coaches coming into the streets to stand to be hired, yet I got one tonight to carry me home.'[39]

Subsequent orders sought not to ban hackney coaches from the streets but to control their manner of driving and to restrict their standing to positions that would not unduly impede the flow of traffic. Over the late seventeenth and early eighteenth centuries therefore, commissioners, justices and, indeed, coachmen worked out minutely calibrated rules to govern the trade in movement. This was not an especially smooth process. Throughout the late seventeenth and early eighteenth centuries, for instance, the wardmote inquest of Cornhill complained of the irregularities of coachmen standing at the Royal Exchange,[40] while frequently individuals were aggrieved by coachmen standing in front of their house or shop. In 1744, for instance, John Bridgen, Professor of Divinity at Gresham College, complained that the hackney coachmen standing in Fenchurch Street 'were a great Nusance' to the houses which he leased from the City, and persuaded the aldermen to command that they move their stand.[41] But the precision of the orders of the Commissioners of Hackney Coaches, such as those stipulating that no hackney coachman was to ply for trade within ten feet of Olivers' coffee house on the west side of the gate leading into Westminster Hall, and that none was to stand within nine feet of the doors of St Paul's Cathedral, helps to explain why the jeremiads warning of imminent gridlock largely died away in the early eighteenth century.[42]

Since the publication of *Discipline and Punish* historians have become increasingly sensitized to the pervasiveness of Enlightenment projects for the regulation of bodily deportment.[43] Yet while licensing and the rules governing the conduct of coachmen clearly sought to produce patterns of orderly behaviour conducive to the efficient functioning of London public space as an arena for trade and polite sociability, they should not be seen as a programme of regimented movement akin to military drill. In the first place they were not simply imposed from above. The Cromwellian regulation of the 1650s was partly a response to petitions from hackney coachmen seeking to structure and thus presumably to protect their trade.[44] Some of the hackney coachmen similarly petitioned in favour of licensing and regulation in the 1660s and the 1690s.[45] This is not surprising. As with any guild or fellowship, unregulated working conditions were not necessarily to their advantage. After all, the owners of the coach licenses made a considerable investment in regulation by paying their initial fee and had every incentive to work together, hiring counsel and lobbying in defence of their rights and working conditions.[46]

Moreover, when the commissioners commanded that hackney coach-men not break rank on the stands in which they had to wait in line,[47] their concerns chimed with coachmen's fraternal ethos, expressed not only by their regular use of the term 'Brother Coachman',[48] but in forms of collective sociability such as a coachmen's cricket team.[49] Something of their solidarities can be glimpsed in an episode retold in the *Spectator*. A young gentleman 'beckon'd a Coach' by Temple Bar. As he was follow-ing the fad among young men at the Inns of Court to drive coaches, he told the coachman to get in and he would drive it. Despite the latter's doubts about his capacity to negotiate the traffic, he managed to get down the Strand (at less than walking pace). There he had to navigate the narrow passage by St Clement Danes church, 'where are always Coaches in waiting'. Seeing this individual, all the coachmen whipped him. The amateur driver 'seem'd at first a little uneasy under the Operation, and was going…to take the Numbers of their Coaches', but his passen-ger persuaded him to keep going. When the correspondent asked the coachmen about their behaviour, they explained that 'it was a Custom among them, whenever they saw a Brother…unstable in his Post, to lend him a hand to settle him again'.[50]

Yet the commissioners did not simply try to ensure that hackney coach-men observed the social niceties of the street and did not block the thor-oughfares. They also regulated the quality of the hackney coachmen's service and the *prices* they charged. Both matters could be contentious. Less than a month after the overseers of hackney coachmen had been confirmed in the City, one of them was stripped of his office and fined for over-charging.[51] Such disputes might even lead to bloodshed. In July 1679, for instance, it was reported that 'a disbanded Officer' had run a coachman through for 'demanding more money than the Gentleman agreed for'.[52] Consequently, from the 1680s, if not earlier, the official rates and orders of London's coachmen were reprinted in handbooks like John Playford's *Vade Mecum*.[53] Indeed hackney coachmen were among the most regulated sections of the early modern economy.[54]

Initially this pricing structure was expressed in fairly rudimentary terms. The 1662 Act of Parliament, for instance, commanded that coachmen were not to charge more than 12*d.* for any journey between the Inns of Court and St James's Palace or places within Westminster not further than Tuttle Street. The vagueness of the last phrase, in which journey lengths are gauged by topographical comparison—distances are like those between the Inns of Court (the plural is revealing) and the Exchange—reveals points of potential conflict between coachman and customer.[55] What exactly was the distance between two points?

Legislation introduced under Queen Anne refined this fare structure by naming prices for particular distances—no passenger should, for instance, pay more than 12*d.* for a journey of under one mile and four furlongs. It thus instructed the commissioners to measure and publish the distances between 'the most noted Places' within the Bills of Mortality. They accordingly spent 43 shillings on 'a Mathematicall Wheel to Measure ye distances of Places' and establish their authority over the streets of the metropolis.[56] As they explained fifteen years later, 'for the better Determination of Disputes concerning the Fares of Coachmen…they have directed, and are frequently still directing, many particular Distances to be admeasured'.[57] Yet, although one contemporary guidebook assured its readers that 'For the better knowing the Distances between the most noted Places in…*London* and *Westminster*, the Commissioners have caused the same to be measured',[58] such measurements did not endow them with some general, quasi-Newtonian, authority over London space. Most of their surveys were specific to one dispute. As they noted ruefully, the knowledge of particular measurements 'is no great general service, Cases exactly the same seldom happening twice'.[59] Nevertheless, they gradually built up their findings. In 1725 their book of 'admeasurements' had grown to 226 folio pages,[60] and by the second half of the eighteenth century such accumulated knowledge of distance and price was being systematically set forth within the public sphere. Texts presenting this information set themselves up as a more reliable authority to London streets than the coachman's often duplicitous claims to local knowledge. As one such guide declared, to 'expatiate on the Usefulness of a Book of Coach-Rates, would be to offer an Affront to the Reader's Understanding; the Impositions of Hackney-Coachmen having long been universally complained of.' Offering the reader (or rather user) 'Above Four Thousand FARES', *The Book of Coach-Rates* consisted of an alphabetical list of possible journeys, their length and cost, beginning with Albemarle Street and concluding with Whitehall.[61]

Far more sophisticated was *The London Companion* (1773), which presented 'upwards of Thirty thousand different Hackney Coach Fares' so the reader could calculate 'almost any Fare'.[62] It comprised a series of seventy-one tables, one for each London coach stand, listing the fares from that stand to 750 possible destinations. Illustration 4 presents the fares from Bloomsbury Square. Under each fare—1s., 1s. 6d. and so on—is a list of numbers, and in the first part of the book is an alphabetical list of destinations, each of which is given a number. So if one wanted to know how much it would cost to take a coach from Bloomsbury to Bethlem, all one had to do was to look up the Hospital in the alphabetical list [illustration 5] and discover that it was 48. By then checking the table for Bloomsbury Square and one would find that it was an 18d. fare.

[xi]

ALPHABETICAL LIST

of all the VILLAGES, SQUARES, STREETS, LANES, &c. to which the Fares are given from the different Coach-Stands, in and about London ; together with the Number annexed to each by which it is reprefented in the following Tables, in order fo. afcertaining the Fare.

A			
A Bchurch-Lane	1	Beak-Street	34
Addle-Street	2	Bèar-Street	35
Adelphi-Buildings	3	Beaufort-Buildings	36
Admiralty	4	Bedford-Row	37
Agoftone	5	Bedford-Street	38
Air-Street, *Piccadilly*	6	Bedford-Bury	39
Albemarle-Street	7	Beech-Lane	40
Aldermanbury	8	Bennet-Street	41
Alderfgate-Street	9	Bentinck-Street	42
Aldgate	10	Berkeley-Square	43
Amen-Corner	11	Berkeley-Street	44
Argyll-Buildings	12	Bermondfey Church	45
Arlington-Street	13	Bernard's-Inn	46
Arundel-Street	14	Berner-Street	47
Afylum	15	Bethlem Hofpital	48
Audley-Street, *North*	16	Bethnal-Green	49
Audley-Street, *South*	17	Billingfgate	50
Audley Chapel	18	Billiter-Square	51
Audley-Square	19	Birchin-Lane	52
Aylefbury-Street	20	Bifhopfgate	53
Ayliff-Street	21	Bifhopfgate-Street Within	54
B		Bifhopfgate-Street Without	55
Bagnigge Wells	22	Blackman-Street	56
Baldwin's-Gardens	23	Blackmoor-Street	57
Bank	24	Black-Friars-Bridge	58
Barbican	25	Black-Heath ; Green Man	59
Barnaby-Street	26	Blackwall	60
Bartholomew's Hofpital	27	Bloomfbury-Square	61
Bartlet's-Buildings	28	Blowbladder-Street	62
Bafing-Lane	29	Bolton-Street	63
Bafinghall-Street	30	Bolton-Row	64
Batterfea	31	Bond-Street, (Old)	65
Battle-Bridge	32	Bond Street, (New)	66
Bayfwater	33	— from Vigo-Lane to Conduit Street	67

4. *The London Companion* (1773), p.xi

Within such publications one witnesses a startling commodification of space. Whereas the nineteenth-century railway timetable rendered the journey between two locations temporally, in these tables distances are expressed in monetary terms. The coach stands of the capital thus mapped out new, commercially generated, topographies which supplemented the mental maps of street and landmark. The visitor or inhabitant oriented themselves with reference to price as well as place. London, one might say, was no longer just a fair city, it was a city of fares.

It is instructive to compare this process with other eighteenth-century

```
      From Bloomfbury-Square Stand.        [7

  ─── Shilling Fares. ───        ─ Eighteenpenny, continued. ─
 2│ 65│153│266│445│521│626     591│618│641│665│692│726│741
 4│ 66│156│269│446│525│642     599│622│652│666│711│727│745
 7│ 78│166│271│454│528│646     611│627│660│697│720│728│746
 8│ 81│168│274│456│544│649        ─── Two Shilling ───
12│ 82│169│284│457│557│667       5│172│311│360│441│587│676
13│ 85│184│290│459│559│677      10│183│312│371│452│588│685
16│ 96│186│321│469│562│681      21│185│313│380│475│596│691
20│100│189│322│470│569│684      26│187│318│381│495│607│694
25│105│192│328│471│570│706      33│207│332│386│505│614│696
27│110│199│331│472│571│707      45│214│338│389│522│623│697
29│118│202│346│477│572│708      55│246│339│393│537│624│709
32│119│219│351│478│573│712      71│277│340│401│541│625│715
34│122│227│353│479│574│713     101│279│341│405│548│672│723
40│126│229│363│487│575│714     109│289│343│407│550│673│724
41│127│232│392│489│576│719     112│293│357│423│564│674│725
42│134│238│394│499│577│721     115│309│358│435│580│675│750
43│135│242│400│500│585│729        ─── Half Crown ───
44│137│243│410│501│589│733      49│170│294│417│552│698│703
58│138│244│412│502│590│738      93│237│320│418│578│699│704
62│139│247│437│503│603│739      94│253│336│535│600│700│718
63│140│251│439│508│604│740     143│254│337│538│601│701
64│152│264│446│512│613│742     145│255│416│540│602│702
   ─── Eighteenpenny ───          ─── Three Shilling ───
 1│ 91│163│268│385│458│517      31│146│273│342│419│551│631
15│ 92│174│280│387│461│523     113│176│333│344│539│553│682
17│ 95│190│291│388│462│524     144│270│334│373│542│630│743
24│103│191│296│395│473│527       ── Three and Sixpenny ──
30│104│204│308│397│476│531         295│306│  │632│693
48│106│205│323│403│480│532         ─── Four Shilling ───
50│114│209│324│408│484│536      6│ 76│233│272│488│490│507
51│116│213│329│409│485│549       ── Four and Sixpenny ──
52│120│215│361│415│486│560            60│  │640
53│147│218│365│422│491│561         ─── Five Shilling ───
77│148│220│366│425│494│563       149│182│263│671│673
79│155│235│382│431│499│565
84│158│262│383│444│504│579
89│159│267│384│455│513│586
```

5. *The London Companion* (1773), p.7

developments in commerce and the control of space. A succession of fine studies has drawn attention to the ways in which measurement and mapping articulated unequal power relations and facilitated political control.[63] But, while these publications of the fare structure clearly provided a means of reducing coachmen's bargaining power, the process by which it came into being was, as we have seen, much more gradual and much less systematic than the ways in which the military,[64] or the excise constructed standardized statistical representations of space.[65] The closest parallel for this kind of pricing of distance would seem to be postal services.[66]

We should, furthermore, be cautious about presenting the regulation of hackney coaches as a 'modern' disciplinary formation, a form of eighteenth-century 'police'.[67] In fact, the rules laid out by the commissioners had many affinities with forms of civic regulation going back to the fifteenth century. In the City the conduct of the watermen and the fares which they could charge had, like the prices and behaviour, and numbers of porters and carters, long been subject to public regulation.[68] When in 1654 the aldermen drew up rules for coachmen at the Council of State's request, they used the City's long experience of drafting regulation for carmen.[69]

Nevertheless, the language of fares did restructure and commodify social relations on the streets of the capital. Everyone who hired a hackney coach was the driver's 'fare'. Thus in 1684 Thomas Cox, coachman, was reported to have 'took up a *Fare* at *White-Hall Gate*, which be [sic] drove into *Water-Lane* in *Fleet-street*.[70] The disquiet about the profound egalitarianism of such commercial terminology was intensified by the unruly reputation of the hackney coachmen. Daniel Defoe wrote that their overcharging and their 'saucy impudent Behaviour' had 'been the Occasion of innumerable Quarrels, Fighting, and Abuses'. Indeed, he noted, several had been killed by Gentlemen 'provoked by the villainous Tongues of those Fellows, beyond the Extent of their Patience.'[71]

To illustrate these traits and to demonstrate the extreme difficulty of getting them to go where they were commanded, Defoe described an incident in which a gentlemen coming out of a Fleet Street tavern one night called a hackney coach. One arrived, but the driver asked him where he was going before he had a chance to get inside the vehicle. The gentleman said he would say when he was inside—suspecting that the coachman would not agree to go to East Smithfield, his desired destination. At this the coachman declared that he would not take him and drove back to his stand. Thereupon a boy who worked in the pub promised to get the carriage for the gentleman. He walked up to it and got in, telling the driver to turn round. As they passed the tavern the boy instructed for him to pull up. Realizing that he had been tricked, the coachman drove on up Fleet Street despite the youth's repeated commands for him to stop. When he finally halted, he tried to drag the boy out of the vehicle. The lad eventually got out and reported the driver to a constable. Unfortunately, however, the offender had already substituted a false set of numbers and so the wrong coachman was hauled before the Commissioners.[72]

Defoe's account highlights how it was the ambiguous nature of the relationship between coachman and passenger rather than the extent of their social difference which was the main cause of conflict. Revealingly, his main concern in *The Great Law of Subordination Consider'd* was the insubordination and laziness of servants. The hackney coachman's obedience to his fare, should, Defoe argued, be as automatic as that of a servant in a well-run household. Every set of regulations for coachmen from the 1650s to the 1770s *required* them to go without question wherever their passenger desired within the Bills of Mortality. Thus for Defoe, among the coachman's infractions was his disobedience of the boy. Despite his youth, he was a fare and ought to have been obeyed.

Yet hackney coachmen were not servants. The holders of coach licenses were generally businesspeople who owned their own horses;[73] in the 1690s many accumulated several licenses despite the £50 entry fine that each required. In 1694–95 Francis Morgan owned at least seven.[74] The men they hired as coach drivers were much poorer, and some, like Robert Salisbury, committed to Bridewell in 1639, and described as having 'no h[ab]itacon nor service but useth to drive Hackney Coaches when he is hired', may have been economically marginal.[75] Yet such employment also required considerable experience in working with horses, which conveyed a certain status.[76] Moreover, drivers seem to have been paid according to their takings and thus had ample opportunity for increasing their earnings through their own initiative.[77] In fact, working as hackney coachmen offered a way for some servants to achieve independence. Among the licensed hackney coachmen in 1664, for instance, was a former coachman of the Earl of Norwich. In 1695 John Verney's coachman handed in his notice, 'not', Verney noted, 'to get a better place, but…to set up a hackney coach and drive it himself.' 'His wife is a proud woman', he continued, 'and he hath a little of it himself, and they think it below 'em to be a servant.'[78]

The Verneys' former coachman might no longer have been a servant, but he still had to take orders. It would not, furthermore, have been in his economic interest to obey some of these orders, for some journeys would not have been advantageous or profitable. As the gentleman that Defoe portrayed well knew, no coachman wanted to take a fare to East Smithfield where there was little demand for hackney coaches—only three of the 400 licensed coaches in 1664 were based there.[79] The potential for conflict when a coachman did not behave as was wished was, therefore, always present. Indeed to climb into a hackney coach was to surrender yourself to the control of another person. The coachmen quite literally held the reins in this relationship; in many ways the street belonged to them, not their more affluent fares. It was said that they made 'Signs with their Fingers as they drive by each other, to intimate how much they have got that Day', and 'can carry on that Language to give Intelligence where they are driving', allowing them to follow or to intercept each other.[80]

An increasing number of cultural historians and sociologists of science now stress how material culture structures social practice. Mimi Hellman, for instance, has shown how objects played an active role in constructing eighteenth-century salon civility. The delicate furniture and fragile china of the Parisian salon, she argues, inculcated patterns of behaviour because they had to be used in certain ways or they would be broken.[81]

The hackney coach similarly structured the spatial practices of the London street, for it functioned as a technology of convenience—permitting patterns of sociability and shopping, work and recreation over more extensive areas of the capital. But it was also a recalcitrant technology with decidedly contradictory effects. It was not just that hackney coaches, their horses and their drivers contributed appreciably to the disorder and the unruly contestation of the thoroughfares. More importantly, it was a form of transport over whose drivers the passenger had only limited control. Although eighteenth-century economic texts regularly naturalized the functioning of trade and the exchange of goods, through the physiological metaphor of circulation, it was never possible to circulate on the streets of London without encountering and negotiating the commercial, spatial and, above all, the bodily practices of people like the hackney coachmen who worked on them.

4. Public Spaces, Private Disputes?

Fights and Insults on London's Streets, 1660–1800

Robert B. Shoemaker

Eighteenth-century understandings of the distinction between 'public' and 'private' were different from the modern distinction between the home and outside the home. Eighteenth-century houses were frequently public spaces, in which a number of people unrelated, perhaps even unknown, to each other could be found; while outdoor spaces, such as narrow courts, alleys, and yards, often had the character of private streets, attracting few passers-by beyond the people who actually lived there. The eighteenth century conceived the public/private distinction in terms of what was sociable as opposed to what was solitary.[1] This intermingling of the 'public' and 'private' in outdoor spaces facilitated their use for the resolution of interpersonal disputes, but it could also enable the wider community to get involved, particularly since personal behaviour at the time was very much seen as a matter of public interest. Early-modern streets were places for expressing and consolidating communal solidarity—not only in official civic and royal processions, but also by neighbourhood policing of individual behaviour, by arresting suspected criminals, defaming those whose behaviour contravened social norms (most often by calling women accused of sexual immorality 'whores'), and supervising fights between men who called into question each other's honour.

During the eighteenth century, however, London's public life was transformed. Visually, houses were built according to the new regular and symmetrical 'Georgian' style, new streets and squares were laid out in rectilinear patterns, and street pavements were cleaned and rendered uniform. New arenas of sociability were established, notably coffee-houses, assembly rooms, and clubs, and more respectable standards of behaviour were expected of those who frequented all these places.[2] Culturally, the increasing availability of printed publications and the decline of press licensing facilitated the development of a 'public sphere' of rational discourse.[3] This chapter will argue that the creation of these 'spaces of modernity' was accompanied by a shift in Londoners' attitudes towards the use of public spaces for expressions of collective opinion, and particularly for the conduct of interpersonal disputes. By examining patterns of public insults and fights, we can assess the extent to which the changes to London's physical appearance and cultural life were matched by changes in Londoners' perceptions of the uses to which metropolitan outdoor spaces should be put.

Defamation

The streets were frequently used in the seventeenth and eighteenth centuries as places for the expression of collective sentiments. The inclusion of crowds of Londoners in celebrations of political anniversaries and military and naval victories was meant to convey the impression that these were expressions of *public* or *community* sentiment.[4] This demonstrates the powerful appeal of the image of a single, all-embracing community opinion in this society. This practice was, of course, not confined to official demonstrations, and there are numerous examples of crowds and individuals at the local level assuming the mantle of collective authority in order to validate their actions: not only in politics, but also when accusing, apprehending, and punishing accused criminals. Londoners were accustomed to responding to cries of 'stop thief!' or 'murder!' by joining in the pursuit of suspected criminals. The practice of shaming their immoral neighbours, particularly women who engaged in sex outside marriage, by publicly summoning the collective condemnation of the neighbourhood, is a similar kind of community policing. This is not to say, of course, that any of these sentiments *were* universal. Celebrations of anniversaries and victories were often used for oppositional political purposes and popular protests frequently expressed contentious views, for example during the weavers' protests of 1697 and 1719–21 or when defending or attacking brothels. The moral standards expressed by defamers were not necessarily universally held, certainly not in the neighbourhoods where prostitutes lived.[5] The streets were a contested terrain, which residents sought to control as a way of claiming overwhelming community support for their point of view.

Defamation was thus very much a public activity in early modern London. From her study of cases brought to the Consistory Court of London between 1560 and 1640, Laura Gowing concluded that 'defamations rarely happened inside private houses, at meals, or within private conversation, but were staged, often in the open, with an audience provided by the witnesses who, hearing a great noise in the street, left their work or houses to investigate or intervene.'[6] Any number of defamation cases in the early modern period could be used to illustrate its public character, demonstrating that insults were made in ways that sought to attract attention, inviting neighbours and passers-by to join in condemning the behaviour of the accused; that people listened and responded to insults, frequently crowding around the defamer and defamed; and that such insults damaged the reputation of the accused.

By the eighteenth century, however, many defamations were no longer conducted on the streets: in a sample of 124 defamation prosecutions at the Consistory Court of London between 1679 and 1792, 19 per cent of the insults took place inside houses; 18 per cent took place in taverns and shops; 33 per cent took place partly indoors and partly outdoors, with the participants standing in doorways or shouting through open windows or doors; 14.5 per cent occurred in yards, alleys, and courts; and only 15 per cent happened in major streets. Often, there was no attempt to publicise the dispute. Insults and accusations that arose in discussions, wherever they took place, were not always attempts to expose the culprit publicly as immoral and destroy her reputation. In 61 per cent of defamation cases the audience which heard the insult was described as no more than the usual two to four witnesses who testified in court. This is not surprising when so many cases took place indoors, even though many households were populated with servants, lodgers, and visitors. Of those that took place inside houses, 96 per cent listed no general audience beyond the specified witnesses. The fact that defamers were twice as likely to be reported expressing passion and anger in incidents taking place inside private houses as outdoors (37.5 per cent, compared to 17 per cent of insults taking place outdoors), suggests that defamers felt less inhibited by what observers might think of their behaviour when they were indoors, presumably because there were fewer witnesses, and they were known to the defamer.

But as noted earlier, some houses, particularly lodging houses, had the character of public places. A 1681 exchange of insults took place entirely in a bedroom, but those present consisted of a married couple and five other unrelated people, including a servant; a lodger; Mrs Hill, who ran the lodging house; and a neighbour, Alice Welthorp. Welthorp testified that 'hearing a noise at one Mrs Hill's...[she] went into the said Mrs Hill's to see what the matter was'—she appears to have been able to enter the house at will.[7] In some of these cases where the insult occurred indoors, the defamer clearly attempted to spread the insult beyond the household, recruiting public support to shame the victim. In 1715, Charles Blew, a bailiff, and a married couple went to the house of Anne and Peter Anderson and argued over a debt. In the kitchen, with a servant and three others present, Charles told Anne 'you are a nasty common whore and a bawdy house whore'. He then repeated the insult in the doorway on the way out, knocking on the door to draw the attention of what soon became an 'abundance of people about the said door who were strangers'.[8] Thus what was already a semi-public dispute was further publicised.

Many insults took place while women and men were standing in their respective houses or shop doorways, relaxing or working. Laura Gowing argues that, from doorsteps, 'women reinforced their position in the house-holds from which stemmed their standing in the community.'[9] In 1701 Elizabeth Butcher and Edward Collins were at their doors in Vinegar Yard, off Drury Lane [illustration 6], when Edward said, 'I wonder you have the impudence to stand at the door.' Asked to explain why, he continued 'because you had a child before you was married'—the clear implication of this comment was that only respectable members of the community were allowed to affirm their social standing publicly by displaying themselves in their doorways.[10] As this example suggests, it was not only women who stood in doorways: 24 per cent of the defamers in doorways were men, and 56 per cent of the audiences for doorway insults were mixed sex.

But in many cases it is unclear whether eighteenth-century insults were intended to have a public audience or not. In the narrow yards, courts, and lanes of preindustrial London, conversations were easily overheard, not necessarily by design. In 1791, James Bealby quarrelled with Mary

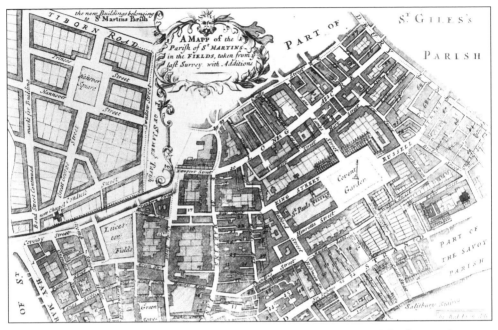

6. 'A Mapp of the Parish of St Martins in the Fields' (detail), from John Strype, *A Survey of the Cities of London and Westminster* (6th edn, 1754). Vinegar Yard is number 66, located just off Drury Lane on the top right of the map

Barke in a yard off a lodging house in Drury Lane, calling her a 'bunter' [whore]. Although he repeated the words 'in a voice loud enough to be heard by any person at a distance', the witnesses stated that no one else was present beyond three women in the house. Two of these heard but did not see Bealby make the insult, and the third was told by Barke as she was coming down the stairs 'mind, he calls me bunter'. (Note that in this case the *victim* sought to publicise the insult in order to ensure an adequate number of witnesses to the case could be presented.) Despite the limited audience, a witness testified that she had subsequently heard the defamatory words 'spoken of in the neighbourhood.' By raising his voice, Bealby may have intended to attract such attention, but he may also just have been angry.[11] In another case, the defamer's intentions were clear: witnesses testified that a woman spoke 'in a public manner with a loud voice' outside a shop, which had the desired effect of raising 'a great mob or tumult of people passing and repassing along the street, who stopped on account of the noise made'; and in another, the defamer followed her victim out of a shop, clapped her hands, called her whore, and 'bid her go home and louse her family'.[12] The implication of these examples is that in other incidents, where no mention was made of speaking in a loud voice, or in a public manner, or of clapping, insults were made without the intention of attracting public attention.

Insults that took place outside achieved varying degrees of publicity. In assessing the significance of these incidents, it is clearly important to distinguish between the various types of outdoor spaces that existed in eighteenth-century London. Clearly the small-scale, often dead-end, yards, courts, lanes and alleys of the metropolis were used and viewed differently from the open streets, with the latter seen as more 'public' spaces, governed by different expectations of conduct.[13] A map of part of the parish of St Martin's in the Fields drawn around 1700 illustrates [illustration 6]—and possibly exaggerates, but that in itself would be significant—the contrast between the wide main thoroughfares of London's main streets and the numerous narrow passages where many people lived and worked.[14] In an account of the celebrations of Admiral Vernon's birthday in 1741, the *Daily Post* noted that it was 'remarkable that at night not only the high streets, but the private ones, nay even the courts and alleys, were illuminated.'[15] As this comment suggests, major expressions of public sentiment, including processions and riots, typically took place on what might be labelled 'public' streets and squares, in contrast to more 'private' spaces. The difference between patterns of social relations in alleys and streets in London is also evident in John Gay's *Trivia*, where the narrator leaves 'the noisie roads' to enter an 'uncrouded' alley:

> Here I remark each Walker's diff'rent face,
> And in their Look their various Bus'ness trace.

The pedestrian can identify not only the trades of the people he encounters but also their emotions, whether it is the 'jealousies and cares' of the broker, or the dissimulation of a 'lavish rake' attempting to avoid his creditors.[16]

As we have seen only 15 per cent of defamation cases were identified as occurring in places labelled as streets, which suggests that such places may have been deemed too 'public' for the kinds of discussions which gave rise to insults; when those standing in their doorways are counted, yards, alleys, courts and lanes were far more common sights of insults. Eleanor Bond was so sure that Joan Latchfield was a whore that she said 'I have proved her a whore and will call her whore wherever I meet her, though it be in Cheapside'—the implication was that to make such an insult on London's biggest thoroughfare would be unusual.[17] The witnesses in another case made a special point of noting that the defamer had spoken 'in a public open manner' and 'in the open street', suggesting that such behaviour in that location was uncommon.[18]

Main thoroughfares had both advantages and disadvantages to defamers seeking to publicise their accusations. On the one hand, they attracted big audiences: 74 per cent of the insults recorded as taking place in streets attracted the attention of 'several' or 'other' people beyond the witnesses who testified in court, compared to only 37 per cent of all the other defamation cases which took place outdoors. On the other hand, the fact that a quarter of street insults apparently failed to attract a wider audience suggests that, as is apparent in novels such as Daniel Defoe's *Moll Flanders* (1722), it was possible to achieve a degree of anonymity or privacy on the street.[19] Moreover, the audiences found on the street were less likely to be local residents and people known to the parties, and possibly were therefore less interested in the dispute, and their opinions may have been deemed less important. Whereas the audiences for insults which took place around doorways and in courts were described as 'neighbours' and 'crowds', those in streets were more often labelled as 'others', as in the phrase 'in the presence of the respondent [witness] and many other persons whose names he does not know'.[20] There is some evidence that defamation disputes on the streets tended to attract a selected audience, a subset of the numerous people passing by: only 44 per cent of the audiences for insults on streets were mixed sex, compared to 65 per cent in all other cases. Only a proportion of passers-by got involved in defamation disputes on the streets and these groups were most often single-sex, though there are equal numbers of all-male and all-female audiences. The fact that eighteenth-century defamers tended to choose spaces where fewer, but more familiar people would be present suggests that they did not seek an entirely 'public' audience.

Fights

Fights that led to a death and an accusation of murder provide the evidence for this section, since these are the best documented.[21] In an age when medical care was poor and violent altercations were common, there are reasons to believe such fights were more representative of everyday violence than they would be today—it was just unlucky that one of the the protagonists died from the wounds received. These assaults, brawls, and duels were, needless to say, very different types of disputes from the defamation cases that were prosecuted at the London Consistory Court. Whereas very little physical violence was used in defamation cases, and they mostly involved quarrels between women (though men account for 39 per cent of the defamers), the vast majority of the fights leading to murders involved only men. Whereas defamation cases prosecuted in the church courts all directly concerned sexual behaviour (although there were often ulterior motives behind the prosecution), fights were prompted by accusations of many different forms of dishonesty. There are also important differences in the way the protagonists used London's private and public spaces.

Many people, particularly men, who committed violence and sought publicity for their actions, used violence as a means of publicly affirming their social and gender identity. The street violence committed by young gentlemen and noblemen in the early eighteenth century, for instance, constituted aggressive public attempts to assert their superiority over the watch, as a symbol of civic government; over the middling sort and the poor; and over women.[22] While the majority of fights (56 per cent of the 210 fights sampled) took place out of doors, in streets and yards, alleys, courts, fields and on the River Thames, there was a big gender difference: disputes involving men were almost twice as likely to take place outdoors as those involving women (83 per cent *vs* 42 per cent).

As Rowlandson's 'Miseries of London' suggests, there were many people who enjoyed a good fight. When fights took place outside, crowds sometimes gathered, placed bets, ensured that fair play was maintained, and encouraged the combatants to continue the fight [illustration 7; atypically, in this print the combatants are women]. Spectators did not actively take sides; they just ensured fair play and enjoyed the spectacle as a form of public entertainment. In 1761, William Smith and William Alsop argued while playing a game involving throwing at oranges. After they exchanged

blows Alsop walked away, but Smith and 'the mob' brought Alsop back
to the field, where the crowd formed a ring and encouraged the two to
fight. As one witness reported, 'they were overpersuaded by their seconds
to fight longer than they would have done, having both of them [had]
enough'. After half an hour's fighting, Smith scored a direct hit and Alsop
fell down and died.[23]

Understandably, however, many disputants sought to avoid such attention. Although many fights started in alehouses and coffee-houses and
continued outside on the street, moving outside was not always a deliberate attempt to publicise the dispute—often it was the reverse. In 1694
Foulke Salisbury and a Mr Cusack drank together all afternoon, first at
Salisbury's lodgings, then in an alehouse. After a disagreement the two,
apparently seeking to resolve the dispute in private, went downstairs, left
the alehouse, and went into Grays Inn Lane. However, to Cusack's frus-
tration, Salisbury's brother Robert followed them. Despite Robert's
unwanted presence, the dispute unfolded: insults were exchanged, swords
drawn, and Salisbury was murdered.[24] Sometimes the parties went
outdoors because the alehouse or coffee-house keeper, seeking to maintain order in his house and protect his premises and customers, ordered
the parties to leave. In other cases, there was no room to fight inside, or
the feuding parties settled their dispute inside, but then the dispute erupted
anew on the way home. In 1721, James Biss and Thomas Crofts 'fell out
at a tavern about a wig, and would have fought, but the witnesses prevented
them'. They then moved to a coffee-house, fought, and were parted. Later
they met again in a mews, where Biss stabbed Crofts and killed him.[25]
There are numerous examples of fights in this period which were broken
up by friends, passers-by, constables and night watchmen. This is why
men who were determined to fight often *avoided* publicity, arranging to fight
in out of the way places, whether indoors or in secluded sites outdoors.

This applies particularly to duels, which despite the fact they took place
in order to assert and defend the publicly recognised 'honour' of the
combatants, paradoxically typically took place in private—though the
participants could expect that news of the duel and its outcome would be
publicised by word of mouth, and, in the case of elite duellists, even in
the newspapers. Thus, duels frequently took place in the private rooms of
alehouses and coffee-houses. In 1718, two men fell out in the City while

MISERIES OF LONDON.

Being a compulsory spectator and auditor of a brawling and scratching match, between two drunken Drabs in consequence of the sudden influx of company by whom you are hemmed in an hundred yards deep in every direction, leaving you no chance of escape till the difference of sentiment between the ladies is adjusted. where you stand you are (that is Invas) closely bounded in front by a barrow of cats meat, the unutterable contents of which employ your eyes and nose, while your ear is no less fully engaged by the Tartarean yell of its driver.

7. 'Miseries of London' by Thomas Rowlandson (1807)

arguing over whether one, William Bowen, 'was the honestest or as honest a man as any man in England'. Unsurprisingly, this led quickly to the other intimating that Bowen was not honest (it was said he had the reputation of a whore and a child, and had drunk the Jacobite Duke of Ormond's health), leading to a challenge. They went to the Swan Tavern, but could not find a 'convenient room' (they rejected a room where others were present), and then went to the Popes Head Tavern, obtained a room, barricaded the door with chairs, and engaged with their swords.[26] But perhaps owing to disapproval from innkeepers (as well as the increased use of pistols), duels were far more likely to take place outdoors, in fields and parks, early in the morning when there were unlikely to be spectators: frequently in Hyde Park, but also 'in the fields between Tottenham Court and Marybone', in Paddington Fields, or 'behind Bedford House'.[27] In 1731, for example, two young gentlemen exchanged 'high words' in a

8. 'The Coffee-house Mob',
Edward Ward, *The Fourth Part of Vulgus Britannicus: or the British Hudibras* (1710), frontispiece. From J. A. Sharpe, *Crime and the Law in English Satirical Prints, 1600–1832* (Cambridge, 1986)

coffee-house near St James, and called a coach which took them to Hyde Park. Unfortunately from their point of view, they were observed, and some others, 'suspecting ill consequences', followed them, and prevented the duel from taking place.[28] In 1771, a dispute occurred between two gentlemen in Kensington Gardens, described as 'a public garden', which led to a challenge being issued, upon which the parties 'retired to a more convenient part of the garden, where in less than five minutes the affair was decided.'[29]

Similarly, altercations which took place in coffee-houses were not necessarily intended to have a public audience, despite the fact that such houses were sometimes conceived of as 'a tool for the construction of a "polite public"'.[30] In an anonymous 1710 depiction of coffee-house life [illustration 8] an argument has erupted in the foreground, leading one participant to throw his cup of coffee in another's face, but those sitting at the other end of the table, and at a table in the background, carry on their discussions and smoking, either oblivious to the dispute or studiously avoiding it. When Joseph Brice and Captain Richard Jasper argued when playing a game in Munday's Coffee Room in 1761, the two 'went to a further part of the room and discoursed', before leaving the room to fight a duel in the private room of a tavern—the two clearly did not want, and were able to prevent, anyone else from becoming involved.[31] Whether the fight ultimately took place indoors or outdoors, combatants found many places where they could conduct their disputes with a degree of privacy.

Was there a 'privatisation' of conflict in the eighteenth century? Throughout this period, even when their disputes took place in 'public' spaces, we have seen that disputants often avoided publicity, or sought to limit their audience. Nonetheless, in a number of cases the participants actively sought attention from passers-by, by speaking loudly, clapping their hands, locating their disputes in a crowded space, or agreeing to fight in front of an audience. There are plenty of reasons why these practices might have waned in the eighteenth century. Not only was the physical environment of London's streets transformed, but early modern notions of community became unsustainable in a rapidly growing metropolis with more than half a million inhabitants. In a society subject to high levels of geographical mobility and fragmentation by religious and political beliefs, as well as emerging class identities, individuals began to ignore public responsibilities and pay less attention to street life. Elites, for example, spent more of their leisure time in spaces with restricted admission, such as assembly rooms, theatres, clubs, and coffee-houses.[32] Concurrently, Londoners played a decreasing role in enforcing the law in this period. They participated in fewer informal shaming punishments, began to rely on 'thief-takers' to apprehend criminals, and they were more likely to hire deputies to act as constables and night watchmen in lieu of serving by rotation.[33]

Many disputes already took place in front of small audiences, and inside houses, at the start of this period. Nonetheless, there is evidence that an increasing number of disputes took place behind closed doors over the course of the eighteenth century. At the London Consistory Court there was a decline in the proportion of defamations prosecuted which took place outdoors, leading to an increase in the proportion of cases taking place inside private houses from 15 per cent in 1679–90 to 25 per cent in 1776–92. More importantly, there was a dramatic decline in the total number of cases prosecuted, which suggests that the defamatory insult itself became less common, or at least it ceased to have the kind of public impact which it had had a century earlier.[34] Similarly, there was a significant decline in the number of fatal fights which took place outdoors, leading to an increase in the proportion of such cases in the sample taking place indoors from 38 per cent in the late seventeenth century to 54 per cent between 1750 and 1781, while those which took place in the open street declined from 34 per cent to 18 per cent. This decline was most marked in cases of deferred violence such as duels, where the number of cases taking place in alehouses and coffee-houses, or in fields, heaths and commons outside the metropolis increased dramatically. It was not only élite behaviour that was changing: in *c.* 1780, the Prussian visitor Archenholz observed that the 'custom' of settling differences by 'boxing match' in which the 'spectators, far from opposing [the fighters], encourage the idea' was not 'so much in fashion as formerly.'[35]

In part, this decline in the use of public spaces for fights was the result of a growing intolerance of violence, and the reduced role played by violence and considerations of honour in dominant conceptions of masculinity,[36] but it was also part of a much broader cultural change, since the decline of public disputation is also evident in patterns of public insult, in which women played a major role. An important transformation took place in the relationship between the individual and the community, in which publicly established reputation and honour became less important in shaping individual identity, and reputations were increasingly shaped by other factors (class, voluntary societies, print, individual consciences). In the second half of the eighteenth century witnesses in defamation cases frequently stated that they were unsure whether the victim's reputation had actually been harmed by the insulting words.[37]

As a consequence of these and other changes, the individual's responsibilities on the streets, and more generally street life came to be viewed differently during the eighteenth century. The streets (but probably not the smaller yards, alleys, courts and lanes) came to be seen as unsuitable for the resolution of private differences, and also as spaces where individuals in their day-to-day lives were not expected to get involved in disputes. People began to abandon their sense of responsibility for policing public spaces. They became less likely to intervene when they witnessed a crime, and they were less likely to rush to investigate when they heard insults voiced on the streets. In defamation cases witnesses started to use the term 'public street' to make the point that the insult had taken place in an inappropriate location. This term was not used in the depositions for the thirty-three late seventeenth-century cases in the sample. It first occurred in the sample in 1715, but not again until the 1770s and 1780s. In 1771, for example, Elizabeth Batchelor reported that she had heard Martha Mictie defame Catherine Shephard many times, but 'particularly the deponent hath heard the said Martha Mictie in the public street several times say and declare that the said Catherine Shephard was a whore and an old bawd'.[38]

Miles Ogborn characterises this new approach to the street by describing it as a public space inhabited by 'privatised individuals'.[39] Such people required more personal space on the streets, and this was reflected in new standards of civility which regulated personal interactions. These new expectations are reflected in the changing language of complaints recorded on Middlesex recognizances for assault, which from mid-century increasingly noted that the victims had been kicked, pulled, pushed, seized hold of, and knocked down. Expectations of the spatial respect required by pedestrians expanded to the point where being pushed and shoved was so intolerable that it was worth complaining to a justice of the peace. Thus, in the 1760s, *but not before*, a number of defendants were bound over for, for example, violently pushing a man about and treading on his toes, 'shoving and pushing' a woman about and 'ill treating her', and seizing hold of a man by the collar and 'ill treating him'.[40] This sensitivity was particularly focused on that locus of individuality, the face. A number of recognizances from the 1760s complained of men and women who spat at, or thrust their fingers, hands, or fists in front of other people's faces.[41]

These new expectations of street behaviour led to a less tolerant view of people gathered together into crowds. As Ogborn suggests, Londoners developed ways of maintaining their individuality, 'of being out in the moving, rushing crowd but not being part of it.' More than before, the 'mob' came to seen as disorderly, fickle, and unrepresentative of the public at large. Its protests were seen as increasingly uncivilised and anarchic. In September 1761, when Queen Charlotte was expected to arrive in London, the *London Evening Post* worried about the disorder and lawlessness of the planned bonfires in the streets, since, the paper asked, 'who can restrain a mob?'[43] Ten years later, when celebrations and illuminations were held on the occasion of the King's birthday, the *General Evening Post* observed that 'the people, at least the *canaille*, filled every avenue, and rendered passing the streets very disagreeable.'[44] Even before the Gordon riots, the violence of which in 1780 'ruptured the partnership between the crowd and the [political] radicals', the press had called the legitimacy of mob protest into question, even on occasions, such as anniversaries, when crowds had traditionally been called upon to join the celebrations.[45]

London's diverse outdoor spaces were used in a variety of ways for conducting disputes. Sometimes antagonists invoked community support for activities as diverse as popular protests, shaming and staged fights, they did not always seek publicity. Over the course of the eighteenth century, new expectations governing conduct in public spaces meant that London's main streets were far less likely to be the setting for private disputes than they had been at the Restoration: both insults and fights were more likely to take place indoors, in narrow courts and alleys, or in fields out of sight of passers-by. Such disputes were now hidden from public view—and, largely, from the view of the modern historian. This transformation was part a broader change in the relationship between the individual and the community, and it led to increasing suspicion of crowd protests, and concern about the way the streets were used for demonstrations of allegedly 'public' sentiments. The reformed fabric of London's streets and buildings had a counterpart in the character of street life: both private disputes and public demonstrations became unacceptable in London's new 'public streets'.

5. 'You bitches...die and be damned'

Gender, Authority and the Mob in
St Martin's Roundhouse Disaster of 1742
Tim Hitchcock

Sarah Bland, Elizabeth Surridge, Mary Wood, Jane Goosberry, Betty Eaton, Mary Onion, Elizabeth Desborough, Sarah Starkes, Mary Innings, Elizabeth Amey, Ann Norton, Mary Cosier, Ann Branch, Elizabeth Beaumont, Mary Maurice, Phyllis Wells, Mary Hammond;[1] these women were arrested on the evening of 15 July 1742 in the parishes of St Paul Covent Garden and St Martin in the Fields. It was a hot Thursday night[2] and Booker Holden, a 'midnight reformer'[3] and the High Constable of Westminster had decided to clear these most disorderly of London's parishes of their population of streetwalkers and beggars. On the authority of a general warrant issued under the signature of Thomas De Veil, and with the aid of an army of constables, beadles and watchmen, Holden swept through the streets in the hours after the watch was set at 11p.m., entering homes and shops and bagnios, picking up both pre-selected individuals, and anyone who had the misfortune to be wandering in the wrong clothes or in the wrong place.

Phyllis Wells had just arrived in London that morning by coach from Deptford, and had spent the day at Kensington.[4] She was on her way to her brother-in-law's house in Heathcock Court with some coltsfoot[5] when she was picked up by Booker Holden himself. She was dressed modestly in a light brown Camlet dress, and Thomas Morris, the watchman who accompanied Holden,[6] tried to convince him that she was 'an honest girl'. But Holden would have none of it, and sent her in the custody of a constable to the roundhouse belonging to St Martin in the Fields.

The roundhouse was sited on St Martin's Lane just south of Duke's Court and opposite the parish church.[7] It was made up of three floors,

9. The holding cell of the contemporary Watch House belonging to the parish of St Marylebone

and a set of stocks capped by an ornate wooden carving depicting one man flogging another, stood in the street outside.[8] The lower ground floor contained two cells, one each for men and women. The women's cell, or hole, was six feet two inches wide, by six feet six inches long. There was a low bench set along three walls, and a privy emptying into an open sewer in one corner. A small barred and shuttered window opened onto the street, and a heavy door, with a cast iron bolt, gave access to a hallway, and stairs to the floor above.[9] [illustration 9]

When Phyllis arrived at the roundhouse she was conducted into the drinking room which occupied the whole of the floor above the cells and acted as a general reception room and office. It was a little after eleven o'clock at night, and a steady stream of watchmen, constables and their prisoners was making its way to the house. Phyllis Well's name was entered in the watchbook by William Bird, the watch-house keeper, while Joseph Akins, the constable of the night, sat beside him at a long table. She was allowed to sit up a few hours, before being forced down into the holding cell below. [illustration 10]

Sarah Bland was 26 years old and had been working St Martin's Lane as a prostitute, when she and her cousin Mary Maurice were brought in at 11:15. Initially they joined the crowd in the drinking room as their names and offences were written down in the watchbook. Mary was of middling height and rather stout, and was dressed in red shoes, a black petticoat and a white gown—clothes which marked her out as a prostitute in the eyes of the authorities.[10] Together, Mary and Sarah formed one of the ubiquitous groups women who plied their trade on the streets around Covent Garden.[11] Sarah was ordered down to the hole almost immediately and Mary Maurice asked to go with her. Here, they joined twelve others, including Ann Branch, a small, crooked woman wearing a red cloak, already confined below. A few minutes later Mary Cosier, who had been picked up in a cook shop, was brought in and taken down to the cells, while in the room above Phyllis Wells, Elizabeth Surridge, Ann Norton, Mary Wood, Elizabeth Amey and Elizabeth Beaumont were allowed to sit up drinking wine.

If you 'behaved civilly',[12] if you looked a bit better dressed than average, if you were old, if you were on the correct side of an ill-defined divide between the respectable and the intolerable, an evening spent in the roundhouse could be a minor irritation. Ann Norton paid six pence to William Bird's wife, Eleanor, for a quartern of Usquebaugh and a chance to remain upstairs for a few hours.[13] While Elizabeth Beaumont, who at 58 was the oldest of the prisoners, probably paid for a bed for the

10. A woman being examined at the Watch House belonging to the parish of Covent Garden

night, and avoided the hole altogether.[14] She was a poor widow, but had been a respectable householder in St Martin prior to the death of her husband Thomas, a staymaker in Burleigh Court.[15] Several Watchmen knew her history, and she was given a range of privileges that night at their behest.[16]

If you were male the overwhelming likelihood was that you would be allowed to sit up stairs chatting to the watchmen, beadles and constable. If you were female, however, you were likely to be treated rather differently, and to be put directly into the hole.

The women picked up that night formed a cross section of the plebeian female population of Westminster. They were servants, a washerwoman and a chairwoman; but most commonly they were beggars and prostitutes. Collectively they were practitioners of that tenuous economy of makeshift lived by the plebeian population of the capital. These were the same women who would later leave their children to the tender mercies of the Foundling Hospital just then under construction a few hundred yards to the east of the roundhouse, or who would enter the Magdalen Hospital for penitent prostitutes.[17] They were the gin drinkers of Hogarthian satire, and the objects of scorn chased and punished by the Societies for the Reformation of Manners.

Subsequent accounts of the events of that evening would stress the women's honesty and misfortune, but for the men who policed the streets, and ran the roundhouse—who arrested, confined and swore at these women—they were the simple embodiment of a powerful disorder, a disorder with a distinctly female complexion which could be controlled only by the violent imposition of male authority, and which was increasingly defined as 'respectability'.[18]

At the roundhouse that night the scene in the drinking room, the all-purpose space which occupied the first floor of the building, was busy and almost convivial. Watchmen would stop and purchase a glass of beer or wine from Eleanor, and several of the women and all of the small number of men taken up, sat around the edges of the room chatting among themselves. But, while on this night the drinking room was lively and sociable, the conditions below stairs in the hole were rapidly becoming intolerable.

By one in the morning, with almost twenty people in the enclosed space, the heat was intense, and the drunken camaraderie which had earlier greeted the women as they came into the cell was transformed into desperation. Stripped down to their shifts or completely naked, they began to struggle for breath, while their clothes became soaked in sweat. Mary Cosier later testified that her handkerchief was as stiff as buckram with perspiration.[19]

At two in the morning Elizabeth Amey and Phyllis Wells joined the women already in the hole. By this time several of the women were in fits and were yelling out for relief. They swore and damned William Bird to hell and began to cry 'Murder' and 'Fire'. They beat on the low ceiling of the cell with their shoes trying to attract attention and cried out that one of them was in labour and needed relief.[20] But mainly they cried out for water: 'For Christ's sake let us have some water'; 'for the Lord's sake a little water'.[21] Many of them had been drinking heavily over the course of the previous evening and as the effects of alcohol wore off and as the heat of the crowded room increased, their thirst rose to a new and insistent pitch.

Between four and five in the morning the final three women to be confined in the hole were forced down the stairs by Robert Bushel, one of the beadles of the parish. He was himself profoundly drunk by this time and quickly returned to the drinking room to report his inability to put any more women in the cell. At which William Bird himself went down and physically forced these last three women into the hole.

As this final triad of prisoners were shoved and jostled the women set up a desperate cry for relief. Along with their curses, they offered what money they had in exchange for water and air and asked that the door to the hole be left open so that a few of them could sit on the stairs. Elizabeth Amey knocked William Bird's candle out of his hand in an attempt to push past him, and Bird, in response, said 'you bitches…die and be damned' before closing the heavy door on the cell.[22]

By this time in the morning, just before sunrise, Booker Holden had long since gone to his bed and the constable of the night and the 43 watch-men and six Beadles employed by the parish were keen to follow.[23] But before they could they needed to secure the prisoners. William Bird's son, eight-year-old Tom, was sent out to close the shutters on the barred windows of the cells and found that the cries and supplications of the women confined below had begun to attract attention on the street. One elderly woman tried to pass a quartern pot of gin through the bars; while Mary Saint heard Phyllis Wells plead, 'For God's sake give me a little water', before William Bird came out of the house and pushed her and the woman with the gin away. He closed and padlocked the shutter on the cell's only window and went back into the house.[24]

Deaf to the cries the women made, at least fifty men, who between them, had rounded up these waifs and strays of St Martin and St Paul, trooped back to the watchhouse, climbing the stairs beside the window to the cells below, and signed off for the night, before going home to their beds. Having closed the windows and shut the doors; having put Elizabeth Beaumont to bed in the spare room; William Bird lay down, still in his waistcoat, on his own bed for a few hours sleep before one of the beadles was due back to present the prisoners to Thomas DeVeil, one of the JPs who had issued the general warrant.

Outside a small crowd continued to gather. One woman tried to use a long stemmed tobacco pipe pushed through the slots in the shutter to pour beer into the parched mouths of the women inside.[25] In the cell Mary Maurice was beginning to feel light-headed. She said to Sarah Bland

'Let me die, let me die, for God's sake,' before laying her head on her cousin's lap and gradually slipping off the bench and onto the floor where her body was discovered the following morning.[26]

Phyllis Wells told a fellow prisoner of her fear of her brother-in-law's reaction when he found her; and as she grew faint, complained that if she 'could get a drop of water…[she] would be better'.[27] Sometime between 5 in the morning and 10 the following day, she slipped from her place on the bench and fell to the floor where she later died.[28] By seven in the morning, Mary Cosier was struggling to keep Ann Branch's crooked frame upright on the bench next to her. When Mary could no longer hold her, Ann fell to the floor where she too died.

The general warrant issued by Thomas DeVeil and Joseph Bromfield the previous day had specified that everyone taken up on its authority should be presented at DeVeil's Bow Street house by eight the following morning. In the event no one came to St Martin's Lane until past ten o'clock. When the cell door was opened the stench was nauseating and three people lay dead or dying.[29] Of the 21 women who emerged 13 of them were marched off to Bow Street, while the rest collapsed on the floor in the drinking room or on the ground outside the roundhouse. A surgeon was called and these eight women were bled, one of them (whose identity was never discovered) died on the ground outside the roundhouse. At the end of a long night of 'reformation' four women were dead, 13 were on their way to being examined by Thomas DeVeil and a further seven were allowed to simply slip back onto the streets of London.

At one level, the events of that night were a simple tragedy. But, at the same time the treatment meted out to these women reflects the growing clarity with which the authorities viewed the highly gendered boundary between order and disorder, the respectable and the intolerable. And draws our attention to the very real conflicts and tensions which characterise the evolution of policing and local government in this period. This was a tragedy made possible by the policies and circumstances of the people who formulated and implemented local government decisions. In this instance, the circumstances of the keeper of the watchhouse, William Bird, who was eventually convicted of the women's murder, and the policies of Thomas De Veil who had issued the general warrant that led to their arrest, created a series of pre-conditions which allowed these women to die.

11. St Marylebone Watch House, Rowlandson and Pugin (1809)

The person most self-evidently responsible was William Bird, the watchhouse keeper. He was one of the growing body of professional clerks who serviced the commercial and bureaucratic sectors of the London economy. By 1742 he had been married to Eleanor for eighteen years. They had seven children, three of whom were still alive.[30] He was appointed to the posts of parochial rate collector and watchhouse keeper in July 1739 and in the process placed himself squarely in the middle of a bureaucratic nightmare.

The parochial government of Westminster was undergoing a revolution in the middle decades of the century. As a result of the Watch Act passed in 1736, the select vestry of St Martin took over control of the nightly watch, and along with the vestries of the other Westminster parishes, began to supersede the Court of Burgesses as the lead institutions in the ordering of the streets.[31] The vestry was given direct management of the watch and the beadles at the expense of the traditional forum for the administration of Westminster, the Court of Burgesses. [illustrations 11 and 12] And while constables continued to be appointed by the Court, the effective organisation of this nascent police force of St Martin fell into the hands of the merchants who monopolised the vestry.[32]

12. A Beadle belonging to the parish of St Martin in the Fields

In any revolution there are conflicts. As early as June 1736, just a few weeks after the Watch Act came into force, a group of watchmen went on strike and were immediately discharged,[33] while the watchhouse keeper quickly found himself at odds with both the select vestry and with the constables still appointed by the Court of Burgesses. He resigned in 1739 and William Bird, now aged 35 and with three children to support replaced him.[34]

The implementation of the Watch Act had re-ignited an ongoing dispute between the populace and the select vestry and precipitated an angry rate revolt. As a result, in less than a year of his appointment Bird's accounts were examined by the vestry and he was discharged, owing the parish £15—a sum he could ill-afford. Knowing that he would be imprisoned for this debt, Bird disappeared in March 1739/40 and the vestry promptly demanded that his wife Eleanor deliver up the keys to the watchhouse to John Tilton, the principal watchman. Eleanor Bird, 33-years old with three children to care for,[35] simply said no, and by August both she and Bird were back in the watchhouse, refusing to either pay the £15 or to leave the building. For the next two years, until the morning of 17 July 1742, the Birds hung on to the one thing they had left—William Bird's position as watchhouse keeper. He wasn't paid but it is clear that William Bird continued to do the work, and while he was not 'properly a constable', he was 'deemed the officer' responsible for the roundhouse by other parish employees.[36]

By the evening of the 15 July 1742 William Bird and his wife had established their right to continue running the roundhouse and could look forward to a long night during which they might recoup some of their financial losses. But, they were nevertheless in a remarkably tenuous position.

The other principal actor in this tragedy was Thomas DeVeil. He had come to prominence in the years after 1729 as one of the few justices willing to implement the ill-conceived Gin Acts of 1729 and 1736.[37] More than this, he took a particular interest in the suppression of political dissent and from 1734 received a £250 government pension from the Secret Service Fund for his activities against Jacobites and anti-government sedition.[38] He was also one of the most important participants in the recreation of local government brought about by the passage of the Watch Acts of 1735 and 1736. It was Thomas DeVeil, sitting above the select vestries, checking on their proceedings and signing off the annual accounts, along with the five or six other active Justices who had survived the government enquiries into the Middlesex Bench of the mid-1730s,[39] who both directed and profited from this newly powerful system of local government.

Robert Bushel arrived at Bow Street with at least thirteen prisoners a little after ten on the morning of the 16th. He had marched his prisoners through the streets south of Covent Garden and Thomas DeVeil immediately set about examining them. The process took several hours and it was not until the afternoon that he discovered the seriousness of the situation. John Maurice was one of the last people to be examined and it was only his statement which contained the vital information that several people had died the previous night.[40]

Realising the likely reaction of the mob, the first thing DeVeil did was to dismiss all the prisoners. But that evening, as DeVeil must have realised would happen, a crowd gathered outside the roundhouse which grew in size and anger. Stones and bricks were thrown and by two in the morning the whole of the front of the house was in ruins. Although DeVeil had a reputation for always being willing to help quell a riot, neither he nor John Bromfield went near St Martin's Lane that evening. And it was left to James Frazer, another JP, to protect Bird and his family, who were still sheltering inside, and to disperse the crowd.

The situation for DeVeil, this 'oracle of the vestry' as his earliest biographer would have him,[41] and the most prominent signatory of the warrant, was a delicate one. Horace Walpole, whose sinecure as Inspector-General of Imports and Exports DeVeil had been awarded in 1738,[42] was so shocked by the deaths that he could exclaim that 'the greatest criminals in this town are the officers of justice'. According to William Shenstone, 'a large number of people of the first fashion went from the roundhouse to DeVeil's, to give in informations of their usage', while he describes DeVeil himself as 'greatly scared'.[43] From DeVeil's point of view it was immensely important that public anger and blame should be directed to the lowly individuals who had staffed the roundhouse, or at the very least the officers appointed by the Court of Burgesses, rather than at the Justices who had authorised the general warrant.

By Saturday, a Coroner's Inquest had been convened which brought in a verdict of wilful murder against William Bird for the suffocation of Mary Maurice and three women, whose names were as yet unknown.[44] DeVeil took this opportunity to further damn Bird in the eyes of the public and to help direct the outrage of the inhabitants of Westminster away from himself by the unusual step of publishing his version of events early the next week.[45] In an advertisement placed in the *London Evening Post* he first of all prominently named Booker Holden as the originator of the warrant and down-played his own role, disingenuously defending the warrant as normal and legal procedure.[46] He then reproduced the warrant itself which specified that 'vagabonds, pickpockets, and other dissolute and disorderly persons' were to be the sole objects of the search, and that its conduct was to be the responsibility of Holden alone. The advertisement then went on to blame the constables (who had been appointed by the Court of Burgesses) for having 'greatly misbehaved' themselves before offering up William Bird as a possible scapegoat. DeVeil then appended two very carefully chosen depositions, one from Elizabeth Surridge, who was described as a washerwoman, and another from Mary Wood, a chairwoman, which served to highlight Bird's role. In the process DeVeil effectively implied that the sweep was conducted in contradiction to the warrant, against working women of all sorts instead of the beggars and vagabonds actually listed. No mention of the legion of parish officers who had participated in the events of that night was made and the statement ended with the provocative note that Bird, Holden and the other constables would be re-examined by DeVeil at his house the very afternoon of publication.[47]

On Tuesday, the keeper of the Gatehouse had to bring Bird all the way around Hyde Park in order to avoid the angry mob which DeVeil's advertisement had brought into being. While after the interview, a loud and boisterous crowd of several thousand people followed Bird's progress to Newgate.[48] With the help of the Coroner's Jury, and through a subtle advertising campaign, when combined with the poor reputation Bird already possessed among the prostitutes of Westminster (something DeVeil would have been quite aware of),[49] the blame for the disaster was placed squarely on the parish employee who was in the weakest legal position. At the same time, the select vestry and the Middlesex Bench were largely absolved of responsibility.

Bird's first trial for murder took place in mid-September, and according to William Shenstone, writing in late July, the prosecution would 'be carried on with violence, so as probably to hang the keeper'.[50] Four experienced attorneys were commissioned to make up the prosecution team, while Bird's attempt to find a defence lawyer met a wall of professional indifference. By the day of his first trial, Bird had failed to locate anyone willing to act as defence council—two claimed to be out of town, two others 'begged to be excused', while a fifth simply returned the brief without explanation. William Bird, whom the trial records describe as a 'labourer', was forced to defend himself against the best legal minds the government could muster.[51]

The first trial was a noisy affair and lasted ten hours.[52] Bird was delivered to the Old Bailey in chains and cut a sorry figure in front of the crowded courtroom. The watchmen, beadles, and constables, the women themselves, and even DeVeil were called to give evidence, with Bird making ineffectual interjections along the way. His papers were lost and his witnesses failed to turn up. And at the end of a long day the jury declared a verdict of 'special', essentially refusing to pass judgement on a technicality. As soon as this was announced the Grand Jury processed indictments on two further deaths, and a second trial was arranged for the next sessions.[53] On this occasion the indictment was drawn up more carefully, avoiding any possibility Bird would get off. After seven hours of evidence he was found guilty and sentenced to hang.[54]

Bird's life, however, did not end on the gallows. Instead, his sentence was commuted to 14 years transportation, and he was shipped to Maryland on 13 April, the following year. The ship, the *Justitia*, was under the command of Barnett Bond, and on his orders Bird was denied food and water. He died of starvation and dehydration before the ship reached

Maryland.[55] Eventually Bond stood trial for murder at the Court of Admiralty held at the Old Bailey and was acquitted. Bird's wife, Eleanor, married a neighbour, Thomas Pettart, a shoe closer at the Fleet a year later, and by the early 1750s was forced, with her four children, into the parish workhouse.[56] Thomas DeVeil returned to Bow Street and continued his life as Britain's first stipendary magistrate. He died of a stroke in 1746.[57]

In the year following the disaster the parish of St Martin rebuilt the roundhouse at a cost of £83.15s; adding piped water and a new set of iron palings, five foot, eight inches high in the process.[58] A year later the parish spent a further £8.19s repairing the damage done to the house by the population of Westminster, and in each succeeding year for the next decade a similar sum was spent on repairs.[59] The Watch was strengthened, and the Watch Act reformed. The role of the beadles was regularised, and they were given new uniforms at the cost of £36.17s.[60] And finally, the salary of the new watchhouse keeper was raised in order to discourage the selling of liquor.

In part the events described in this chapter were brought about by the commonplace failings of incompetence, venality and drink. But they also reflect one of the points at which both local and central government, the petty bureaucrats who ran an increasingly complex system, and the people who made their living on the streets of London came into conflict, illuminating in the process a complex map of gender and class relations. The night of the 15 July 1742 represents one of a series of moments when a narrow strand of male London society sought to impose its sense of order and regularity upon the chaotic largely female and traditional society which heaved and jostled around it. For the prostitutes and beggars who were confined in the hole that night, it was part of an ongoing struggle against a newly intrusive authority—a moment when the traditional cry of 'murder', that singular appeal to authority previously available to all the inhabitants of England, was found to fall on the deaf ears of an increasingly stratified society.[61] For the army of men who hoped to turn their new-found literacy and numeracy to account in the growing monster of local government, for that cadre of civil servants who implemented elite male policy, it was a moment when their ultimate powerlessness was made manifest. For the householders of St Martin it was a moment when their distrust of government was vindicated; when the population of Westminster was transformed into the dangerous leviathan of public opinion which would haunt the aspirations of later eighteenth-century governments.[62] For the smug vestrymen, and vain JPs, for DeVeil and his creatures, it was a moment of supreme panic—one of those rare occasions when the shimmering mask of control projected by these men onto the records of parochial and judicial administration slipped to reveal the naked fear and corruption which lay beneath. And for London, it was a point of transition between the collective, if oppressive, policing associated with the Societies for the Reformation of Manners, and the institutional edifice which would become the Metropolitan Police.

And if the events of that night did not really change anything; if they were quickly forgotten by contemporaries and justifiably ignored by historians, they still exemplify the complex relationships of gender and class, of authority and power experienced by eighteenth-century Londoners.

6. 'Every lane teems with instruction, and every alley is big with erudition'
Graffiti in Eighteenth-Century London
Lisa Forman Cody

Few urban artefacts seem as modern as graffiti. And aside from some activists and artists who consider this genre both aesthetic and political, many more treat these urban, spray-painted tags as the annoying signs of an economic underclass, disaffected youth, and the obsessively territorial in an alienated postmodern world. Graffiti, however, does not belong to our century alone; nor has it always been viewed in such a pejorative light. Londoners scribbled marks in public places long before they suffered from modern anomie. Perhaps even more surprisingly, some eighteenth- and nineteenth-century citizens even celebrated graffiti, presenting these public scrawls as a delightful and democratic language that all could share.

London's early modern graffiti was created by a surprisingly broad socio-economic cross section, and was distinguished by a striking juxtaposition between high and low culture. Our best catalog of eighteenth-century graffiti, the popular, four-part pamphlet series, *The Merry-Thought: or, The Glass-Window and Bog-House Miscellany* (1731), collected together both classically inspired poems written with diamonds in tavern windows and limericks written—sometimes with shit—in privies. Conflating diamond-sporting élites with *hoi polloi* produced a fairly obvious political argument: people of all ranks obsessed about the same visceral aspects of life—eating and eliminating, copulating and cuckolding. *The Merry-Thought* argued that Londoners, whether rich or poor, loved to scribble their witty (and witless) thoughts on sex, love, money, Catholics, class, and culture anywhere somebody else could read them, sometimes in Latin, and often in explicit Anglo-Saxon.

It is impossible to gauge how much graffiti the streets of eighteenth-century London actually possessed, but some asides in the press suggest it was very common. A tongue-in-cheek correspondent to the *Connoisseur*, for example, wrote in 1755 that he had learned how to read from seeing the words and signs that assaulted him in every street: 'Every lane teems with instruction, and every alley is big with erudition [even] though the ignorant or incurious passer-by shuts his eyes against that universal volume of arts and sciences, which constantly lies open before him in the highways and byeplaces; like the laws of the *Romans*, which were hung up in the public streets'.[1] In the eyes of this observer, graffiti and other written words on handbills, and in newspapers piled up at printers' shops and coffeehouses spelled out thousands of messages—a perhaps strange phenomenon in a city where so many could not read.

Eighteenth-century graffiti, even when produced by the well-heeled, was extraordinarily visceral. Not only did scribblers write about sex and defecation and draw smutty doodles, they also wrote in earthy materials: charcoal, mud, and faeces. When we think of where this graffiti was—on streets, outdoor walls, and the windows of coffeehouses and inns—it contradicts our image of what the eighteenth-century 'public sphere' actually looked like. We have inherited an image of the eighteenth-century public as especially refined, marked by politesse, sophistication, and cumbersomely elegant hoopskirts and coats that would seem to prevent writing on outhouse walls with one's own waste.[2]

The reality of public life, however, was rougher and much more bodily than this. Effluvia, foul manners, and fisticuffs were everywhere. To live in London was to experience odours, cacophony, and alarming sights. The early modern world was a stinky one, rich with the smell of sweat, urine, human and horse faeces. Housewives and housemaids dumped chamber pots out of windows onto the heads of walking day-dreamers. The streets ran with waste, and many neighbourhoods housed huge and permanent piles of dung and worse. Animal corpses, hides, and bones littered countless roads and choked the Thames. Criminals' decapitated heads remained on pikes at Temple Bar until they rotted off. Eighteenth-century Londoners revelled in the details of their bodies, avidly discussing their warts and poxes in letters and quack advertisements which littered newspapers and plastered walls. As John Black describes in chapter 7 of this volume, couples occasionally copulated in extremely public venues, too, providing titillating (or perhaps disturbing) spectacles for all who wandered into the streets. To this public sphere of smells, sex, disease, and dung, we must add a superabundance of words and pictures scribbled on the outside of buildings, in outhouses, on fences, and scratched into doorjambs, often invoking bodily products and pleasures.

The evidence for graffiti
The Italian word, 'graffiti', literally meaning 'scratches', was coined in 1851 by archeologists, and specifically referred to the writings on the ancient walls of Pompeii. But long before there was a word for it, people did it, and even collected and commented on it. From the ancient Greeks onward, the practice of marking one's name and opinions on other peoples' property continued uninterrupted. In the middle ages, the English carved all over churches, motivated in part by the folk belief 'that cutting one's name or initials in a church brought luck'.[3]

Despite its apparently universal human appeal, locating graffiti in any one specific time or place—namely in London from the 1660s to 1870s—is maddeningly difficult. Unlike letters, printed media, and even other forms of ephemera which can be boxed and saved in an attic or archive, graffiti has been rarely preserved. Unless it was carved, it washed away over time, leaving historians to find examples only by chance. Given the elusiveness of graffiti, then, we must acknowledge that little has survived, and recognise that a history of the subject is, in part, a speculative one, at least for London in this period.

Very few British artists depicted graffiti, even iconographically, but archeological evidence and written accounts provide tantalising evidence that graffiti was far more common than the pictorial record would indicate. A wide variety of useful sources, from blasé asides in legal records to snobbish critiques in the *Spectator*, from newspaper reports to plaster casts of Newgate's stones preserved in Europe's only graffiti museum, all testify to the many forms and functions that eighteenth-century graffiti took.[4]

The forms of eighteenth-century graffiti
In its most basic form, London's pre-twentieth century graffiti must be considered functional. Writing on the wall with charcoal or chalk would

have been the easiest, cheapest way to leave a note before the twentieth century, as recorded in the following 1688 criminal case. James Lorraine, a surgeon from the parish of St James's, Westminster, testified that he went to the house of Dennis Hobry 'and missing [him], left a Chalk upon the Door, of Direction where [he] might come'.[5] That such an aside was an unremarked upon part of the narrative suggests how perfectly common a form of leaving a memo this was. This chalk message happened to survive only because this particular piece of testimony helped pinpoint when Dennis Hobry's wife Mary murdered him.

Another commonplace form of graffiti included children's first attempts at writing and their games of hopscotch, hangman, and doodles. We find such examples recorded in first-century Pompeii, seventeenth-century Dutch paintings, early nineteenth-century French prints, and American photographs from the 1940s.[6] William Hogarth's 'The first stage of cruelty' (1752) offers a well-known example of street boys drawing a game of hangman on the wall. Although Hogarth can be considered no more transparent a recorder of the written landscape than any other satirical graphic artist, his purpose, particularly in this image, was to comment on the world as it *was* rather than should be. 'The four stages' was aimed at the lower orders, showing them the barbaric effects of their uncouth manners. True, the game of hangman drawn on the wall symbolised the eventual demise of the series' central figure, Tom Nero, yet the print could only educate the illiterate if the key signs were 'realistic'.[7] Eighteenth- and nineteenth-century folklorists who preserved traditional English games confirm that such chalked games as 'Scotch Hoppers' and 'Tray Trip' were ancient and commonplace.[8]

The correspondent writing to the *Connoisseur* in 1755 who described a London rich with words in every street and alley claimed he learned how to read by 'follow[ing] the example of the ancient *Peripatetics*, who used to study walking: and as I had not the advantage to be brought up a scholar, I have been obliged, like the *Lacedaemonian* children, to the public for my education'. His very first lessons, in which he learned letters and simple words, came from graffiti: 'those elegant monosyllables, which are chalked out upon walls a[n]d gates, and which (as pretty books for children are adorned with cuts) are generally enforced and explained by curious hiero-glyphics in *caricatura*'.[9] This description of simple words and rude signs actually worked as a *double entendre*: naturally, monosyllables were the words little children first wrote, but 'monosyllable' was also slang for female genitals. Another eighteenth-century newspaper laughingly lamented children's precocious doodles:

> But now, alas! E'en children name
> Without a blush, their parts of shame.
> In wicked sport, they rudely scrawl
> Unseemly words on ev'ry wall
> And underneath the well-spelt line
> The parts themselves at large design;
> Cause maids to blush behind the fan,
> To languish, sigh, and wish for man.[10]

These commentators were not the only ones to describe graffiti as dirty. In fact, the richest source for English graffiti, *The Merry-Thought* series, focused almost exclusively on sex and defecation—sometimes fusing the two as in this piece of outhouse lust from Hampton Court recorded in 1703:

> Oh! that I were a T—d, a T—d,
> Hid in this secret Place,
> That I might see my *Betsy's* A———,
> Though she sh—t me in my Face.

(Such scatological doggerel begged for a response; 'Written under this in a Woman's Hand', 'E. W.' remarked: ''Tis Pity but you had your Wish.')[11]

More than just cataloguing the smutty and often violently misogynistic content of contemporary scribbles, *The Merry-Thought* series of pamphlets reveals some other patterns about graffiti, including its location across London.[12] To authenticate examples of graffiti, the editor, 'Hurlo Thrumbo' usually identified where and when it was recorded. Though this presentation was highly selective—it tells us where he and his *readers* drank and micturated, *not* where all Londoners actually scribbled publicly— mapping his examples does reveal significant facets of London's graffiti culture. [illustration 13]

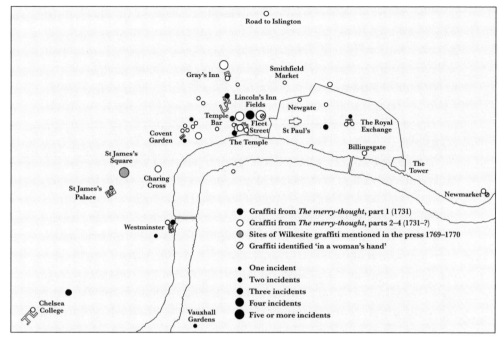

13. Map of graffiti

Our map indicates that London examples from the first edition came predominantly from Fleet Street, the Temple Bar, Westminster, and the western hamlets of Chelsea and Hampton Court. The first two places were in the publisher's neighbourhood of Warwick Lane and the centre of the city's book trade. The latter three areas were places commonly visited by the city's literati. Some of the Westminster examples were either in Greek, Latin, or 'dog-Latin', reflecting the surrounding population of clerics, school-boys, and members of parliament, all eager to show off a little classical wit, even it was rather silly:

O mirum Fartum
Perigrinum Gooseberrytartum.[13]

Subsequent editions of *The Merry-Thought* included examples submitted by readers from Smithfield Market, Billingsgate, docklands, and Southwark. Many new examples arrived from areas surrounding the publisher's own neighbourhood of Warwick Lane, including the Inns of Court, the Temple, Covent Garden, Charing Cross, and more from Fleet Street and Temple Bar. (Graffiti on Temple Bar must have been quite amusing to compete with criminals' decapitated heads displayed on pikes.) Some graffiti reflected its location: Covent Garden examples, for instance, decried prostitutes, while the Temple examples denounced lawyers. One Charing Cross example pined over a certain lovely but unnamed seamstress of the neighbourhood.

Yet we must wonder what sorts of graffiti 'Hurlo Thrumbo' excluded. He records no examples of personal attacks, a single dirty word, the clearly political, atheistic, incendiary or even topical. He includes only one bit of graffiti from Newgate—although most prisons were actually deeply carved with prisoners' marks—and only a couple of examples of misspelled, semi-literate attempts at wit. Overall, the effect of *The Merry-Thought*, since it selected many literary, classically inflected, and witty examples, was to elevate graffiti as a literary form. And like Joseph Addison in the *Tatler* and other eighteenth-century authors who compared high and low writing, he sometimes found them remarkably alike.[14]

According to Daniel Defoe in *Moll Flanders*, couples sometimes courted each other by taking turns writing a line of seduction (or carping complaint) in tavern windows with a diamond ring (or even 'a diamond pencil', in the case of the Earl of Chesterfield).[15] *The Merry-Thought* also suggests that they used privies for lovemaking, and left their triumphant post-copulatory remarks on the walls. A 1718 example from the outhouse at the Bush in Carlisle boasted:

Reader,
Within this Place two ways I've been delighted;
For here I've f—, and likewise here have sh—d.
They both are healthful, Natures's Ease require 'em,
And though you grin, I fancy you desire 'em.[16]

(And if one were tempted to read 'f—' as merely passing gas, the doggerel from a string of respondents, both disgusted and delighted, made clear to the reader of *The Merry-Thought* that the first writer had made a sexual, rather than a flatulent, boast.)

It does not take an historian to tell us that women also went to the toilet in the eighteenth century, but *The Merry-Thought* series reveals that women wrote on many more public spaces than we might expect. Several examples of both the élite diamond writing from tavern windows and the more plebeian privy poems are described as 'in a woman's hand'. These tend to be smart ripostes to earlier graffiti, presumably by men, usually about women and their bodies, as the example above by the Hampton Court hack wishing to be a turd demonstrates. Examples of feminine graffiti remind us that even if women did not frequent coffeehouses in great number,[17] they did spend time in taverns and in the privies of 'public' neighbourhoods including Covent Garden and Fleet Street. 'Hurlo Thrumbo' only specified where a handful of feminine words were located; instead he described women's marks as from 'a window of a Private House', from 'a Lady's Dressing-Room', from outside London, 'From an hundred Windows', all of which reveal the editor's heavy hand.

The Merry-Thought collected general forms of *ad hominem* attacks (without naming names, except in the cases of women toasted in the diamond-engraved glasses that were also included in the collection). Doubtless, these examples represented only a fraction of the city's graffiti boasting of having cuckolded this or that husband. Written attacks maligning one's enemies were extraordinarily common from the seventeenth century onward, and these examples imply that sharp words were everywhere, both in print and in chalk. Compared to surviving examples of chalked graffiti, however, an extremely rich record of printed attacks survives in the archives and the press. Newspapers printed not only spurious stories lampooning the great, but also advertisements placed by the libeled and slandered who wished to silence rumours, as in this case from February 1680. 'A certain Lady of Quality in London' alerted the public that she had not 'lately been brought to bed of an untimely squint-ey'd Female Child' as had 'been maliciously and most industriously reported' throughout the metropolis.[18] A few printed examples have survived in archives when the maligned took legal action and the attack became part of the court's record. Mr Firth of Sheffield took his case to the King's Bench because a handbill libeling him as 'Dr. JURA, ALIAS DR. INK. (Surgeon & Man-Midwife to his Holiness the Pope)' had been 'posted & distributed in every part of the Town'.[19] In the 1770s, the surly, irascible journalist,

A Man hanging for Love, drawn when Painting was in its Cradle, with his Dog barking at him, viva voce. *From the three Pigeons at Brentford.*

14. 'A Man Hanging for Love', *The Merry-Thought*, 'Hurlo Thrombo', Pt II, p.17

Philip Thicknesse, was lampooned by James Gillray as a 'A vicious old dog' in a faux lost-dog handbill he had printed up and posted throughout Westminster.[20]

We might distinguish chalked marks from printed satirical attacks, but contemporaries seemed instead to lump these genres together. The correspondent to the *Connoisseur*, for example, linked graffiti to quack handbills, street-corner oratory, and to his own labours, first at a newspaper 'where my business was to invent terrible stories', and then as an editor of 'works that required a great fund of erudition, such as bog-house miscellanies'.[21] The correspondent to the *Connoisseur* mocked the overabundance of lowbrow language in the city, lumping all of it together. In so doing, he also criticized the notion that simply learning to read and write made one a literary figure, particularly if one only ended up compiling collections of graffiti.

Yet graffiti did differ from printed media, as a symbolic or hieroglyphic language. As a collection of stick figures, numbers, and doodles of genitals and other things, graffiti could be understood and created by the illiterate. Hieroglyphs built a language not only understandable to nearly *anyone*, but also capable of being deployed by *all*. At the same time, however, these signs could remain obscure in their meaning. One part of *The Merry-Thought* included an odd pair of stick figures, one hanging from a gibbet, the other wearing a pointy hat. [illustration 14] 'Hurlo Thrumbo' included the many graffiti speculating on the meaning of this odd scene of a man, a dog, a woman, and a noose, including one signed by 'Mary Worthless' suggesting the dutiful man hanged himself because the 'Cruel She' ordered him to. Another argued quite contrarily that the caption should read: 'Hang me, if I will *hang* for any Woman'. And yet another simply found the drawing to signify the equality of all:

No Matter if the Man is longer than the Gallows,
He smokes and drinks his Glass like honest Fellows.[22]

As vague as the doodle might have been, its malleability contributed to its democratic potential. Anyone could find meaning in it, even if it was personal, non sequitorial, or downright wrong.

Political graffiti

Political graffiti is especially difficult to document, but records of it do survive. A church pillar in Hitchin, Herfordshire, for instance, is still inscribed with a decapitated head and the word 'royall', said to be carved in 'reference to the unhappy fate of Charles I' in 1649.[23] *The Loyal Protestant*, a paper in the pocket of Charles II, the loyal son of Charles I, recorded a bit of northern graffiti in November 1679:

> It is reported, that his R. H. being entertained at a Person of Qualities house in Yorkshire, took special Notice of the following Lines, Engraved with a Diamond in a Glass-Window; which words were engraved, as is affirmed, by that blessed Martyr, King Charles the First, the Letter C.R. being set under them.
> Errours in time may be redress'd,
> The shortest follies are the best.[24]

Though commemorative, reporting this particular incantory-sounding graffiti also made a contemporary, veiled political threat against the parliamentary enemies of Charles II in a year of deep and ominous political division.

We have records of more insurrectionary graffiti from the 1760s forward. In the day of John Wilkes, that charming, xenophobic man of the people, his supporters attacked his political enemies not only with printed works, but also graffiti. In April of 1770, for instance, 'several places in St James's Park, and on the walls in the neighbourhood of the Parliament House' were 'covered in letters near a foot long declaring "Impeach the ———s mother— Impeach the D———r—Impeach her!"' It was not only the mother of George III, the Princess Dowager, who was threatened, but perhaps more ominously, the wall of St James's palace was inscribed with the following lines:

A Prophesy.
A cold winter
A mild spring
A bloody summer
A dead ———'[25]

Such graffiti threatening to end the reign of George III like that of Charles I was potentially treasonous. But unlike some other forms of political language, successful graffiti was anonymous.

Wilkes's supporters had a particularly efficient sign that they could quickly leave anywhere and everywhere: the number '45'. They obsessively commemorated the 45th issue of his opposition paper, *The North Briton*, by invoking the number in every possible way, from making forty-five toasts to serving forty-five pound plum puddings. Occasionally, Wilkes's supporters foisted a '45' on the less politically committed by chalking it on the cloaks of passers-by, and even carving it into the doorjamb of a magistrate who had sentenced one of these chalkers to two years' imprisonment.[26] The cheery *Wilkes's Jests, or the Patriot Wit* (1770) told of 'an honest Hibernian' writing '"Wilkes and Liberty forever!" on a slitch of bacon'. (Incidentally, the man's landlord 'ate a slice and "declared it was the best bacon he had ever eat [sic] in his life".')[27] This record perhaps hints that Wilkes's supporters posted this catchphrase and the '45' on many more surfaces than the merely edible. In fact, one cartoon from 1770 depicted a '45' and a portion of Wilkes's name scrawled on an alley wall in the background.[28] Sources into the nineteenth century continue to document graffiti used by those opposing the state, the status quo, and rival political factions.[29]

One question these traces of political graffiti raise is whether they functioned in the same way as other forms of popular politics such as processions and the wearing of party symbols. John Brewer has argued that the Wilkesite use of the '45' differed dramatically from traditional spectacles and nationalistic political culture. Pope burnings and parades, for instance, were often sponsored by the state as part of a traditional community ritual. But chalking a '45' on magistrates' clothing erupted from below, and was directed against the state. And unlike the momentary spectacle of a pope burning or pagent, Wilkes's supporters' omnipresent writing of 'Wilkes and Liberty' and '45' on shaving mugs, ladies' ornaments, sides of bacon, and

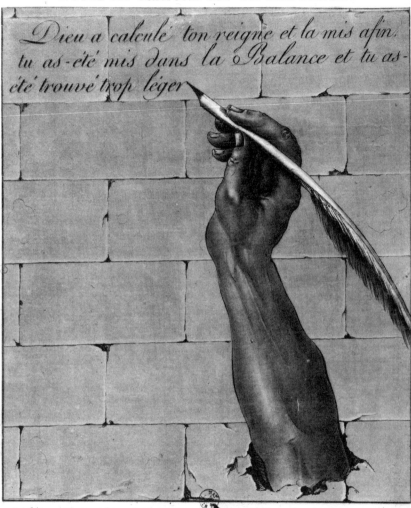

15. 'Louis le traître lis ta sentence'

door-jambs created a more transcendent form of political culture,[30] which suggests how some graffiti contributed to a lasting political landscape in the city, long beyond the political moment itself.

A later, French print, '*Louis le traître lis ta sentence*', which was sold in London's printshops in 1793 after Louis XVI had been executed, suggests that graffiti could be seen not merely as ephemeral, but as of more lasting importance.[31] [illustration 15] Here, a black hand bursts out of what must be a prison wall and writes the nation's damning sentence for Louis to read on the stones. Of course this image does not document actual graffiti, but rather suggests that contemporaries believed the permanent and historically transcendent to be written on the wall, as the cliché would have it. In turn, the print suggested that graffiti bore witness to and was one of the means through which a political moment was preserved for posterity.

Satirical artists also used graffiti within certain scenes to make a fleeting moment within a single image connect to a larger narrative. Graffiti could foreshadow events within a print series, as in the case of William Hogarth's 'The four stages of cruelty' and 'A Harlot's Progress', or even outside the picture frame in the 'real' world, as in James Gillray's '*Un petit souper a la Parissienne.—*or a family of *sans-culotts* [sic] refreshing after the fatigues of the day' of 1792. [illustration 16] Here, we see Parisian radicals enjoying a cannibalistic feast. On the wall behind them we see two childishly scrawled bits of graffiti. Above the fireplace (in which an infant is roasted on a spit), a stick-figure holds an axe in one hand, and a decapitated head in the other, and is flanked by the words, '*Vive la Liberté*' and '*Vive le Egalité*' [sic]. To the right, a fat and stuffy little man holding a sceptre and sporting a ribbon on his chest, 'Seurs le Grand', has lost his head. Gillray's central scene of the cannibals eating piles of mutilated bodies represents the recent September massacres. But the graffiti also portends events: 'Seurs le Grand' with his little scepter could well be Louis XVI who, in reality, had not yet lost his head, but soon would to the sans-culottes of Paris.

When Gillray and Hogarth used graffiti in these images, they also damned the character of scribblers. *The Merry-Thought* and eighteenth-century periodicals presented graffiti in a generally positive, if risqué light, as being created by people of all classes. Hogarth and Gillray, on the other hand, made it signify the savage, and in doing so pointed the way to our own twentieth-century irritation with graffiti as criminal vandalism.

16. 'Un Petit Souper a la Parisienne', James Gillray, *The Works of James Gillray*, vol. 1, p. 87.

As inflammatory as the huge, painted letters on the side of St James's Palace threatening the mother of George III were, London's authorities apparently failed to prosecute graffiti writers for vandalism until the twentieth century. City magistrates of course periodically brought charges against rioters, especially the anti-Catholic rioters of the 1780 Gordon Riots, for destroying property. But nobody who had simply scrawled 'No Popery' on a wall was prosecuted that term at London's central criminal court, the Old Bailey. Unlike wearing a pro-Wilkes badge or carrying an effigy of a politician, graffiti was an anonymous and subterranean act, and thus difficult to prosecute. As *The Times* complained in 1788 about some damage done in Kensington Gardens:

The offence that is offered to the eye of Majesty, and which so disgraces some of his subjects, who have transferred the filth of their polluted minds to his seats and alcoves, deserves a most severe castigation; and it is highly probable some of these scribbling fools will be caught in the fact; and by a few well drawn lines on their backs, be taught that he who offends the eye of delicacy, merits punishment as much as the man who offends the ear.[32]

In the eighteenth century, writing on walls or in windows was not in itself regarded as criminal, perhaps because people from all walks of life did it (writing specifically on Westminster Bridge, however, was added to the late Georgian 'Bloody Code' as a capital offence).[33] When contemporaries did describe graffiti as criminal or immoral it was because the particular *content* offended them. In the nineteenth and twentieth centuries when it was increasingly believed that only certain anti-social types scrawled on walls, then the very act itself became criminal alongside other acts of vandalism (so criminal in fact that although the Queen of England is today offered dispensations to commit many crimes, this does not extend to graffiti).[34] Another reason why graffiti may not have been criminally pursued in the eighteenth century was because almost the only acts of graffiti that really destroyed property were committed by the well-off who could afford to scratch with diamonds. The less well-heeled usually used more ephemeral writing materials—chalk, charcoal, and faeces which did not cause lasting damage.

The nineteenth-century 'discovery' of graffiti, or the Pompeii effect

The English state may not have brought charges against graffiti writers before the twentieth century, and private citizens who had a '45' chalked on their property may not have prosecuted defacers, even though they would pursue window breakers.[35] But élites had other ways of culturally silencing the subversive potential of graffiti. They romanticized it and turned it into an *historical* or antiquarian artefact.

Around 1814, John Claude Nattes (1765–1822) painted the perhaps only plausibly accurate image of actual graffiti in London. [illustration 17] This small watercolour depicted the inside of the Temple of Concord in

17. 'View from inside the Temple of Concord, Green Park, *c.* 1814'

Green Park and highlighted both the graffiti and fallen masonry, invoking the ruins of Italy and Greece. (This was exactly the sort of defaced monument that *The Times* complained about in 1788.) Nattes's work epitomized the British Romantic movement. His imagery captured the lovely, but decaying ruins of ancient peoples—or sometimes he simply made more modern monuments, such as the Temple of Concord, appear ancient. Although the Celtic fringes of the British Isles from the Scottish Highlands to Irish bogs had been viciously conquered by the English during the seventeenth and eighteenth centuries, Nattes and many other Romantics depicted this cultural conquest in melancholy and wistful tones. Nattes portrayed many of Britain's landscapes and ruins, which had actually been very recently destroyed, as old as the classical world, and in so doing helped efface a recent and brutal political history.[36] The Temple of Concord in Green Park is of course not one of these ethnic buildings felled by English troops in the Celtic Fringe. But Nattes's depiction of this

London monument eliminates the subversive and potentially political aspects of graffiti by presenting it as a classical ruin. Natte represented London's graffiti as antique, as a sign of a lost and crumbling past, essentially equivalent to Pompeii itself.

And indeed, no scribbles from the past generated more excitement than those of Pompeii, particularly by the mid-nineteenth century, thanks to Raphael Garrucci's monumental and widely acclaimed *Graffiti de Pompeii* (1856). Carved scribbles in the classical world had been known from such ancient authors as Pliny, but Garrucci's work revolutionized how the British press and literati viewed historical graffiti.[37] Almost suddenly, commentators emphasized how the writing on ancient walls provided a social history which both illuminated a specific, unique moment and at the same time linked the present to the past through this 'universal' phenomenon. Pompeii's graffiti intrigued Victorian commentators because it revealed the lived reality of beloved ancient authors, but also offered an opportunity to discuss the dirty by condemning it:

> The very worst…revelations, it must be confessed, are borne out by the graffiti. Many of the persons who form the subject of their strictures are described as making immorality their profession…. while the sentiment of some of the graffiti themselves exhibits a cynicism at once so gross and so unblushing that we can only understand their presence in a public place by supposing the whole tone of the public mind to be sunk to those lowest depths of hideous and unnatural depravity, of which so awful a picture is drawn in St Paul's Epistle to the Romans.[38]

In other words, grafitti for all its charm, historiographical potential, and transcendental ability to link generations, was a lowbrow and deviant phenomenon, not because it was vandalism, but because vandals expressed their necessarily depraved opinions.

The great Victorian humour magazine, *Punch*, mocked the recent scholarly enthusiasm for graffiti through a satirical review of an imagined book, *The Graffiti of London*, by Sir Cannibal Tattoo, an imaginary Polynesian scholar.[39] In this pretend essay for 'the *Polygamic Review*', Mr Punch describes how he accompanied Sir Cannibal Tattoo throughout London as they visited landmarks marked by graffiti and other written signs. The graffiti of Pompeii was often incomplete since time destroyed individual letters; similarly Punch and Tattoo found London's graffiti to be partial and puzzle-like. Both wildly miss guessing the real meaning of such half-visible chalkings on the Mayor's residence as

I -M THE- K-N- -F -HE -ASTL-
-ND YOURA D—TY R-SCA-
Tattoo insists this reads:
I am the Knife [which] the Astley
Hand[ed] your [ ]. A Dirty Rascal.

The results of such mock scholarly myopia was to make all the graffiti of London utterly nonsensical of course. Such misreadings created an entirely fictional and ridiculous history of London (or Pompeii). By lampooning the scholarly tendency to over-read, *Punch*'s satire really satirized contemporary authors for projecting their own values into the ancient, and largely unknowable urban landscape of Pompeii.

Perhaps the most interesting aspect of *Punch*'s sendup was the humour editors' inventing the cannabalistic, primitive scholar who was shown to be wiser than the fictional Mr Punch. It is Mr Punch in fact who turns the most obvious signs, such as 'M-ND T-E PAIN-' which is posted outside the Temple one day, into the utterly ludicrous:

May we venture a guess? Is it *Mind the Pain*, and has a preceding word dropped, which was *Never*? If so, we think we see a solution. The Temple, as has been said, was famous for its Jews, who, again, were the most celebrated dentists of old times, and who, all schoolboys will remember, were sent for to draw the teeth of KING JOHN, about 1666 [sic]. Well, was this inscription, like the Roman *Salve*, the address to visitors to a Temple dentist?

Tattoo, on the other hand, suggested 'the last word was *Paint…*'. Mr Punch dismisses Tattoo's interpretation as 'a happy conjecture, but we give it *valent quantum*'.

On the one hand, the fictional Sir Cannibal Tattoo turned cultural

hierarchies upside down. He not only made the graffiti of London primitive by making it a topic for anthropological inquiry, but he also was
represented as more pragmatic than the native Londoner, Mr Punch. But
on the other hand, Sir Tattoo symbolized graffiti: the savage, cannabalistic and superstitious culture of the tattoo. Ultimately, *Punch's* lampoon
marked graffiti as primitive and marginal, by representing it as cryptic, but
highly banal. In the end, misreading graffiti as our satirical scholars do,
was perhaps the best way Victorians could efface the real graffiti of London.
Mr Punch and Sir Cannibal Tattoo celebrate the anonymous and potentially political, anti-Catholic and hungry scribbles of 'NO P-PE-Y' and 'I
AM STAR-ING' as simply jolly fun, and in doing so *Punch* rendered graffiti nonsensical and politically harmless.

7. Illegitimacy, Sexual Relations and Location in Metropolitan London, 1735–85

John Black

> Tuesday 17 May [1763]….so I sallied to the streets, and just at the bottom of our own, I picked up a fresh, agreeable young girl called Alice Gibbs. We went down a lane to a snug place, and I took out my armour, but she begged that I might not put it on, as the sport was much pleasanter without it, and as she was quite safe. I was so rash as to trust her, and had a very agreeable congress.[1]

This laconic sexual episode in the life of the young James Boswell has in many ways come to typify modern historical depictions of eighteenth-century metropolitan sexuality.[2] Boswell's early evening carnality with a prostitute in a London street, along with similar sexual encounters in the parks, alleyways, and alehouses of the metropolis, has become familiar, if not overly familiar, to the readers and writers of metropolitan history.[3]

The impression conveyed by Boswell's writings of a nocturnal city where every available public and semi-public space was the site of sexual assignation still appears to hold historians in its sway, this chapter will explore the more mundane realities of eighteenth-century metropolitan sex. It will demonstrate that while public spaces, such as parks, streets, alleyways, and even hackney carriages, were used for illegitimate heterosexual (and homosexual) encounters, it is in the semi-public spaces of the alehouse, tavern, inn, coffee house, and lodging house, and above all within the confines of the private household, that illicit sexual activity took place. At the same time, this chapter will provide a broader context for our understanding of pre-modern sexual behaviour. It will go beyond an examination of the world of commercial sex inhabited by men like Boswell, to look at the social, class and power relations which underpinned sex outside of marriage, in this most sexualised of urban spaces.

By law every mother of an illegitimate child was obliged to swear out a brief account of her sexual history before a magistrate.[4] Thousands of such sexual transcripts survive for eighteenth-century London. Some are only a few words long, while others can run to several pages. For the purpose of this study the bastardy statements sworn to by mothers of illegitimate children in five metropolitan parishes have been used; the West End parishes of St Clement Danes[5] and St Mary-le-Strand,[6] the eastern parishes of St Botolph Aldgate[7] and St Leonard Shoreditch,[8] and the western suburban parish of St Luke Chelsea.[9]

Bastardy statements were depositions given mainly by mothers of illegitimate children before parochial and magisterial administrators.[10] These statements were solicited in an attempt to ascertain the name of the father and the parish whose responsibility the child was likely to become. The bastardy statements detailed the settlement history of the mother, the occupation and residence of the father, and the circumstances of the birth of the illegitimate child—if the child had been born by the time the deposition was taken. Between the mid-1730s to mid-1780s, most, though not all, statements recorded in London parishes also gave a brief sexual history of the relationship between the mother and father of the illegitimate child, frequently including a note of the place where sex first occurred.[11]

Between them, the five parishes assayed here provide a cross section of the geographic and socio-economic map of London. The large West End parish of St Clement Danes was a centre of consumerism, law, and leisured pursuits, while the smaller parish of St Mary-le-Strand was the home of the more traditional gentry. In the east, an impoverished population of weavers, as well as other manufactures dominated the populous parish of St Leonard Shoreditch. St Botolph Aldgate was the permanent or temporary berth for mariners and those who worked the river. On the western fringe of the metropolis, the inexorably urbanising parish of St Lukes Chelsea was an aristocratic and gentry resort at the beginning of the eighteenth century, as well as being an important area for market gardening. Increasingly throughout the century, manufacture and a more socio-economically variegated population entered its boundaries.[12]

While Boswell provides one blinkered view of London's sexual landscape,

Sexual Location	St Clement Danes, 1740–85	St Mary-le-Strand, 1740–85	St Lukes Chelsea, 1735–66	St Botolph Aldgate, 1742–61
Type	(%)	(%)	(%)	(%)
Public Space	3	2.5	5	0
Eating/Drinking Establishment	15	4.5	16	17
Lodging House/ Private Lodgings	26	33	19	17
Private Household	56	60	60	66
Total	100	100	100	100
	(N=395)	(N=82)	(N=72)	(N=30)

Table 1: Location of Illegitimate Sexual Relationships in London (1735–85)

the picture that emerges from the bastardy examinations is both more believable and prosaic. Very few of the sexual encounters recorded in the depositions took place in the parks, gardens, streets and alleyways of the metropolis. Not one sexual incident in the open air is documented in St Mary-le-Strand or St Botolph Aldgate. [For all statistics quoted, see Table 1.] In St Clement Danes, a mere 3 per cent of illicit sexual relationships were sited in a street, field, barn, shed, or hackney carriage. Even in the suburban, more sparsely inhabited, parish of Chelsea, only 5 per cent of sexual unions were staged in a place of public access. Of the 450 cases of bastardy recorded in the eastern parish of St Leonard Shoreditch, only one cited sex as taking place in a field.

Even among this small number of *al fresco* sexual encounters, the majority took place in the fields and woods of the still rural hinterland around London. They percolated in and around the satellite villages surrounding the capital. These were snatched episodes of sexual gratification found in fields, barns, outhouses, and parkland, with very little obvious social or geographic connection between the participants. On 7 July 1773, Elizabeth Dickinson, a twenty-eight-year-old married woman, gave her bastardy statement before the parochial officers of St Clement Danes. In her deposition, she related that her husband, a merchant seaman, had been at sea for a year, before she embarked on an extremely short-lived affair with John Gray, the proprietor of the Pinner stagecoach. This sexual union consisted of one act of intercourse in a field in Pinner.[13] There is nothing in Elizabeth Dickinson's deposition that openly portrays this sexual relationship as one of prostitution, but several of its details suggest that this might have been the case.

The same possible link to prostitution is found in the story recounted by the widow Elizabeth Ellis in December 1739:[14]

> Who saith that she is now pregnant of a bastard child or children, which was unlawfully begotten on her body by one Richard Spragg, now a carter living with one Mr Randall at Uxbridge in the country of Middlesex aforesaid. Who had carnal knowledge of her body by the first time in a barn opposite to the sign of the Hogs Brought to a Fair Market at a place called Shepherds Bush near Acton in Middlesex aforesaid, and several times after in the said barn.

Again, there is a good possibility that this was a sexual relationship based on money. In most bastardy statements, there is a sense that the female examinant belonged to a specific place or parish, whether as an employee or a lodger, but this is not the case with these two women, or the majority of women who confessed to illicit sexual encounters of a similar nature.

Only one deposition involving sex in a place of public access, given before the Chelsea parish officers, even hints at the possibility that the sexual relationship was actually based on some more usual form of social relationship than that encompassed by prostitution. On 17 March 1741, Mary Steward, a single woman, stated that she was pregnant:[15]

> by one John Pink, the gardener to the Right Honourable the Lady King, at Ockham Mill in the county of Surrey (where this examinant lived a hired servant). Who had carnal knowledge of her body the first time in the month of September last in the tool house in the garden belonging to the said Lady King aforesaid, and several times after in other places…

That Mary Steward both continued the relationship over an extended period of time, and was conscious of the social connections of her partner suggests that she and John Pink were engaged in something more than a quick financial transaction.

When sexual episodes staged in the rural areas around the metropolis are discounted, the proportion of illicit carnal relationships within a public setting in the urbanised areas of the metropolis is negligible, and all of these were recorded in the bastardy examinations of the single parish of St Clement Danes. Less than 2 per cent of all sexual relations that led to the birth an illegitimate child, and where sexual location was stated, took place on the streets of London. These were most definitely casual sexual affairs, with the scent of prostitution always near, if not baldly stated. Alice James was a twenty-year-old domestic servant who had been out of service for one year when she had sex on two occasions with John Lock, a private in the Grenadier Guards, 'under a gateway near Arrundel Street, Strand'.[16]

Almost half the sexual relationships conducted in the streets of the capital were actually played out in the passenger space of a hackney carriage. In most cases the sexual act was performed only once. In the early 1740s, Elizabeth Bowman worked for two years as a tavern servant at the Ben Johnson's Head in Little Russell Street—a tavern whose clientele were characterised, if not caricatured, as 'all the Rakes, Gamesters, Swindlers, Highwaymen, Pickpockets and Whores'.[17] She named James Airey the younger as having 'had Carnal knowledge of her Body on the 24th Day of May last [1743] being Whitsun Tuesday in a Hackney Coach at which time he got her with Child.'[18] At no other time did they have sexual intercourse. This incident may have been instigated by the general bonhomie associated with the celebration of Whitsun, or a simple case of prostitution.

Another female examinant portrayed sexual relations in a hackney carriage as a seduction of a domestic servant by a gentleman.[19] Though the events recounted here occurred outside the time-scale of this study, the details merit attention:[20]

The Voluntary examination of Judith Page spr aged near 22 years/Middlesex and Westminster} (to wit) The Examinant Judith Page upon her Oath saith that she never was married. And That on or about the 16th Day of January last this Examinant having leave of her Master with whom she then lived servant to go to see a Play at Covent Garden House she went & whilst she was waiting at the Door to go into the House a Person appearing to be a Gentleman of small stature rather lusty dressed in a Black Coat with a great coat over it with his Hair dressed Powdered and tied in a que introduced his discourse to this Examinant and she being afterwards sitting in the Pitt the sd. Gentleman sat by her & discoursed with her. And after they came out of ye House he over persuaded her to go with him which she did and when they got as far as St Paul's where he called a coach this Examinant when she had got into it told the Coachman to drive to Catherine Street in the Strand and whilst the Coach was going from St Paul's to Catherine Street the said Person had carnal knowledge of this Examinant and at the same time begot on the Body of this Examinant the Child or Children with which she is now pregnant….And this Examinant further upon her Oath saith that the sd Gentleman was a stranger to her she having never seen him before or since that night She was so connected with him. And that he called himself (on her asking his name) Frederick Jones and saith that the sd. Person is the only and true father of the sd Child. Taken & Sworn the 30th. Day of Sepr 1793….[Signed Judith Page.]

This account of plebeian womanhood openly and persistently seduced by an elite libertine fits neatly with the pre-occupations of both Boswell and the historiography of eighteenth-century sexuality, as do the other depositions relating carnality in a public setting.[21] However, they still represent only a tiny minority of the sexual encounters recorded in the examinations. In other words, while open air sex can be found in the detailed records of plebeian lives, while Boswell's prostitutes can be found here, they do not represent the normal experience of sex, as reported by plebeian women in parochial records.

The reality of sexual behaviour in the semi-public worlds of London was both more complex, and perhaps less brutal than Boswell and his modern chroniclers may have led us to believe.

Almost 15 per cent of all bastardy examinations recorded in St Clement Danes in the period 1740–85, where sexual location was indicated took place in an alehouse, tavern, inn, or coffee house. In Chelsea for the period 1735–66 the equivalent figure was 16 per cent. In St Botolph Aldgate 14 per cent of all illegitimate relations recorded from 1744 to 1762 were initiated within an inn, tavern, or alehouse. While in the smaller parish of St Mary-le-Strand this figure was a mere 4 per cent.

The exact nature of the social relationships upon which these sexual unions were based was convoluted. Almost half of the sexual relationships in Chelsea, Clement Danes, and St Botolph Aldgate were between men and women who had no apparent connection to the place of business in which the act took place. They appear to have been no more than customers. The rest of the sexual relations in Chelsea, Clement Danes, and Aldgate, which took place in these locations were formed between the women employed as servants in these eating and drinking establishments and male customers, employees or lodgers. Male inn servants and female customers, male owners of the premises and their female servants, male and female servants, and men and women for whom the inn or tavern was the setting for an explicitly stated cohabitation can all be found in these records.

If we look exclusively at sexual relationships between the customers of these establishments, i.e. if we exclude people identified in the examinations as servants, owners and lodgers, the picture that emerges seems to support the current historiography, in suggesting a prominent role for inns and alehouses as sites for prostitution.[22] Certainly Boswell's encounter with two amateur prostitutes in a London alehouse could be fitted alongside some of the incidents recorded in the bastardy examinations.[23] But none of the women who gave birth to an illegitimate child openly stated that they used these semi-public sites as venues for paid sex. While in examinations such as that of Mary Parker, given before the magistrates of St Clement Danes in 1790, a clear distinction was made between Mary's role as an inn servant and her later employment as a prostitute. She stated that while she had been an inn servant for two to three years at the Lyon and Cat in Carey Street in Clement Danes, it was only later that she became a prostitute and worked 'the Town as a Street Walker and [therefore] cannot tell who is the Father [of her child]…or begot the same'.[24]

The impression, however, that a proportion of the sexual encounters between customers, and sited in the eating and drinking establishments of the capital, were characterised by the exchange of money remains, and is further supported by the reputations of the houses most frequently mentioned. In the bastardy examinations of St Clement Danes, the majority of the inns, coffeehouses and alehouses mentioned as sites of sexual activity, can be demonstrated from other sources to have had an unenviable reputation as fronts for bawdy houses. Susanna Manning, a widow of no stated occupation, had sex on several separate occasions in

September 1782 with William King, a tidewaiter, at the Rose Tavern in Covent Garden.[25] At the beginning of the eighteenth century the Rose Tavern was already notorious as 'the Resort of the Worst Characters in Town, male and female, who make it the Headquarters of Midnight Orgies and drunken Broils, where Murders and Assaults frequently occur'. By the 1760s, the Rose had become the home of striptease and flagellation shows.[26]

The names of bawdy houses and brothels such as the King's Head Tavern in Russell Street, The King's Arms in Catherine Street, and the White Horse in Covent Garden are commonly recorded in the bastardy examinations of Clement Danes as venues for sexual relations.[27] More than this, several of the taverns mentioned in the examinations appear on more than one occasion. Although historians have not identified the Bull and Gate in Holborn as a site of prostitution, it formed the stage for three different illicit affairs in the space of only a few years. More often than not the couples involved in these relationships had sex on only one or two occasions. And while it remains possible that these sexual relationships did not involve the exchange of money, alehouses like the Bull and Gate appear to have lent themselves to the needs of prostitutes and their clients.

The character of the sexual relationships involving the female servants and the male owners, customers, lodgers, and servants of these eating and drinking houses is, however, a different matter. And while there remains the possibility that these relationships involved the exchange of money, this cannot be determined with confidence. As noted previously in the case of Mary Parker, some women identified themselves as both prostitutes and inn servants. But, if we cannot come to a firm conclusion from these records about the financial aspects of the relationships recorded, it is clear that the relationships between inn servants and their male contemporaries do reflect the existence of misogynistic and sexually dismissive attitudes on the part of the men who were customers of, lodged at, worked in, or kept the urban alehouses, inns, and taverns of eighteenth-century London.[28] The most extreme examples of misogynist attitudes can be found in the behaviour of the masters of eating and drinking houses, particularly victuallers. On 14 May 1762, Elizabeth Woodfin, servant to Thomas Yates, swore to the parish officers of Shoreditch, that:[29]

about nine days before Bartholemews Tide last pass as near as she can now recollect as to the time one Thomas Yates a Victualler who keeps the three Pidgeons in Hammersmith placed this Examinant on a large Table in the parlour of his house there and then and there, had carnal knowledge of her body and also about a Week after had in the said parlour and on the said Table a second time carnal knowledge of her said body and is the said father of the said Child or Children with which she is now pregnant And this Examinant also farther saith that since she found herself with Child she acquainted the said Thos. Yates therewith who then offered her six Guineas if she would swear the Child or Children to any other person or marry any young man she liked & pulled out three Guineas and desired one Evans then present to hand him three more who offered to lend him the whole six but this Examinant refused to swear it to any other person but sayd [sic] she would take the six Guineas and he never should be troubled on account of the child but he refused to pay the money unless she this Examinant would swear it to some other person and hath threatened to present this Examinant & put her in the pilory or transport her if she should offer to trouble him on account of getting her wth. Child.

Most sexual relationships between female inn servants and their lodgers, customers, fellow servants, or employers, involved a number of acts of intercourse, over a relatively long period of time, six to nine months. The female servants were single and aged between twenty-one to twenty-seven years old, the optimum age for marriage among the plebeian population of the capital. The male sexual partners were of a similar socio-economic background to the women, and included waiters, journeymen tailors, butchers, and even victuallers. Both the age and social background of the individuals involved point to the possibility that at least some of these sexual relationships were viewed as part of a courtship process. However, the overwhelming impression left by the depositions, as illustrated by the deposition of Elizabeth Woodfin, is of casually entered into short-term sexual affairs.

As with alehouses, the evidence for the nature of sexual relationships sited in lodging houses is complex and ambiguous. 26 per cent of all mothers whose experience was recorded in the examinations for St Clement

Danes gave a lodging house as the place where sex first took place. In St Mary-le-Strand, 33 per cent of all illegitimate sexual relationships occurred in lodgings, while in Chelsea the figure was 19 per cent, and 17 per cent in Aldgate. The more miserable lodging houses of London feature prominently within the historiography of metropolitan sexuality as the home of prostitution and casual carnality.[30] Though the bastardy statements provide examples of prostitution and casual sex taking place in lodging houses, they also provide a more varied image of the sexual uses to which this particular type of location was put.

At one end of the spectrum there are depositions such as that sworn before the parochial officers of St Clement Danes in January 1786 by seventeen-year-old orphan Mary Browne. Mary had worked as a prostitute since the age of eleven, and her evidence would appear to support the contention that many low lodgings were little more than bawdy houses. Mary Browne explained:[31]

> That during the time she has been upon the Town, she has frequently lodged at the House of one Mrs Davies in Jackson's Alley Bow Street, where she has been received as a Lodger, the said Mrs Davies knowing that she was a Prostitute, and that she has frequently with that said Mrs Davies's Knowledge and Consent brought home with her and entertained Men for the purposes of Prostitution—and that several other young women who are common Prostitutes on the Town continually lodge there and are encouraged by the said Mrs Davies in the habit of Prostitution…

Although it is possible that Mrs Davies had organised the house as a brothel it is more likely that the encouragement she gave her female lodgers to bring customers home, revolved around a concern to collect the rent, and the extra fee that would come with each client.[32]

However, closer study of the cases of illegitimate sex in lodging houses undermines any clear connection between prostitution and these particular semi-public spaces. The majority of these lodging-house relationships seemed to have evolved out of a more normal social connection between the sexual partners. Among the majority of individuals involved, whose social position was nearly equivalent, there is compelling evidence to suggest that these sexual encounters were a part of courtship. The age structure of the participants in these relationships between plebeian male lodgers and the female servants who worked in the lodging houses suggest that at least the women viewed them as disrupted courtships. Most of these relationships lasted for upwards of a year before the parochial officers discovered the relationship, generally on the birth of the child, or the desertion of the mother-to-be by her lover. Sex took place a number of times. The women were all unmarried, and tended to be in their late teens or early twenties, suggesting a certain sexual vulnerability and emotional naivety on their part.

Sexual relations involving female lodgers also had the socio-economic indications of being courtship relationships. The majority of illicit sexual relations involving female lodgers were between plebeian men and women, though a minority were also between plebeian women and a minority of males of middling status. Most of the women were female domestic servants, plus several milliners, seamstresses, and a cook. A socio-economic indication, perhaps, that a number of these relationships were part of a courtship process.

Johanna Chapman, a twenty-three year old single woman, who had sex in her lodgings in Wandsworth with William Powell, a blacksmith, during the month of April 1784, did indeed marry her sexual partner in the parish church of St Mary-le-Strand on 18 October 1784—two months after she had sworn to her deposition describing the circumstances of her illegitimate pregnancy.[33] It is not recorded if pressure was brought to bear on Powell by the parish to marry his bride, but it would appear not.

Mary Breech, a twenty-eight year old widow of unknown occupation, thought that her sexual relationship with John Russell, a journeyman staymaker, would end in legitimate marriage, not an illicit pregnancy. In a bastardy statement recorded in St Mary-le-Strand on the 17 December 1741 she stated that John Russell 'through Insinuating and promises [sic] of Marriage had frequently in the Month of April last and at Several times Since Carnal Knowledge of her Body in the Room where she then Lodged at one of which times He did beget on her Body the Child or Children she is now with…'[34]

The sexual relationships between men and women of similar socio-economic backgrounds tended to last longer, with a substantial number having had social relations for one to four years before their first sexual intercourse occurred. This suggests the possibility that at least one of the sexual partners believed themselves to be in a courtship relationship. On 2 July 1764, Elizabeth Marsden, of single marital status, related to the parish officers of St Mary-le-Strand that:[35]

> About Four Years ago she became acquainted with William Wise a Journeyman Baker And that about the Middle of the Month of March in the Year of our Lord One thousand Seven Hundred and Sixty Two he the said William Wise upon a Bed at his then Lodging in a Front Room up Two Pair of Stairs in a House in Drury Lane nearly opposite Vinegar Yard and at divers other Times and Places before that Time had carnal Knowledge of the Body of this Examinant...

However not all illicit sexual relations between plebeian men and women, which were set in lodging houses, were necessarily part of a courtship relationship. The lodgings of plebeian putative fathers could also be the site of more casual sexual episodes. In October 1782, Margaret Harwood, a twenty-eight year old domestic servant of single marital status, had sex with a black mariner, Phillip Warren, in his lodgings at Angel Court in the Strand. When Margaret Harwood swore her deposition four months later her relationship with Phillip Warren was already at an end.[36]

Symmetrical sexual relations staged in lodging houses could also be adulterous in nature.[37] Elizabeth Milkin married her husband Paul, a sailor, on 13 May 1742. Paul Milkin left his wife and child in March 1743 to board ship. By the end of September 1745, Elizabeth Milkin had met Daniel Field, a wharfinger, and begun a sexual relationship with him at her lodgings. When Elizabeth Milkin gave her deposition in March 1746, she was some months pregnant, and named Daniel Field as the putative father.[38]

Though casual sexuality, sexual exploitation, and adultery featured within the illegitimate sexual relations between plebeian men and women conducted in lodging houses, it would appear that for the most part these were relationships that, for one of the sexual partners at least, had been intended as part of the courtship process.

At the same time, a substantial minority of depositions grew out of socially asymmetrical relationships where the possibility of courtship seems less likely. These reflect a different set of expectations and behaviours on the part of the participants. In relationships where the male sexual partner was drawn from the middling sort or gentry, including the officer-class and professionals, a more exploitative set of attitudes can be seen, which reflect the powerfully unequal positions of elite men and plebeian women.

In keeping with Boswell's attitude to the female servants who worked in the metropolitan households where he lodged, the relationships between gentry, professional, and middling order men and female lodging house servants seem to have entailed a strong presumption that these women were sexually available or fair game for seduction. These illicit sexual unions were shorter lived than those between socially equal partners by several months, with a significant number containing a mere one or two sexual episodes.

On 3 August 1776 Ann Wilson, a twenty-three year old widow, swore to a bastardy statement in which she named a physician, Mr Gilbelkausen, as the father of the illegitimate child with which she was a few months pregnant. Ann Wilson had worked as a domestic servant for Mr John Perins, a watchmaker in the Strand, since November 1774. It is not known how long Gilbelkausen had lodged with John Perins, but sometime in January 1776 he seduced Ann Wilson and had sex with her at the lodgings for the one and only time. By mid-July 1776 it was discovered that Wilson was pregnant, and promptly dismissed by her master.[39] When Wilson's bastardy statement was recorded Mr Gilbelkausen was still lodging with John Perins.

When the seduction of female lodging-house servants by gentry or middling order lodgers resulted in an illegitimate pregnancy, the fathers were quick to disavow any emotional, legal, or financial responsibility for the mother or child. This was true in the case of Hannah Bradly, a twenty-eight year old domestic servant who had sexual relations with Thomas Leigh, an attorney's clerk, who lodged with Bradly's employer, a Mrs Ballester who lived in Warwick Street near Golden Square in St James Westminster. Hannah Bradly had worked in Mrs Ballester's household for five months when she first had sex with Thomas Leigh in the spring of 1760. When Bradly discovered she was pregnant she:

applied herself to the said Thomas Leigh for aid and assistance for her lying-in, she not having the wherewithal to maintain her self and the child. He answered, if one single half penny would save her and the child that he would not give it her, and pushed her out of his office…[40]

These asymmetrical sexual relationships could also be coloured by an even more sinister and threatening atmosphere, emphasising the vulnerability of female domestic servants working in the metropolitan household.[41] Elizabeth Butler worked as a domestic servant for a milliner named Mrs Giles, in whose house Richard Tisdell, a 'gentleman', had lodged. In her bastardy statement recorded by the parochial officers on 13 February 1741, Elizabeth Butler related that:

he the said Mr. Tisdell lodging in the same House & coming home late one night in the Month of June last [1740] & locked her in his Room & with Force had Carnall knowledge of her Body at which time he got her with the Bastard Child or Children she is now pregnant.[42]

Some time between the act of rape and the recording of Elizabeth Butler's bastardy statement, Richard Tisdell absconded.

Not all illicit relations between elite men and the female servants who worked in the lodging houses of London involved sexual violence, or even libertinism. At least one or two such sexual unions seem to be relatively long-lived relationships based on an emotional attachment between the individuals involved, even if they did not ultimately lead to marriage. Sir James Carnegie, a Scottish Baronet, first employed Christian Berrychill as a female servant at his home in Nairn. Christian later migrated to London, taking up a place on 16 December 1751 with Mr John Beuermen, a tailor living in Great Suffolk Street, St Martin's-in-the-fields. Though not specifically stated, it would appear that James Carnegie and Christian Berrychill had been lovers before Berrychill left his employ in Scotland. On 8 January 1752, three weeks after Berrychill began her service in London, James Carnegie took lodgings with John Beuermen. The next day, Carnegie 'had carnal knowledge of the body of this Examint. [Christian Berrychill] and several times after in his said Lodgings between that time & the Middle of the next Month'.[43] It is not known if the relationship between James Carnegie and Christian Berrychill continued, whether permanently or temporarily, but on 19 October 1752 Berrychill gave birth to an illegitimate son baptised by the name of James Carnegie.

Although semi-public spaces were the setting for a significant proportion of illegitimate relationships, undoubtedly the majority of illicit sexual unions were conducted within private households, whether this was the home of one or other of the lovers, or that of a relative of the male or female sexual partner, or the household within which either or both lovers were employed. 56 per cent of all sexual relationships in Clement Danes took place in these categories of social settings. In St Mary-le-Strand and Chelsea, private households were the setting for 60 per cent of all illegitimate relationships, and 66 per cent in St Botolphs Aldgate. These households were far less likely to be the setting of exploitative or perfunctory sexual relationships. In the main these were sexual relationships that grew from prolonged social contact between men and women of similar social status.

Nearly one quarter of all sexual relationships recorded in St Clement Danes, St Mary-le-Strand, and St Luke Chelsea were between fellow servants or fellow employees. In St Mary-le-Strand the men were chiefly shopmen or fellow domestic servants. Similarly, the fathers in St Clement Danes, who had affairs with female servants, were male domestic servants, journeymen or apprentices from the manufacturing and retailing trades. These were men who had reached, or soon would reach, that stage of the male life-cycle where they were most likely to wish to marry and set up as a master in their own right. At the same time, these male sexual partners were mainly in trades and occupations in which men could comfortably establish themselves as a small master using the savings accrued by a female domestic servant.[44] They were also men in occupations that often relied upon the labour of the spouses and families of journeymen.[45] It is in these types of social and spatial settings that the majority of sexual relationships evolved. One case history stands proxy for many. During the mid-1780s, Sarah Walker and William Walker worked together for several years for a Mr Johnson who kept an Alamode Beef Shop in Blackmoor Street, St Clement Danes. At some point Sarah and William began a relationship that resulted in the birth of a daughter in October 1787. Atypically, William did, in fact, marry Sarah five weeks after the birth of their child. As far as can be ascertained there was no pressure from the parochial officers of Clement Danes to do so. What is more relevant is that Mr Johnson continued to employ William after the couple married, thus ensuring some form of financial security for the newly formed family.[46]

That is not to say that private households were without sexual exploitation and sexual danger for the women who worked and lived in them. Almost one-in-ten illegitimate sexual relationships in Aldgate, Chelsea, Clement Danes and St Mary-le-Strand were recorded as taking place between a master and his female servant in a private house. And while the socio-economic status of masters involved in such illicit unions were plebeian or middling order in character, with one or two professionals, and only one gentleman, there remained a reslutely exploitative character to the relationships they pursued. The men and women engaged in these relationships were of similar or proximate social status, at least suggesting that they could be viewed as courtship relationships by one or other of the sexual partners. However, even relatively humble masters of female domestic servants in the Georgian metropolis did use their patriarchal power and position to entice or browbeat the women in their employ into sexual relations with them. On 13 October 1750, Elizabeth Bussell described one such extreme misuse of power at the hands of her master Samuel Firmin:

Elizabeth Bussell, single woman, aged 26 years, maketh oath that she lived with Mr Firmin of the parish of St Clement Danes, button seller, as a hired servant about three years and a half, …And this examinant voluntarily says that on the Sunday night the riot happened in the Strand (which was on 14 Apr. last) her young master (Mr Samuel Firmin) then took an opportunity, there was only an errand boy besides themselves in the house, to lock him out of the room where they were, and forcibly lay with her, this examinant, which was effected by his taking a penknife out of his pocket and threatening to kill her if she refused. With which she was so much terrified and weak by struggling, [she] was obliged to comply against her will. And this examinant also says that the said Samuel Firmin several times afterwards lay with her frequently. And one time in particular he beat her so much about the eyes, which were so bad, she was obliged to apply to one Mrs Dean, an oculist, for a cure. And this examinant further says that she believes she had a miscarriage by her young master, as Mr Stammers (Mrs Firmin's father) very well knows. For she says that

Mr Stammers often persuaded and prevailed on her to drink warm ale in which she had great reason to believe he had put something extraordinary, for it always soon after made her sleep very much. And says that Mr Stammers himself has used her very ill, and often attempted to get into her room when she was in bed to lay with her. And this examinant says that in her conscience she really believes that the illness and unhappy disorder she has lately been under in the said workhouse was occasioned wholly by the base and unkind treatment both of young Mtr Samuel Firmin and the said Mr Stammers.[47]

Despite this catalogue of callous, pre-meditated sexual and psychological abuse against a female servant by her master, not all master-servant sexual relationships were of this character. They could also originate from a mutual affection, leading to marriage or a marriage-like relationship. One such example was sworn to by Ann Winter. Ann Winter, a servant to James Hemlock, a druggist, cohabited with her master at his house on Snow Hill in the parish of St Sepulchres in the City of London for at least ten years during the 1760s and 1770s. From 1770 to 1775, Hemlock fathered three illegitimate children by Ann Winter: named John, William, and Charlotte. When the parish officers of St Clement Danes recorded the deposition of Ann Winter on 20 June 1779, it was not made clear whether the cohabiters had separated.[48] As she was in the position of giving such a deposition, it can only be assumed that somehow, whether through death or estrangement, their relationship was at an end, but it is likewise apparent that it had been a relatively strong one, while it lasted.

It is clear that the streets and alleyways of London were not the main stage for the collective sex-life of metropolitan inhabitants, and that the current historiography is wrong to emphasise the extent of public sex on the streets of eighteenth-century London. The major portion of open-air illicit affairs, which were recorded in the bastardy statements of the five parishes assayed here, actually took place outside the main urbanised areas of the capital. Those instances of carnality recorded as being set in places of public access tended to be either acts of prostitution or casual sexual relations, but in either case, were relatively uncommon. In the semi-public space of the inn, tavern and alehouse, where a notable minority of carnal affairs were conducted, these illicit sexual acts emerged from a variety of

social contexts. Though it would appear that at least some of these relations involved prostitution, the picture is complicated by the existence of
a large number of relationships which seem more like courtship than
commerce. At the same time, it is clear that these semi-public sexual
settings witnessed a range of sexually exploitative and misogynistic behaviours. In cases where lodging houses (these most public of private spaces)
formed the locus of the relationship, an even more variegated picture
emerges. In the main, these were sexual relations between men and women
of the same social standing, who for the most part appear to have been
involved in a courtship relationship. At the same time, one can also find
prostitution, casual sexual affairs, and sexual exploitation. Undoubtedly
the main site of illegitimate heterosexuality was to be found in the private
households of both eastern and western parishes. Sexual relationships
were founded mainly amongst men and women who lived and worked
within the same household. Though emerging from different social contexts
and social relations, it was within both the semi-public and private sphere,
but most especially the private, that eighteenth-century metropolitan
heterosexual relationships were most commonly conducted.

8. The Spatiality of the Poor in Eighteenth-Century London

John Marriott

Street cleaning

The opportunity radically to rebuild the capital along planned and rational lines after the great fire of 1666 was squandered. Major thoroughfares were widened and large numbers of houses and public buildings reconstructed, but the medieval palimpsest was preserved, and much of the capital's public space remained irregular, haphazard and dirty. This lack of vital space for London's citizens to meet, converse and relax in a secure and congenial environment hampered the development of these new publics of privatised individuals, in response to which determined attempts were made to know and hence civilise its streets. In what follows I wish to investigate aspects of this exploratory and civilising endeavour, and assess its impact on the dynamics of what was arguably the most intractable problem faced by reformers, namely, the dogged persistence of the poor in the known and unknown spaces of London's topography.

In the course of the eighteenth century legal, parochial and literary authorities attempted to appropriate the streets of London, and hence transform spatial conceptions of a city fast emerging as the great centre of world trade and empire. It was against this backdrop that urban improvement gathered momentum. Plans were outlined by John Spranger in 1754 which heralded a cultural geography of Westminster appropriate to its status as the locus of an ascendant commercial power:

> In all well-governed Countries, the first Care of the Governors hath
> been to make the Intercourse of the Inhabitants, as well as of
> Foreigners, sojourning in the Country, safe, easy and commodious,

by open, free and regular *Highways*. This is more especially incumbent on *Trading* Nations, as, without a free and safe Intercourse between Place and Place by Land as well as by water, *trade* cannot subsist, much less flourish.[1]

Spranger proposed that in order to overcome the piecemeal reform by local bodies which had so stifled effective action, authority should be invested in commissioners to make by-laws, raise funds through the rates and punish offenders. The resultant Act, 2 Geo 3 cap.21, provided the power and finances to adopt systematic programmes of improvement, thereby guaranteeing an unprecedented uniformity in paving and street lighting. Such improvement was dependent, however, upon a systematic knowledge of metropolitan topography; it was in this period that London's expansive physical body became known.

John Strype's edition of Stow's *Survey of London* appeared in 1720. It was the product of nearly twenty years' labour, but contained so much obsessive detail that Stow's personal stamp was almost entirely lost.[2] Strype meticulously mapped London's topography through descriptive travelogues, interrupted by historical detours into churches, monuments, dignitaries and charities, but in the process revealed little more than the physical streetscapes of individual wards:

Then turn back again through the said Postern lane to *Moor lane*; which *Moor lane*, with all the Allies and Buildings there, is of this Ward. After that is *Grub street*, more than half thereof to the streightening of the Street. Next is *Whitecross street*, up to the end of *Beech lane*; and then *Redcross street* wholly, with a part of *Golden lane*, even to the Posts there placed as a Bounder.[3]

This was a venture made possible by the active involvement of commercial and political interests. The mayor and court of the City of London, to whom Strype dedicated the work, offered practical and financial support from the outset, and the list of subscribers' names included attorneys, goldsmiths, merchants and gentlemen. Most significant, however, were booksellers and printers, who numbered forty-three out of a total of 272. The control of cultural production was passing from the hands of personal patronage to the local state and the metropolitan market.

These interests were also evident in the publication of John Rocque's great maps of London. Published in 1746 as twenty-four imperial sheets making a map measuring thirteen by six and a half feet, they represented the first systematic cartographical survey of London since 1682.[4] Rocque also had the support of the City, and among the four hundred subscribers were counted Horace Walpole, government offices, and academic institutions. The map, drawn with an unmatched intricacy and precision, was intended both as a reliable guide to the 'street traveller' and an accurate record of London's world status. In the event its form rendered it difficult to use; it remained, like Strype's survey, little more than an ordered inventory of names and shapes without interpretation.

Something of a transition was heralded by the publication in 1766 of the Rev. John Entick's weighty and detailed record of the metropolis.[5] Combining history, sociology and topography, Entick attempted a totalising vision of the labyrinthine complexity of London's spaces previously beyond the purview of detached observers such as Strype. In this, he drew upon earlier surveys, particularly Stow's, but by implicit references to street life, Entick anticipated the survey of Charles Booth over a century later:

> *Grub-Street*, as far as *Sun-Alley*, is in Cripplegate-Ward; but it is not either well-built, nor inhabited better than *Moor-Lane*. Nevertheless, it contains a number of courts and alleys, as, *Lins-Alley, Honey-Suckle Court*, well built; *Fleur de lis Court, Little Bell-Alley, Flying horse-Court, Oakley-Court, Butler's Alley, Crosskeys Court, Great Bell Alley*; all very mean.[6]

These surveys opened up Westminster and the City to the bourgeois pedestrian and traveller; all they now needed were clear street names:

> Whereas, were but the names of Streets cut on white Stones, the Letters blacken'd, and set up at every Corner, the Greatest stranger might, with the assistance of a small pocket Map, find his Way to any Part of these contiguous Cities and their extended Liberties.[7]

The attempt to know London's physical and social topography was paralleled by the literary appropriation of metropolitan space. The London of Daniel Defoe was akin to that of Strype and Rocque. Evident in his *Tour Thro' the Whole Island of Great Britain* and novels such as *Moll Flanders*, it was one of a featureless, formless and two-dimensional inventory of street names and buildings, conveying a sense only of an anonymous and ceaseless traffic.[8] More significant was the topography that came to be revealed in the work of Augustan satirists. Pope, Gay, Swift and Hogarth provided dense maps of the city and its inhabitants that were not only reliable guides to its intimate topography, but simultaneously gazetteers of a distinct cultural geography in which the infested courts, alleys and markets became symbolic sites of a sombre regime. Their moral symbolism, therefore, was located not in some vague, Miltonic pandaemonium, but on the congested physical landscape of London.[9]

As a result of these various impulses, in the latter half of the eighteenth century London streets became straighter, better paved, lit, and known, more closely surveyed, cleaner—in short, more civilised and modern. Thus constituted, they formed urban spaces fit for bourgeois intercourse and conviviality, but also a communications infrastructure opening up the new sites of relaxation—parks, shops, coffee houses and theatres—to a wider public. It was a process integral to metropolitan modernity.[10] But who precisely inhabited these spaces, and for what reasons? Corbyn Morris' close analysis of the growth of London supplied some of the answers:

> Multitudes of adult Persons are continually called to *London* from various Parts, by occasional Business. To instance Particulars,—Many of the Courts of Justice…Others by commercial affairs; as foreign and provincial Merchants, Tradesmen, Captains of Ships, Grazers, and all sorts of apprentices—Great numbers by Attendance upon the Court and Parliament, as Persons from different Counties, interested in publick Acts, Officers naval and military, and others soliciting Preferment.[11]

This for the most part was a bourgeoisie working, living and moving in a metropolis at the centre of commerce, empire, the law and government. Here was a forum for their activities, an environment containing unparalleled opportunities for exchange with like-minded people, even if strangers. Here too were unprecedented concentrations of material and cultural resources at their disposal that promoted one of the most dynamic features of urban modernity, namely, consumption. London was the 'showcase capital city' of a country thrust into the vanguard of consumer culture through possession of the appropriate material and intellectual preconditions.[12]

There remained, however, a continued threat to this modernisation. Streets could be known, and then cleansed and straightened by the determined removal of physical detritus; human forms proved rather more stubborn. Beggars, vagabonds, and criminals of various descriptions were drawn to London, and as long as they contested its streets and found refuge in its innermost sanctuaries, bourgeois public space was never likely to be entirely secured, modernised or cleansed.

Publick beggars

Vagrancy emerged as a problem in early modern England. The decline of agrarian capitalism, implementation of poor laws, demographic dislocation attendant on enclosure, and increases in population swelled the ranks of so-called masterless men, many of whom were compelled to wander around the country in search of work.[13] As potent symbols of transgression in a society that valorised protestant virtues of sobriety, hard work, thrift and respectability, vagabonds and incorrigible rogues were subject to an extraordinarily brutal repertoire of sanctions from whipping and branding to transportation and execution.[14]

Toward the end of the seventeenth century the problem of vagrancy eased. Enhanced economic prospects and increased poor law expenditure forced fewer into transient poverty. This was accompanied by a less harsh disciplinary regime. Vagrants were less likely to be punished as vagabonds. Instead, under settlement laws, they were removed to their place of origin where they could receive statutory relief. By 1700 the vagrant population comprised largely itinerant Scots, Irish, gypsies, entertainers and the ex-military.[15]

Our understanding of vagrancy in later periods is flimsy, but it is evident that even if the number of vagrants fell, the problem persisted in the public imagination throughout the eighteenth century. It continued, for example, to command the attention of the legislature; at least twenty-eight statutes were introduced between 1700 and 1824 to mitigate the problem.[16] And the vagrant was endowed with a certain literary status, inspiring the writings of social commentators, novelists, poets and play-wrights. The metropolis, inevitably, was the focus of this imagination:

> The number of Beggars increases daily, our Streets swarm with this kind of People, and their boldness and impudence is such that they often beat at our Doors, stop Persons in the ways, and are ready to load us with Curses and Imprecations if their Desires be not speed-ily answered.[17]

London acted as a magnet for those displaced from the countryside. Here concentrations of untold wealth were available to be tapped by those with the various skills of begging, fraud, theft and trickery. Relatively little could be done under extant legislation to remove the migrants. In small City parishes it was possible to control immigration by readily identifying newcomers, but in the larger out parishes constant surveillance was impos-sible. Confusion between the operation of the poor and vagrancy laws, lack of suitable local officials to enforce them, and the constant worry about costs of removal to places of settlement or incarceration meant that for many parishes the easy option was to allow migrants to reside until they became a financial burden.[18]

Without employment and rights to relief vagrants were forced to turn to begging and crime. Indeed, in the metropolitan context (and we have to be sensitive to region) the two were so closely articulated as to appear were synonymous:

> The first sources…of the many robberies committed in our streets…is the prodigious and scandalous encrease of publick beggars….[T]here are more publick beggars in London and Westminster alone than in all the great cities of Europe put together, tho' the revenue collected for the use of the poor in these cities exceeds the revenue of some very respectable sovereign states….That greatest part of these vermin, live better in their secret retirements, and carry home more money at night, than most working trademen, is a well known truth; that most of them are thieves, is doubted by very few.[19]

Encapsulated here was a range of concerns about the metropolitan poor, ill defined though that constituency was.[20] Financial appropriation by, and the spatiality of begging were singled out for attention, growing significantly its symbolic importance.[21] The links between theft and begging, however, were tenuous. Women formed the large majority of those indicted for vagrancy in eighteenth-century London. Widows, out of work servants and abandoned mothers—among the more precarious and vulnerable—featured prominently in the records.[22] Of indicted male vagrants between 1757 and 1776, more than half were over forty years of age, made up for the most part of veteran soldiers and sailors, unemployed artisans and the infirm.[23] These were neither stereotypical beggars, nor those likely to threaten unduly the might of finance and commercial capital.

It was the appropriation by beggars of public space that troubled middle-class London. Given that such space was of critical significance to modernisation, the perceived threat from a population seen as a barrier to progress had to be taken seriously. Space was foregrounded in vagrant laws and in various reforms to drive beggars from the streets and better survey the haunts to which they retreated at night. But of greater significance were the ways in which space both informed and was informed by the discursive construction of the London poor more generally.

Tricks of the town

The eighteenth-century literature of metropolitan roguery had an historical lineage traceable to the Satirical pamphlets of Renaissance London. In a climate of rising of urban pathology attendant on the period of destabilising growth toward the end of the sixteenth century, a metropolitan readership had sought in rogue literature solutions more permanent and valid than those available in dominant religious and feudal perspectives.[24] With the emergence of new political and economic settlements in the latter half of the seventeenth century, this literature fragmented and declined; by the eighteenth it comprised tediously reworked taxonomies of criminal activity, and shameless plagiarisms of familiar formulae.[25]

The tone was set by the publication in 1699 of *The Country Gentleman's Vade-Mecum*, which brought together a number of letters written to a friend to dissuade him from coming to London.[26] It sold poorly and was of little significance, but was resurrected after 1735 in a series of bowdlerised editions, thereby establishing a genre which continued well into the nine-teenth century.[27] Unimaginative though this genre was, it revealed some-thing of the nature of contemporary concern about public space in the metropolis. *A Trip Through the Town* stated:

> The Town of London is a kind of large forest of *Wild-Beasts*, where most of us range about at a venture, and are equally savage, and mutually destructive one of another:…the strange *Hurries* and *Impertinencies*; the busy *Scramblings* and *Underminings*; and what is worse, the monstrous *Villainies, Cheats* and *Impostures* in it.[28]

The passage was reproduced in subsequent versions and used to good effect by Henry Fielding in his *Enquiry into the Causes of the Late recent Encrease in Robbers* (1751). The untamed forest thus became a familiar trope to capture a sense of threat experienced at a time when the metropolitan streetscape began to be surveyed for the first time. It also signalled a depar-ture from previous attempts to map London.[29] As we have seen, Strype's edition of Stow's *Survey of London* had charted the physical topography of its streets, and the built environment of church, monarchy and state had been described in publications such as *The Foreigner's Guide*,[30] but these failed to access the sociological, even when faced by apparently troubling presence of poverty. Now moral baedeckers[31] attempted to describe the life encountered on the author's peregrinations around metropolitan streets. Beggars were singled out as a source of particular concern:

> Turning out of *Covent-Garden* to go to the *Strand* I was accosted by several Beggars, maim'd, lame and lazy. As Pity is so often by our selves and in our own Cases mistaken for Charity, so it assumes the Shape and borrows the very name of it; a *Beggar* asks you to exert that Virtue for *Jesus Christ's sake*, but all the while this great Design is to raise your pity… People not used to great Cities, being thus attacked on all sides, are commonly forced to yield, and cannot help giving something, tho' they can hardly spare it themselves.[32]

These sentiments were those of a metropolitan bourgeoisie forced to contemplate the logical inconsistencies of its moral universe. Beggars were a challenge not because they constituted a serious material threat but because they were able to touch directly the moral and aesthetic sensibilities of a metropolitan elite *in public*:

> When sores are very bad, or seen otherwise afflicting in an extraordinary manner, and the Beggar can bear to have them exposed to the cold air, it is very shocking to some People; 'tis a shame they cry such Sights shou'd be suffer'd: the main reason is, it touches their Pity *feelingly*, at the same time they are resolv'd, either because they are covetous, or count it an idle Expense, to give nothing, which makes them more uneasy. They turn their Eyes, and where the Cries are dismal, some would willingly stop their Ears, mend their Pace, and be very angry in their Hearts, that Beggars shou'd be about Streets.[33]

It was a peculiarly modern challenge (one which many of us still find familiar and uncomfortable) whose symbolic importance seemed to gain force as London emerged as a great commercial and imperial centre. The threat posed by beggars to bourgeois space was transcoded to the nation. Take, for example, Joshua Gee's *The Trade and Navigation of Great Britain Considered*, first published in 1729, and reprinted many times subsequently. This was a substantial thesis on the 'mighty consequence' of trade, and the threat posed to 'vast riches' by the 'want of due regard and attention'. It described in detail Britain's trade with various countries around the world, and outlined proposals for increasing its share. Among the chapters, however, was one entitled 'Proposals for better regulating and employing the poor'. This seeming incongruity makes sense only when the location of the poor within empire is understood:

> But not withstanding we have so many excellent Laws, great numbers of sturdy beggars, loose and vagrant Persons infest the Nation; but no place more than in the city of London and parts adjacent. If any Person is born with any defect or deformity, or maimed by fire, or any other casualty, or by any inveterate distemper, which renders them miserable Objects, their way is open to London; where they have free Liberty of shewing their nauseous sights to terrify People, and force them to give money to get rid of them; and those vagrants

have, for many years past, removed out of several parts of the three kingdoms, and taken their stations in this Metropolis, to the interruption of Conversations and Business.[34]

Desarts of Africa or Arabia

It was in Henry Fielding's *An Enquiry into the Causes of the Late Encrease of Robbers*, however, that we can see the most determined attempt to think through metropolitan poverty and street crime, in the course of which he emphasised another space of concern.[35] Descriptions of the poor drew upon the language of contemporary pamphlets. The identification of 'expensive diversions', 'drunkenness' and 'gaming' as the sources of crime, for example, reflected arguments repeated constantly in literature, courts, churches and parliament. And his approach to the nature, rights and impact of the poor was informed strongly by conventional economic, religious and legal thought.[36] It was a work of awkward synthesis rather than originality, and one replete with conceptual confusion. But it had the merit of recognising that London was assailed by distinct problems which contemporary writings had failed to illuminate.

Using a conventional taxonomy he divided the poor into those 'unable to work', 'able and willing to work', and 'able to work, but not willing'.[37] Beggars, most of whom were recruited from the first two classes, were not of particular concern. If in England 'should be found more Beggars, more distress and miserable objects than are to be seen thro-out all the States of Europe', this was owing to the virtuous humanity of 'all men of Property' who are 'so forward to relieve the Appearance of Distress in their Fellow-creatures' they fail to appreciate that they are encouraging a nuisance.[38] More threatening were the vagabonds, who were unwilling to work, preferring to find their way to London where they could thieve while avoiding detection. The 1740 Vagrant Act (13 Geo 2 cap. 5) designed to deal more effectively with the 'idle and disorderly, rogues and vagabonds, and incorrigible rogues' had dubious relevance to the conditions found there:

Now, however useful this excellent Law may be in the Country, it will by no means serve the Purpose of this Town: for tho' most of the Rogues who infest the Public Roads and Streets, indeed almost all the Thieves in general, are Vagabonds in the true Sense of the Word,

being Wanderers from their lawful Place of Abode, very few of them
will be proved vagabonds within the Words of this Act of Parliament.
These various Vagabonds do indeed get their Livelihood by Thieving,
and not as petty Beggars or petty Chapmen; and have their Lodgings
not in alehouses, etc. but in private houses.[39]

In securing the nexus between poverty and crime, Fielding spatially
reordered the criminal geography of the metropolis. Public spaces inhabited by beggars were not the principal sites of concern for they provided
the metropolitan bourgeoisie with an opportunity to display their chari-
table virtues. Of greater significance were the congested courts, rookeries
and alleys where vagabonds found refuge. These were seen as the sinks of
lawlessness, rendered even worse by the fact that they were private, gothic
and unknowable:

> Whoever indeed considers the Cities of *London* and *Westminster*, with
> the late vast Addition of their Suburbs; the great irregularity of their
> Buildings, the immense Number of Lanes, Alleys, Courts and Bye-
> places; must think, that, had they been intended for the very Purpose
> of Concealment, they could scarce have been better contrived. Upon
> such a View, the whole appears as a vast Wood or Forest, in which a
> Thief may harbour with as great Security, as wild Beasts do in the
> Desarts of *Africa* or *Arabia*. For by *wandering* from one Part to another,
> and often shifting his quarters, he may almost avoid the Possibility
> of being discovered.[40]

As a reforming magistrate who encountered directly those unfortunates
who were unable to avoid 'discovery', Fielding displayed a predictable
tendency to criminalise the streets. The ordering of criminal and poor space
in the metropolis was, however, complex and dynamic. It was intimately
related to perceived distinctions between criminal and pauper activity, and
their structural underpinnings. 'The nature and importance of illegality
were in part defined by its social location', argues McMullan,[41] but the
process was reciprocal—space was also powerfully formed by its crimi-
nalisation. Criminal enclaves persisted in the bourgeois imagination as
proximate antitheses of its own space in the City and Westminster, but at

particular moments of economic depression, bourgeois space itself was seen as threatened by incursions from the only too visible presence of beggars.

We understand little of this dynamic. What is apparent is that much of the writing on metropolitan poverty and crime during the eighteenth century was consciously or otherwise an attempt to understand this spatial reordering. Inevitably, the previous era of metropolitan history exerted a formative influence. In the period from 1550 to 1700 distinct criminal enclaves emerged with a powerful sense of territorial independence that persisted until the mid-nineteenth century.[42] Thus the Clink and the Mint in Southwark, Whitefriars and Alsatia at the City's south-eastern boundary, Spitalfieds and Whitechapel, and the Newgate-Cripplegate area entered into popular imagination as congested zones of criminal activity. Here were defensible spaces where thieves, prostitutes, cheats and beggars found refuge from the law and public surveillance. The complex networks of alleys, lanes and stairs made pursuit difficult, made even more so by strategies of mutual protection adopted by their inhabitants to discourage intruders.

This unknowability contrasted sharply with the only too visible presence of beggars on the main thoroughfares. Stationary beggars adopted strategies that relied on distinct appropriations of space.[43] Sites offering privileged access to pedestrian and carriage traffic were occupied and jealously guarded. Thus the Royal Exchange, St Paul's, the Strand and Charing Cross were favoured. Here beggars could prey upon the sensibilities of large numbers of passers by without undue risk of apprehension under the vagrant laws. The least mobile had to claim their pitch early in the morning; over time they became familiar figures in the metropolitan streetscape.[44]

Beggars and petty thieves, then, were perceived as less of a threat than hardened professional criminals such as thieves, footpads and highwaymen. Beggars may have jostled and disgusted bourgeois pedestrians, but they rarely posed a danger to personal and material well being. And draconian as the vagrancy laws were they could hardly compare with the murderous judicial regime created by the litany of capital statutes introduced at the beginning of the century under which minor acts of theft commanded the death penalty.

For the most part, beggars were seen as an inconvenient and unpleasant presence on metropolitan streets. At particular moments, however, when their numbers increased dramatically, more serious concern was expressed in the literature. The extent of begging was determined by the state of the labour market. It was linked, therefore, to the trade cycle, and if it were possible accurately to chart its course correlations could be made between economic recessions and concern over begging. The eighteenth-century picture, however, was complicated by the frequent interruptions of war.[45] Although the effect of war depended upon the particular stage in the trade cycle when it broke out, what is not in doubt is the impact that the cease of hostilities had on unemployment. As war ended, tens of thousands of ex-soldiers and sailors were dumped on the streets to survive as best they could; many did so through begging and crime. 157,000 men were discharged in 1713–14 (War of Spanish Succession), 79,000 in 1749–50 (War of Austrian Succession), 155,000 in 1764–5 (Seven Years' War), 160,000 in 1784–5 (American War of Independence), and 350,000 after 1815 (Napoleonic Wars). Unsurprisingly, these were the moments of the most intense anxiety about the state of metropolitan streets, when the putative links between beggars and crime were stated most forcefully.

The distinction between roguery and villainy was also evident in popular literature.[46] Rogues were rascals, generally without malice, who lived and worked on the peripheries of the criminal underworld. From the seventeenth century, their culture was described in the picaresque literature of jest books, canting verses and lexicons, travelogues and biographies. In this literature had appeared the first attempts to know the underworld of early modern London, but during the eighteenth century the genre created by Greene and Harman degenerated into tedious formulae. Previous works were pirated, canting lexicons repeated with little variation. Similar trajectories were apparent in fictional and dramatic representations. Richard Brome's *A Jovial Crew* and John Gay's *A Beggar's Opera* have long been recognised as among the most popular and significant plays about roguery. In seeming to celebrate the comparative freedom of beggars from the economic and moral restraint of the time, they touched on a range of contemporary concerns.[47] But these concerns were not around beggars. First staged during the extreme tensions of 1641, *The Jovial Crew* used a familiar narrative of redemption to expose the hazardous and circumscribed liberty of anyone denied property and political rights in an arbitrary and savage regime. And *The Beggar's Opera*, performed in the aftermath of the bloody regime heralded by the introduction of the Black Act and the troubled economic climate created by the South Sea Bubble fiasco, used a London gang of highway-men and thieves (not beggars) to expose the hypocrisy and corruption of upper-class rule embodied in the Walpole regime.

Rogue fiction in the remainder of the eighteenth century possessed little of this critical capacity. Colley Cibber's production of the *Beggar's Wedding, The Beggar's Pantomime* (1736), and the revival of a traditional tale in *The Blind Beggar of Bethnal Green* (1741), were examples of fanciful cele-brations of the putative exoticism and gaiety of outlaw life. All these were eclipsed, however, by the extraordinary success of *An Apology for the Life of Bampfylde-Moore Carew* first published in 1745 and republished in various editions until well into the nineteenth century.[48] It recounted the story 'taken from the mouth' of Carew, the son of a Devonshire gentleman, who fell in with beggars. Like most other rogue literature of the eighteenth century it was a clumsy compilation of extracts from other publications, including Dekker's *Belman of London* (1608), Harman, Fielding's *Tom Jones* and canting dictionaries. Its success, concluded Chandler, 'was dispro-portionate to its merit'.[49]

This literature stood in sharp contrast to the extraordinary output of criminal biography in the same period. In excess of two thousand narra-tives were published in the seventeenth and eighteenth centuries.[50] They appeared suddenly, effectively displacing the prominence of earlier genres of rogue literature found in the metropolis. Purporting to describe the lives, misdemeanours and dying confessions of villains, the accounts served a rather more serious function than providing vicarious and sensational drama for the reader. The biographies of highwaymen, thieves, murder-ers and burglars may have differed in their narrative and mythical struc-tures, but at a time of social and political instability they revealed 'not only the justification of God and the vindication of man but the strengthen-ing, too, of an increasingly favoured conception of society'. In the second half of the eighteenth century, as their social and political significance receded, so the publication of criminal biographies fell. By the 1770s, even highwaymen were forgotten. It was as if attempts to gain access to or even register the presence of the criminal poor in the metropolis had been abandoned.[51]

The eighteenth century thus witnessed a protracted and largely unsuc-cessful attempt to confer order on the spatiality of poverty in the metropolis. At its close it was apparent that in spite of numerous topographical and literary surveys ignorance of the criminalised underworld still prevailed. Concern surfaced from time to time over the presence of beggars and vagrants in public spaces, but their affront was to the sensibilities rather than material and physical welfare of bourgeois pedestrians

In contrast, the gothic haunts of Westminster and the City that provided sanctuary for the more vicious elements of the metropolitan underworld remained unknown, uncontrolled and feared. Occupying identifiable criminalised spaces proximate to the public spaces claimed by the metropolitan bourgeoisie, this was a culture beyond the gaze and reach of travellers, pedestrians, parochial authorities and the law. Not until the mid-nineteenth century was it reached by the determined efforts of evangelicals and urban travellers. What they wrote, and the Dickensian fiction it inspired, perpetuated the significance of the metropolitan underworld in the bourgeois imaginary.

In the troubled decade of the 1790s other mythical sites were constructed. Equally feared, they overlapped with older criminalised spaces, but for the most part were located in the newly-constructed riverside areas of East London. These were the sites inhabited by the casual residuum, first identified and defined by Patrick Colquhoun when he turned his considerable energies to the alleviation of metropolitan poverty and crime.[52]

Back to the jungle

In a lively celebration of the modern urban odyssey, Penelope Corfield has argued that in spite of the claims of 'Hanoverian satirists and Victorian reformers' that city streets were unchartered tracks through lawless jungles, they were 'known arteries of public communication in an expanding public network'.[53] I remain sceptical, for the attempt to survey and thereby know the metropolitan streetscape during the eighteenth century was faltering, contradictory and incomplete. Even at its close, the sites of poverty, thought to provide refuge for petty and more serious criminal cultures, were little understood.

This is not to deny modernising impulses in the metropolis; on the contrary, it is better to appreciate them. The mode of vital existence that is modernity is replete with seemingly contradictory dimensions; it is both an affirmation of empowerment—an excitement in the potential of social and productive development—and a fear of danger posed by its more destructive guises. The metropolitan bourgeoisie who attempted to create public space did so as part of its modern vision, but it never forgot the antithetical presence of forces that seemingly defied modernity. Beggars and vagabonds may have been migrants, often ingenious in their negotiation with metropolitan codes and rhythms, but they fiercely resisted the legal, temporal, spatial and moral imperatives of bourgeois modernisation throughout the eighteenth century. And they continued to live in the jungle and the desert.

In the course of the nineteenth century, more intense policing, the development of harshly efficient mechanisms of poor relief, and improvements in the economy reduced the numbers resorting to the streets, particularly around the streets of Westminster and the City. Redevelopment and slum clearance schemes helped to assuage the threat from proximate criminal enclaves. The fulfilment of bourgeois public space in Westminster and the City, if not realised, must have appeared realisable for the first time.

But the antithetical spectre of a low other could not be excised totally. The casual residuum, defined and located by Colquhoun, had by mid-nineteenth century emerged as the principal, racialised object of fear and disgust.[54] When it eventually broke out of the confines of East London to rampage public spaces in the City, fears of the metropolitan bourgeoisie reached levels of intensity rarely previously witnessed.

9. Private Crime in Public and Private Places

Pickpockets and Shoplifters in London, 1780–1823

Deirdre Palk

The streets of London have long provided ripe opportunities for a variety of thieving activities. Shoplifting and pickpocketing are obvious examples. At the end of the eighteenth century and the beginning of the nineteenth century, shoplifters and pickpockets were active in the capital's streets, squares, rows, lanes and alleys. This chapter reflects on some of the cases tried at the Old Bailey Sessions, which provide insights into metropolitan street life and the ways in which male and female thieves used street space for their operations. It focuses on these two capital crimes—stealing privily in a shop (shoplifting), from 1780 to 1823, and stealing privily from the person (pickpocketing), from 1780 to 1808.[1]

Despite contemporaries' views about the prevalence of these crimes,[2] only a small proportion reached court. One reason for this was their precise legal definition. This is considered first in this chapter, which will then look at who was involved, and at how and when the men and women who came before the court at the Old Bailey[3] went about their business on the streets of London. Gender differences in these activities will be seen to be significant, raising questions about men's and women's use of space, time and opportunities.

The capital crimes of shoplifting and pickpocketing were difficult and costly to prove in court, with the result that relatively few went to trial at the Old Bailey Sessions, representing only a small tip of the large iceberg of these types of larceny.[4] Shoplifting—private larceny in a shop—became a capital crime in 1699[5] when the statute makers responded severely to public perception of shoplifting as a growing phenomenon in the later

years of the seventeenth century, going hand in hand with the development of shops in the streets of towns and cities, particularly in London.[6]
A shoplifter was one who 'at any time… in any shop… privately and feloniously' stole 'Goods, Wares or Merchandises, being of the Value of Five
Shillings or more'. Above all, shoplifting was a 'private' crime. This meant
that a shopkeeper was unlikely to be successful in prosecuting a shoplifter
if there had been any 'cognizance by another person' that the offence was
about to be committed. 'The slightest glimpse of the taking, or even a suspicion of it, seemed to obviate the capital part of the charge'.[7]

The major transformation in retailing in London during the seventeenth
and eighteenth centuries resulted in greater opportunity for theft from shops.
Theft was made easier by increased display of goods in shop windows and
showcases to make them more attractive, and by the way that merchandise
spilled out over street space—hanging in shop doorways or displayed on the
pavement—to tempt the casual shopper. Shop windows were seen as street
ornamentation and new wide pavements enabled crowds to stop and inspect
'the thousands of inventions and ideas' which were available for sale.[8]
However, defrauded shopkeepers had great difficulty in showing that a theft
had been 'private'. London shopkeepers and their staff were wary and alert,
deeply suspicious of every customer they did not know. They kept their eyes
open to comings and goings in the streets outside their own and their neighbours' shops, and, if trade allowed, mounted watch on their neighbours'
premises. For instance, when a clothes seller had hurried to bring inside his
shop his stock—shoes and clothing—from the pavement outside for fear of
a fire in another part of the street, his first concern was to instruct his shop
lad to watch Eliza Nash who had been eyeing the clothes in the doorway.
However, it was his neighbour opposite who brought Nash back a short while
later, with a stolen great coat stowed under her petticoats.[9] The cases heard
at the Old Bailey show how busy the London shops were, full of customers
waiting to be served—anything from a dozen to sixty, if witnesses are to be
believed—and full of people observing others.

Shoplifting was a crime that provoked conflicting emotions. On the one
hand, small shopkeepers expressed desperation about 'the daily depredations'[10] they suffered. On the other hand, some of the more prosperous
traders deplored the new commercial methods being used by their rivals—
knock-down prices, 'sales', and other retail gimmicks, which were deemed

unfair enticement of the ordinary person, particularly the 'ordinary woman'. Evidence given to the 1819 Select Committee on the Criminal Law claimed that shopkeepers' goods are 'flying in the face of every miserable woman who is going past'.[11] Women were significantly involved in this crime; although only thirty or so shoplifting cases were brought before the petty jury at the Old Bailey each year, 54 per cent of defendants were women.[12]

Pickpocketing—larceny '*clam et secrete*' from the person—had been a capital crime since 1565; the crime of feloniously taking any money, goods or chattels worth twelve pence or more from the person of any other, privily, without his knowledge.[13] The sixteenth-century law-makers had in mind a particular crime, which involved:

> certain kinds of evil-disposed persons who do confeder together, making among themselves as it were a brotherhood or fraternity of an art or mystery, to live idly by the secret spoil of the good and true subjects of this realm. [This they did] at time of service or common prayer, in churches, chapels, closets and oratories, also in the Prince's palace, house, yea, and presence, and at the places and courts of justice, in fairs and markets, and other assemblies of the people…and at the execution of such as [sic] been attainted of…murder, felony or other criminal cause, ordained chiefly for the terror and example of evildoers…without respect or regard of any time, place or person, or any fear or dread of God…under the cloak of honesty of their outward appearance, countenance and behaviour, subtilly, privily, craftlily…to the utter undoing and impoverishing of many.[14]

Such a description applied to masculine activities. Contemporaries perceived pickpocketing as a crime perpetrated by boys, and the stereo-typical character of the London streets was the young male who 'displayed a demeanour of assertive, precocious, masculinity'.[15] However, when it came to cases of private stealing from the person tried at the Old Bailey, of the only thirteen to fourteen pick-pocketing cases tried each year in this period, 55 per cent of the defendants were female. The great majority of these were described as women of the town, or 'unfortunate women'; many had committed the offence in the course of sexual encounters.

Pickpocketing, like shoplifting, was a more common crime than the number of prosecutions suggests. Newspapers frequently reported such thefts at public gatherings, fairs, playhouses, processions, and —in outraged astonishment—at executions,[16] but not in lodgings at the end of courts, nor in dark alleys and park gateways where the trial evidence suggested that the majority actually happened. Society was warned of 'expert genteelly-dressed men and women' who went to public occasions to plunder watches, purses and pocket books.[17] However, it was most unlikely that one of those genteelly dressed women would reach court at the Old Bailey as a defendant, and very few such men either.

Pickpocketing was even more difficult to prove in court than shoplifting. Legal commentators advised that:

> The act [statute] was intended to protect the property which persons by proper vigilance and caution should not be able to secure—but does not extend to persons who by intoxication have exposed themselves to the dangers of depredation, by destroying those faculties of the mind by the exertion of which the larceny might probably be prevented.[18]

Although the words of the statute clearly stated that it covered all private theft from the person 'in any place whatsoever', doubts seemed to have arisen about places which might be excluded. When two women tried to empty the pockets of a coachman asleep in his carriage in the street as he waited for a fare at the door of a brothel, the judges ruled that it was not the intention of the statute to find this sort of action worthy of capital punishment. They considered (contrary to its written words but much in its spirit) that the statute was 'intended only for the protection of persons in public meetings and places of proper resort'.[19]

It is almost impossible to state with certainty the status and background of the women who appeared as defendants. Their occupations are rarely mentioned in court or in other official records. It would be an over-simplification to say that the vast majority of women indicted for pickpocketing were prostitutes. Nevertheless, the evidence of both victims and accused showed that private stealing from the person happened as an adjunct to sexual activity or 'treats', in encounters on the streets of London in the dark hours.

The views held by judges and juries about the life-styles of poor women who found themselves on trial made a link with prostitution almost inevitable.[20] It is not surprising that the court records suggest that 76 per cent of female pick-pocketing defendants were, or were seen as, prostitutes, streetwalkers, whorehouse owners, or young women out for a 'good', preferably lucrative, time in male company. In a few other cases, alternative means of earning a living were mentioned—fruit or watercress sellers, market traders, pot scourers, washerwomen, out-of-work housemaids, a needleworker, a woman who ran a greengrocer's shop. All were typical of the marginal, insecure world inhabited by urban women, where boundaries were blurred between servant-hood—whether domestic or in casual trades—and the service of male sexual appetites. Prostitution, characterised by its transitory, seasonal and part-time nature, may have been on the increase on the London streets in the late eigh-teenth-century as other employment opportunities for women declined.[21] Relieving 'clients' of their personal belongings was a benefit to be derived from a package of treats and sex and was a better way of earning a living than relying solely on the small amounts of money negotiated with them solely for sexual activity. The number of women who found themselves at the Old Bailey for so doing was significantly in excess of their proportion among those accused of any other property crime in London.

The world of the streets of London, as described by witnesses in the Old Bailey pickpocketing trials, might appear to have been filled with rapacious and amazonian women. Women like Sarah Strickland, who at 11 o'clock at night carried her drunken victim to her apartment in Moffatt's Court.[22] Or Hannah Hadley whose victim, James Vernon, complained, 'this here woman laid hold of me and brought me down a court [in Wych-Street between 12 and one in the morning] and was pulling me about.'[23] Mary Ann Fisher's victim, encountered in Grays Inn Lane, said 'she clapped her hand on my breeches and was very active about that part'.[24] And Elizabeth Quinn, whose respectable attorney victim said of their 3 a.m. encounter in the Strand, 'She was very loving and she would clench about me—I could not extricate myself.'[25]

Female shoplifters presented rather different characters. There was a sprin-kling of ladies' maids, married women, mantua makers, a children's pump maker, a toy maker, and, amongst them, women who dressed well, for appro-priate dress was important for the shoplifting enterprise. Appearances counted in other ways. When eighteen-year old Mary Palmer, carrying her baby, stole two shirts from a linen-warehouse in Holborn, the 14 year-old shop assistant said he was suspicious of her because 'I did not much like her appearance, she looked like a girl of the town.'[26] Overt sexuality and problems with alcohol were also indicators arousing suspicion. Frances Elliott was unlucky to be spotted by a shop owner as she solicited clients in Covent Garden, wearing a fur tippet she had stolen from his shop next to St Ann's, Soho, the day before. He recognised the hat, not the woman, since his sister had been looking after the shop when the hat had gone missing. He expressed interest in her services, made her get rid of the other 'girls' standing around with her, and asked her to go with him. This she did happily, until shortly they arrived at the Bow Street police office where she was charged with shoplifting.[27] Shop assistants giving evidence would often describe their reactions to women who did not seem sober. 'Difficult and troublesome', or 'hard to suit' are frequent descriptions, matched, equally frequently, with the excuses 'I was much in liquor', 'I had a drop in my head'.[28]

The accounts of the Old Bailey trials suggest purposefulness about the activity of shoplifting. There is evidence of well-planned forays, some of which involved returning to a shop on several days in order to choose the propitious moment. Or substantial part payments for some goods, whilst the rest were secretly lifted. Or down payments on account, though Hannah Mumford's deposit of a bunch of turnips and a muffin on the gown length she said she wanted was a little unusual.[29]

Description of the occupations of most male defendants are given, albeit perhaps unreliably, in court records and, up to about 1805, in the Criminal Registers.[30] Male pickpockets and shoplifters appear to have inhabited the lower end of the occupational spectrum, the largest proportion described as 'labourers', with trades such as shoemakers, carpenters, printers, watchmakers, and jewellers, soldiers, and sailors well represented.

The most striking difference which emerges between the ways in which men and women went about their criminal activities on the streets of London lies in the 'where' and 'when' of the commission of the crime of pickpocketing. Table 2 summarises the place, the time and the environment of the alleged crime as the victim and defendant presented these facts in Court.

	WOMEN	MEN
1. Private lodgings, rooms, apartments, and whorehouses, at night	38 (31%)	2 (2%)
2. Private rooms in public houses, drinking clubs, boxes in public houses, any time	9 (7%)	0 -
3. In coaches, any time; in the watch-house cage at night	1 (1%)	6 (6%)
4. In yards, alleys, dead ends of streets, park gates, public house lobbies, at night	26 (21%)	0 -
5. In the street, in the hours of darkness	22 (18%)	4 (4%)
6. In supper-houses, wine vaults, in a shop, in the open in public house, by the fire, in the tap room	3 (2%)	12 (11%)
7. Openly in the street by daylight, people around, no large crowds	5 (4%)	39 (39)
8. In public places with crowds, fairs, theatres, opera house, processions, watching events and people, Custom House, Tyburn etc.	7 (6%)	30 (30%)
Unknown (cases where, for instance, the prosecutor did not turn up to court and the evidence was therefore not brought)	12 (10%)	7 (7%)
Totals	123 (100%)	99(100%)

Table 2: Place, Time, Environment of Pickpocketing Cases—Old Bailey Sessions (1780–1808) (17 years)

The differences in 'where' and 'when' between the men and the women appear so great that they beg the question as to whether they were committing the same crime. The evidence has been presented in Table 2, in an order: from 1.—the most private, enclosed and dark, to 8.—the most public, open and light. The division is, of course, subjective, but appears reasonable. We may see the half-way point between dark and light, private and public, coming after group 5—the street in the hours of dark. By this point, 78 per cent of the women's activities have happened, and only 12.5 per cent of the men's. From group 6 onwards into the more public areas, 81 per cent of the men's activities have happened and only 12 per cent of the women's. The inversion of the method, place and time of operating between men and women is virtually complete.

Darkness and light concerned the court at the Old Bailey, as it concerned all who were anxious about street crime and effective policing. Views about street lighting and the watch were intimately joined.[31] In court proceedings, it was essential for a victim to be able to identify the perpetrator of the offence, and questions about candles and lamps formed part of the ritual of the courtroom evidential catechism. They heard that Sarah Strickland's Turnbull Street apartment was candle lit;[32] Mary Ann Deochean ran off with the candle from her room at No. 6 Elbow Lane leaving her victim, whom she had met on the Ratcliffe Highway, stranded in the dark;[33] Henrietta Spencer's victim held a candle to see her face in a dark court off East Smithfield;[34] John Jones sent out from Mary George's room in Star Alley 'for soap, coals and a candle to see by'.[35] Sara Smith's victim said there was a very bad light in her room at Cross Lane, Holborn, and there was no candle.[36] Everet Martin, picked up by Mary Partridge whilst he was urinating at the coach stand in Fulwoods Rents in Holborn—one of the most popular pick up points for both men and women—said that all the time he was with her it was so dark he could not see her face.[37] The watchman had to call the lamplighter to assist in searching the ground for the watch that Mary Ann Fisher was accused of stealing from Thomas Cook in Grays Inn Lane.[38] St James's Park gateway thefts were invariably said to have taken place by starlight. The sad victim of Charlotte Walker, who had asked her to see him safe home but had found himself minus his valuables in a sordid room in Parker's Lane, when asked who had brought him there, said, 'Eh! Eh! A woman in the dark'.[39]

Women operated widely at night in the areas we might expect. The Strand and Holborn predominate, together with the whole of St Giles, Covent Garden, Seven Dials, and still, significantly, the City of London. St James's Park and Tothill Street were the women's main working areas to the west. Defending Mary Smith in 1803, her Counsel feigned incredulity when the victim alleged he had met her in St Paul's Churchyard, having walked from the theatre in Drury Lane. 'Do you mean to say you walked from Drury Lane to St Paul's without being accosted or speaking to any woman?'[40]

A THREE BOTTLE BUCK.

THE WAY to STANHOPE STREET.

Watch. *Hollo there ___ What are you after now ? Arrah do you mane to pull down the Watch Box.___* Buck *Not I my old Boy I_I_ only want the _ the _ way to STAN—OP—STREET.___* Watch. *STAND—UP—STRAIT! Indeed honey you may say that with your own pretty mug.*

308   Publish'd Aug.st.8.1803 by LAURIE & WHITTLE, 53, Fleet Street, London.

18. 'The Way to Stanhope Street'

There *were* cases of women operating in public, brightly lit space, and men in private, dark spaces [see Table 2]. The few cases of women or girls operating in public, open space include some who operaed with male companions—one in a public house tap room in Tothill Street,[41] one in Oxford Street on a summer afternoon,[42] and one in the crowds in Queen Street on Lord Mayor's Day.[43] Another picked a pocket in the Royal Theatre where her client had fallen asleep with his head in her lap, and another stole from a country girl newly arrived in London, persuading her to join a group of drinking friends in an Oxford Street public house.[44] A group of young girls was involved in tricking two different women in the street, the first in Artillery Street, and then in High Street, Shoreditch, informing them that their petticoats were trailing and offering help to pull them up, on each occasion stealing purses and money.[45] Another group of girls had their fun in Ludgate Hill, jostling an old woman as she watched children going to St Paul's School.[46] Conspicuous for their unusual female behaviour were Hannah and Mary Wheeler accused of stealing a purse and money from a woman in a large crowd at Charing Cross at 3 o'clock in the afternoon, as she looked at a building which had burned down the night before.[47] Particularly unusual was Hannah Findale, who stole a pocket book containing a well-fitted-out manicure set from a woman in the Bow Street entrance to the Covent Garden Theatre as a small crowd waited for the doors to open for a matinée performance. She cut the woman's petticoat down the length of its pocket, turned the pocket inside out, removed the pocket book and manicure set, and was apprehended as she went into the pocket a second time, attempting to remove a watch which she had detected there. [48]

There was another unusual feature about the few women who stole in ways more likely to be associated with male activity; all but one of them stole from other women, whereas men were invariably women's victims when they operated in their private, dark territory. Men were usually the victims of both male and female pickpockets in this period—90 per cent of the victims bringing cases to the Old Bailey were men. The remaining 10 per cent who were female—a varied handful of married and unmarried women, servants, a lodging housekeeper, and a few genteel ladies on outings to shops and houses in various parts of the capital—were fairly evenly the victims of male and female thieves. Amongst the majority male victims, no group or class predominated, regardless of whether the thief was male or female. The men who tangled with women of the town and were prepared or persuaded to prosecute them for a capital pickpocketing offence were from a wide-cross section of the less financially flourishing members of male society—tradesmen, artisans, labourers, shopkeepers, clerks, servants, a farmer, surprisingly few soldiers and sailors, an attorney, and a small number who said they lived on inherited money. The people around the streets of London who were most vulnerable to the women's attentions, and the most threatened by such criminal activities, were porters and similar types of servants—from grocers' shops, hotels, restaurants, coffee houses, the post office, livery stables, and East India and West India company offices—men who had to earn their living by being able to move around the streets of London at all hours, and to demonstrate reliability and honesty with money and other goods entrusted to them.

Male victims of male pickpockets came from nearly as wide a cross-section of society as the females' victims, although with a higher representation from the slightly better-off merchant and gentry groups. His Excellency Baron Kutzleben was relieved by Lucius Hughes of his valuable gold watch, seals and chain as he came out of the Opera House in Covent Garden.[49] The infamous George Barrington, self-styled gentleman, stole a purse and more than 23 guineas from Havilard le Mesurier, member of a well-connected city family, as he made his way through the excessively crowded lobby of the Drury Lane Playhouse.[50] John Johnstone, Esquire, strolling one afternoon with a group of officers and gentlemen in New Bond Street had his pocket book removed by William Atkinson.[51] However, overall, the cases brought against pickpockets were not often brought by victims in a higher station in life. The gentry and the successful middling sort were usually wise enough not to get involved in prosecutions which could easily damage their reputation and their standing as respectable family men. Perhaps any loss they might have sustained would not be sufficiently significant to them. Further, it was much less likely that they would have found themselves caught up in the sorts of crowds or in the type of streets and alleys in which they or their belongings might be at risk.

As a rule men and boys did their private stealing among crowds watching processions, at public hangings, at fights, in crowds watching the quality pass by, at horse fairs and in theatre foyers, and were pulling handkerchiefs from pockets in the streets in broad daylight. Women on the other hand were taking fair advantage of inebriated, importunate, and unwise men in dark alleys, public house yards, dead ends, up against walls, at park gateways, and during sexual activity in more private places. They took men to their lodgings, through dark alleys and lanes, and in total darkness or by candlelight, relieved them of money and watches, breeches on or off, having ensured the men had been plied with alcoholic beverages, and making sure that they had a female friend near at hand to receive the items removed from the men's persons or clothes.

Differences between men and women in their shoplifting activities are not as significant as those which have been shown for pickpocketing, but are

Methods		Females cases described	% female	Males cases described	% male
In clothing	Cloaks	60	31%	0	
	Petticoats, skirts, gowns, shawl	58	30%	1*	0.5%
	Under coat, waistcoat, shirt	4	2%	31	1%
	In or under apron	22	12%	14	10%
	In loose or fitted pocket	13	7%	12	8%
	In muff or glove, up cuff	6	3%	2	1%
	Down bosom, up stays	7	4%	0	–
	In hat	0	–	8	5%
	In breeches	0	–	5	4%
Otherwise:	In hand	7	4%	9	6%
	Under or in arm	12	6%	33	23%
	Under sack or wrapper	0	–	3	2%
	In bag, basket, pillow case	2	1%	5	4%
	Worn on body	0	–	3	4%
	Carried on shoulder, over arm	0	–	14	10%
	Drawn on a string, on stick	0	–	2	1%
	Taken as delivery agent	1	0.5%	1	0.5%
Total		192	100%	143	100%

* in a country man's smock

Table 3. Methods of Concealing Stolen Items (Where Recorded) in Shoplifting Cases—Old Bailey Sessions (1780–1823)

nonetheless interesting, revealing clear differences in methods of operating.

Table 3 highlights the importance of clothing to the female enterprise—especially the cloak—and the space under petticoats, skirts and aprons. When this is compared with the men's *modus operandi*, there is a significant difference. Men's methods were split roughly equally between their use of clothing, and no concealment at all, small items hand held, larger items tucked under the arm, and larger objects like carpets thrown over the shoulder—suggesting a touch of brazenness. For women, clothing was a crucial hiding place, accounting for 88 per cent of their methods of operating.

Shopkeepers and their assistants, were suspicious of women in cloaks—a common article of clothing for women, rather than men. The court was often keen to establish, at the start of hearing a case, the presence of a cloak. Asked what sort of cloak a woman was wearing, whether it was long or short, a linen draper's brother said it was grey and 'such as women commonly wear',[52] but, confronted with women in long red cloaks, a hosier immediately thought them 'strange'[53]—red cloaks excited heightened suspicions in shopmen.[54]

In 1808, when Maria Smith was charged with stealing eleven shawls from a linen draper in Ludgate Hill, the court was antagonistic towards the shopkeeper since his 'was the shop to which so many people were thronging to purchase goods' that he needed nine assistants to deal with the fifty or sixty people in the shop at any one time. How could he suspect any particular person of shoplifting? The shopkeeper knew exactly how he could—she wore a red cloak and a straw hat. Did people in red cloaks excite suspicion? The shopkeeper thought red cloaks and straw hats were 'fashionable' and they certainly made him suspicious. The court suggested he should have more reason to suspect a woman in a genteel dress, rather than a woman who, as they perceived, was dressed in an un-necessarily flamboyant style.[55]

A poor old woman, Sarah Pine, indicted for stealing 21 yards of printed calico from a shop in Beech Street, Barbican, was wearing two cloaks. A witness reported that:

> She stooped to pick up a half-penny and I observed she was longer than necessary in that posture; when she arose from stooping I observed a kind of bulk under her cloak that I had not observed before... I told her that I thought she had taken away with her more than her own; she threw back her cloak immediately...she seemed very ready to be searched; she had got two cloaks on, a black one and a red one.[56]

Ann Cochran wore a large red cloak down to her heels when visiting a linen draper in Clare market, but she also

> had a singular manner which created a suspicion that she had some evil intention. She wanted to put money down on a gown piece, but I wouldn't allow her—and in a kind of shuffling she ran towards the door complaining that there'd be others who would.

Twenty-one yards of printed cotton were removed from under her cloak.[57]

Witnesses recall items being put under cloaks, cloaks being lifted or flung aside to reveal stolen goods, cloaks rustling suspiciously, bulging shapes under cloaks, cloaks of women tangling together, and a cloak being passed over a woman's face ostensibly to smother her cough. A picture is presented of a female world of flowing clothes, rustling skirts, a confused dance of concealing movements, adjustments of dress, shuffling, waddling, and shopkeepers' hands feeling under petticoats, prodding bosoms, and swathes of textiles emerging from secret places under women's clothing, some still warm from the places where they had been hidden. 'It is hot, quite warm, as if I had been holding it by the fire for about five minutes', said the shop lad who unburdened Elizabeth Stevenson of her booty.[58]

Catherine Drew and Catherine Carney in 1804 were charged with shoplifting as much as 54 yards of printed calico from a linen draper in Holborn. They had come to the shop on two consecutive days to buy calico, on neither occasion producing enough money for the piece which had been cut and set aside for them. On the second day, the shopman saw Drew

> stoop down in pretence of tying up her stockings. I perceived her making a great bustle which excited my notice; when she arose up, she took both her hands, pretending to draw up her petticoat....I perceived the sides of her waist to have increased very much, nearly double to what it was before, which induced me to go round the counter immediately; her eyes were fixed on me; her sides decreased and I picked up a piece from beneath her petticoats.

While he was thus mesmerised by Drew and distracted by all the bustling, Carney was waddling out of the shop with the fifty-four yards of calico cited in the indictment.[59]

The reports of the court hearings at the Old Bailey are full of talk about women's clothing, and there is every reason to suppose that it was of importance to the court's perception of the person.

Some interesting questions are raised by these stories of the different ways that men and women shoplifters and pickpockets operated around the streets of London. They might contribute a further dimension to the public/private distinction which has become an important concept for historians of gender.[60] The late eighteenth century and early nineteenth century have been seen as crucial to the development of the ideology of 'separate spheres' for men and women, an ideology, however, which does not seem to have much explanatory power for the lives of the urban poor. Here we have seen some of the actors on the stage of the London streets, which were at times public, open, busy, noisy, and brightly lit, and, at other times, private, sinister, enclosed and dark. The paths of women and men crossed and collided as these plebeian folk, labourers, servants, women of the town moved about, making ends meet, acquiring as good a living as they could, doing what they could, when they could, and, not surprisingly, doing it differently, at different times and in different places. It is not only that 'spaces, places and our senses of them (and such related things as our degree of mobility) are gendered through and through',[61] but that public and private space may be interchangeable depending on what is done there, who does it and when it is done.

By discretely studying something of the shoplifter's and the pickpocket's way of operating on the streets of London, a clear divergence can be seen between men and women, in style, in occupation, and in how they went about achieving their ends. To some extent, *all* pickpockets moved in a public sphere, even if it was in a darkened street or alley, the closed interior of a coach, or a woman's lodgings—her workplace. Shoplifters too manoeuvred in public space, in shops, and the crowded streets. But both crimes were by definition and essence 'private', without 'cognizance', unseen, unfelt. The public and private spaces of the London streets belonged to the men and the women together, but they could be, and were, used differently.

The public space of the streets which becomes private, and the private action which becomes public, the blurring and blending of the differences, are a theme of many of these stories. The blending is most apparent in the way that day and night, dark and light, had a decisive impact on what men and women did and where they did it. The London night streets were the setting for a different sort of life, a different emphasis in gender relations, a different sharing of space. The eighteenth century saw the dark and private streets of London in which women worked and where they were on home territory gradually becoming lighter and more public.

By the end of the century, not only had many parishes, concerned at the prevalence of street crime at night, raised rates to light more of their streets and dark places, but public offices had been established to deal with apprehended malefactors and the watch had been strengthened.[62] These developments may have made these women more vulnerable to control, as private space became more public, yet their stories show that the night changed the controls of the day.

In daytime, these men and women operated differently from each other, in different shops, in different locations, used different support networks and even moved in different ways. In the dark, at night, the controls on space and behaviour seem to change. Men's behaviour was changed by a different way of sharing public and private space with women. However, women were able to make the spaces their own, to extend their territory and influence, move around more freely and get on with their work. In the day time, women targeted the shops in the public streets of High Holborn, Holborn Bridge, Drury Lane, The Strand, St Martin's Lane, Long Acre, Oxford Street, Fleet Street, and men aimed for the pockets of the crowds outside playhouses and theatres, in the squares and spaces outside the houses of the aristocracy and gentry, in Cheapside on Lord Mayor's Day, at street fights in the Strand and in St James's Street on the Queen's birthday. But at night, in Goodman's Fields, Parker's Lane, Star Alley, Johnstone's Court, the end of Wardour Street, Shepherd Street, the passage leading to the French Horn in Holborn, and in many another little lane, court or alley, women had their way.

10. Mean Streets

Criminality, Immorality and the Street in
Early Nineteenth-Century London

Heather Shore

> A dirtier or more wretched place he had never seen. The street was
> very narrow and muddy, and the air was impregnated with filthy
> odours. There were a good many small shops; but the only stock in
> trade appeared to be heaps of children, who, even at that time of
> night, were crawling in and out at the doors, or screaming from the
> inside. The sole places that seemed to prosper amid the general blight
> of the place, were the public-houses; and in them, the lowest orders
> of Irish were wrangling with might and vain. Covered ways and
> yards, which here and there diverged from the main street, disclosed
> little knots of houses, where drunken men and women were positively
> wallowing in filth; and from several of the door-ways, great ill-look-
> ing fellows were cautiously emerging, bound, to all appearance, on
> no very well-disposed or harmless errands.[1]

Dickens's snapshot of the Field-lane rookery near Holborn contains many
elements of the fear felt by early Victorians for the rookeries and slums
that, it was believed, blighted their metropolis. Thus in the streets and yards
of St Giles, Saffron Hill, Seven Dials, and the highways and alleys of
Bethnal Green, Spitalfields and Whitechapel, Dickens and his contemporaries saw filth, disease, drunkenness, and poverty living in concert with
the over-breeding, cacophonous Irish and criminal classes. In the early
decades of the nineteenth century such streets were at the heart of discussions about crime and poverty in the metropolis.[2] The presence of the disorderly poor, vagrants, delinquent youth and prostitutes on the streetscape
was a continuing irritant to respectable residents, but also to the city fathers

increasingly anxious about the public face of London. However, street-life had long been seen as an annoyance.[3] In the late seventeenth and the eighteenth centuries moral reform groups such as the Societies for the Reformation of Manners had waged campaigns to 'move-on' the idle and disorderly from the streets of London.[4] Yet while the spirit of moral reform was still detectable in the early nineteenth century, in this period the theme was to be reprised with a set of agendas and concerns that differed from the previous century.

This chapter considers the ways in which certain streets and alleys come to be redefined as criminal districts in this period. In these areas the relationship between the street and indoors, the public and the private, is much more intimate than elsewhere, and by the early nineteenth century there were a variety of terms by which to describe these physical manifestations of the 'underworld': rookeries, alsatias, slums, stews.[5] Moreover, there were a number of markers by which it was believed, they could be recognised. The presence of establishments like low public houses, dubious pawnbrokers, old-clothes shops, and dolly-shops marked these streets as criminal milieu in the eyes of the authorities.[6] Police and magistrates perceived such establishments as fronts for receivers of stolen goods.[7] Flash-houses and disorderly houses were believed to operate as centres for theft, fencing, and prostitution. This inter-relationship between street-life and sites of crime formed a central part of the police project of the early nineteenth century, and were major concerns of the 1816 and 1817 parliamentary select committees on policing in the metropolis.[8] In these committees the issue of police reform was set in the context of the rise of crime in London, visibility on the London streets, the institutions of London's criminal 'underworld', and the way in which crime was policed both on the street and indoors.[9] While the control of individuals and institutions was undoubtedly an issue, London crime was discussed largely in terms of localities, and more specifically streets. Hence in 1816 Patrick Colquhoun stated to the committee:

There are certainly in the district of Westminster several houses that are *notorious as the rendezvous of criminal persons*: those in the *higher scale generally go to the houses about Drury-lane and parts adjacent, all of which are well known*; they are an inferior class of petty thieves who generally frequent the houses in and about what is called the city of Westminster.[10]

The interplay between policing, public concern and street cleansing in the early nineteenth century suggests a number of subjects of significant historical interest. First, how did contemporaries think about the 'underworld'? Second, is it possible to map this world—or perhaps more prosaically, contemporary perceptions of what London's 'mean streets' were, and where they were located? And third, how does the development of this reality and these perceptions relate to the re-structuring of London's law enforcement agencies and the fears about a post Napoleonic-war 'crime wave' which gave impetus and point to that restructuring. Having explored these issues, this chapter will then look at one particular institution of the 'underworld' through the lens of the substantial but seldom used manuscript records which survive: the flash-house. These establishments were low public houses of great concern to the participants of the police select committees of the 1810s.[11] By examining how this one component of the broader problem of the 'mean streets' of London were discussed and controlled, and how their existence and identification helped to shape the streets and neighbourhoods in which they were located, this chapter will describe why and how some areas came to take on a new and sinister reputation.

By the early nineteenth century there were five neighbourhoods which collectively contained the most notorious of the capital's streets and alleys: the Westminster rookery known as Devil's Acre, covering the area around Tothill Street, Orchard Street and Pye Street; St Giles, to the east of Oxford Street, extending southwards to Seven Dials; the Saffron Hill and Field Lane areas of Holborn, close to the Fleet ditch; and to the north of the City, an area comprising parts of Whitecross Street, Golden Lane, and Grub Street; and finally the eastern nexus of parts of Whitechapel, Spitalfields, Bethnal Green and Shoreditch.[12] Beyond these areas clusters of mean streets could be found in the Borough, and further east in Ratcliff, Shadwell and Wapping, while streets like Drury Lane and Haymarket had their own infamy, due to their links with the vice trade.[13] Many Londoners believed their streets to be notorious. The chair of the 1816 Police Committee could rhetorically ask, 'Do you know that amongst the great capitals of the continents, Paris in particular, no such evil as exists in the streets of London is to be found?' and be confident that his audience was already fully aware of this damning comparison.[14]

How were such streets and neighbourhoods identified? What was it about them that led to the authorities and elite commentators to view them as 'mean streets'? Overwhelmingly these were areas characterised by poverty, by Irish and Jewish immigration, by high mobility, by the culture of low-lodging houses, penny gaffs, brothels, and public houses.[15] Some of these clusters of streets were historically home to the under-classes, for example, in Westminster there was the area known as 'broad sanctuary', a traditional place of refuge for fugitives from the law.[16] More prosaically, clusters of streets formed and held a particular shape through the forces of economic and demographic change—the slums of east London, the river-side alleys of Shadwell, Wapping, and Ratcliff, the manufacturing areas like Shoreditch, Clerkenwell and Bethnal Green.[17] Thomas Beames' *Rookeries of London* from the mid-nineteenth century was typical in its portrayal of the admixture of poverty, drink, and vice asso-ciated with such streets, 'With such a neighbourhood are connected the lowest prostitutes and the worst public houses—for in these two species of enjoyment, the unhallowed gains of felons are wasted, scattered profusely, rather than spentt...'[18] In these criminal areas, according to the mythol-ogy of the underworld, the corrupters and corrupted lived side by side in venality and misery. Contemporary analysis of criminal networks, whether envisaged as real or imaginary, tended to concentrate on a model of an 'underworld', a cultural phenomenon with its own driving force, its own momentum. In Dickens's account of a night's tour of metropolitan low-life with Inspector Field, the palpable sense of decent into the underworld is manifest:

'Close up there, my men!' says Inspector Field to two constables on duty who have followed. 'Keep together gentlemen; we are going down here. Heads!'

Saint Giles's church strikes half-past ten. We stoop low, and creep down a precipitous flight of stairs into a dark close cellar. There is a fire. There is a long deal table. There are benches. The cellar is full of company, chiefly very young men in various conditions of dirt and raggedness. Some are eating supper. There are no girls or women present. Welcome to Rats' Castle, gentlemen, and to this company of noted thieves!'[19]

The 'underworld' then, was portrayed as something separate, detached from respectable society—an otherworldliness reinforced by the use of the jargon of cant language, secret codes, connections and networks inherent in both contemporary and historical discussions. Whether we interpret the underworld as a rhetorical veneer imposed upon the makeshift economies of the poor; as the shifting strategies of the labouring classes; as the street-life and culture inhabited by a criminal and deviant underclass; or as a product of middle-class fears and anxieties—that otherness remains. Yet arguably by 1815, a very substantial set of concerns had developed which were fostering the construction of the 'underworld' from above.

In 1815, at the end of the Napoleonic Wars, debate focussed on the criminal and disorderly behaviour of the lower-orders. In part this was a response to the vagaries of the post-war period; in part the culmination of a variety of tensions and forces that had been gathering in the preceeding years. The metropolis was the subject of periodic moral panics, and at various points in the eighteenth century 'the late increase in crime' had fuelled both governmental debate, and more parochial conflicts.[20] In a number of cases the re-emergence of debate coincided with an increase in indicted crimes, and a period of peace following the end of the war. Clive Emsley has suggested that in the eighteenth century the press positively created heightened anxieties about disorder at the end of wars, by switching from war-time military reporting to peace-time crime stories.[21] Certainly, there was a sharp increase in arrests and prosecutions in the period following the Napoleonic Wars, which closely corresponds with the early nineteenth century debate about crime and punishment. As a result some contemporary commentators drew direct causal links between the end of war and the rise in offences. For example, Patrick Colquhoun remarked in 1816, 'with regard to the lowest ranks of society, I think there has been a progressive retrograde from the commencement of the revolutionary French war...in the course of the last twenty-four years'.[22] However, much of the post-war discussion was focussed on the apparent increase in juvenile crime, rather than the supposed depredations of disbanded soldiers and sailors. Concern about juvenile offenders was fundamental to the debates about street-life, and the 'underworld' in this period.[23] The flash-houses, for example, were seen as a major force for corruption of the young. As the Middlesex magistrate J. T. B. Beaumont commented in 1816, 'and when in the next stage of their education they are introduced to Flash-houses, they there see thieves and thief-takers sitting and drinking together on terms of good fellowship; all they see and hear is calculated to make them believe they may rob without fear of punishment'.[24]

While crime reporting and the conditions associated with demobilisation undoubtedly contributed to elite concerns about street life, the existence and activities of the Societies for the Reformation of Manners and their imitators was also important. These soceities, dedicated to the private prosecution of immoral behaviour, had been an important component of late seventeenth- and early eighteenth-century London life, and had been temporarily revived in the 1760s, and again by William Wilberforce in 1788.[25] But, while these revivals had a fairly limited impact, their descendent, the Society for the Suppression of Vice founded in 1802 was still active in the early nineteenth century, and could number Patrick Colquhoun, the police reformer, amongst its vice presidents.[26] Local groups were also active in St Leonard's Shoreditch and St Luke's Middlesex; while the London-wide Guardian society concerned itself with the reformation of prostitutes and the preservation of public morals.[27] This Society was specifically concerned with what it saw as the ineffectualness of the laws regarding prostitution and the streets, 'We understand that even where prostitutes are walking the streets and using the most obnoxious and obscene language, they are not cognizable to the law, without an actual breach of peace'.[28] As in the earlier period of moral reform, concern focussed strongly on the visibility of the poor and disorderly on the streets, the prostitute being a key protagonist. However, the rhetoric of street reform was accompanied by a growing concern with the 'houses of resort' or 'flash-houses' on the existence of which a street's reputation might hang.

By the 1810s the relationship between crime and the London streets had qualitatively changed. By the early nineteenth century the 'underworld' was moving increasingly from the street to 'indoors'. In the early eighteenth century, discussion of crime in London concerned ridding the streets not only of the 'idle and disorderly', but of highwaymen, street robbers, riotous assemblies, and the Tyburn procession through the London streets.[29] By the early nineteenth century street-life was still a central concern, but the locations of crime had moved into the low-lodging houses, the flash-house, the disorderly-house, and as the century progressed, the penny-gaffs and the gin palaces. There remained a connection between the streets and the 'underworld'—if anyone was a doyen of the street it was the pick-pocket— but contemporaries talked less in terms of individual streets, from which they could move on the vagrant, the idle and disorderly, and more in terms of areas, of clusters of streets, of localities. In the early nineteenth century, the language of the rookery came into its own. What prompted this move from criminal individuals *on* the streets, to institutions of criminal fraternity *in* the streets was in part, as we have seen, the continuing concerns of moral reformers, but even more important, and certainly novel in this early nineteenth-century period, was the development of a new form of policing in London. The 1810s were a period when the Watch, perhaps the main link between the authorities and the street, was increasingly under attack.[30] Concerns about corruption and venality in the nightly watch were high on the agenda of the post-war select committees.[31] One of the major issues in 1816 and 1817 was the method of policing the streets, and the nature of relationships between the police and the policed. For example, in 1816, Sir Nathaniel Conant, Chief Magistrate at Bow Street, was asked about the 'sort of understanding uniformly kept up between the Police officer and persons of that description, thieves, at houses of this kind, so that when they want them, they know where to find them'.[32] Law-enforcers then, were accused of actively encouraging disorderly houses and flash-houses as a means of surveillance and control. As Patrick Colquhoun told the committee:

> It has been frequently stated that the existence of such houses is necessary for the purpose of enabling the Police officers to know where to find criminal persons accused or suspected of having committed specific felonies; and it must be acknowledged that it frequently happens that the landlords or occupiers of those houses do give useful information to the officers.[33]

This view was confirmed by an Officer from Queen's Square, John Nelson Lavender, who was asked:

> Is it your practice to frequent those public-houses which are called flash-houses, for the purpose of looking after thieves, and persons of bad character, whom you may want to find?—Certainly it is.
>
> Do you consider the existence of those houses as facilitating that object?—They are certainly a necessary evil; if those houses were done away we should have the thieves resort to private houses and holes of their own, and we should never find them.[34]

However, the collusion between law enforcement officers and disorderly house keepers/patrons, may have had more pragmatic roots. The Webbs, in their *English Local Government* (1906), pointed out the short-sightedness of an administration which placed the supervision of the licensed houses under the control of the High Constable.[35] The High Constable had to attend the Licensing Sessions of the justices, and report on the conduct of the publicans within his division, a duty for which he received no stipend.[36] As a result the High Constable was often accused of being in cahoots with the publicans, as the Webbs remarked, 'If the publican kept on good terms with the High Constables, there was no excess that might not be committed with impunity'.[37] According to the Webbs, by the early nineteenth century the office of High Constable had been completely transformed, 'The vast amount of business and the odiousness of the work in the densely crowded Divisions of Middlesex, led to the office being avoided by every respectable citizen, and sought after only by those who would make a profit out of it'.[38] Thus the corruption of the High Constable, and by association the petty constables, still the only type of police active in most of the metropolis, was an almost inevitable effect of the widespread corruption amongst the magistracy. For example, in 1790 a committee of the Quarter Sessions reported to the court the case of a justice named Blackborough, who had used his position to threaten the constables who tried to arrest thieves and prostitutes who were his tenants. Blackborough was also accused of accepting money in return for publicans' licenses.[39]

Another key factor was the changing nature of recreational drinking. Since the gin drinking spree of the early eighteenth century, described by

Dorothy George as an 'orgy of spirit-drinking', there had been substantial changes to the brewing and distilling trade, but also to the way people drank.[40] While the Gin Act of 1751 and a run of poorer harvests had profoundly affected the distillation of gin—the culture of drinking was fundamentally changed. Both spirits and beer were popular drinks in the later eighteenth century, and the production of both was increasingly monopolised by manufacturing industry. While restrictions on the distillation of gin had tightened up, the laws around licensing and beer production had become markedly lax. Partly this was a response to the gin-drinking epidemic, and the perception that beer was a traditional, and safe beverage. This was also encouraged by the establishment of large breweries in both London and other parts of the country. Large industrial breweries encouraged the growth of tied public houses as an outlet for the sale of their product.[41] By 1815 the twelve major brewers of London produced around two million barrels a year, representing a fifth of the national output.[42] Increasingly, in London, the breweries monopolised the public-house trade. Moreover, as a response to the concentration of the alcohol trade in the breweries' hands, from the mid-eighteenth century the number of public-houses in the capital, as well as the traditional ale-houses and inns, increased rapidly. By 1815 brewers like Hanbury and Truman's in East London had ensured that the public house had become a common sight in the urban landscape. One of the results of the changes outlined above was a polarisation between licensed, respectable public houses and unlicensed, smaller, often poorer houses. The unlicensed houses had little incentive to become 'respectable' since so much of the market was dominated by the brewery-tied houses. The increasingly strict monopoly exercised by the breweries over the supply of beer encouraged the independent houses to turn to the sale of spirits. By the 1810s there were a significant number of disorderly public houses and spirit shops operating without licenses, but perhaps of even more concern to the Police Committees were the number of disorderly houses and flash-houses operating *with* licenses. And it is at this point that the interests of the brewers coincide with concerns about the streets of London.

Mr Robert Henderson, solicitor and partner to one of Tower Division's licensing clerks outlined the problems of the competition for monopolisation of public houses as he saw it, 'As the most profligate houses are frequently the most profitable, they will have the benefit of the brewer's interest and protection'.[43] What Henderson and a number of other contributors to the committees argued, was that a system had developed where it was in the breweries' interests to maintain disorderly houses because of their profitability. This, they argued, was colluded at by certain licensing magistrates who were said to have financial interests in either the property or the brewery. The prime example of this was in the east of the city, in the parishes of Shadwell and St Matthew's, Bethnal Green. St Matthew's became the object of a long running battle between local residents and moral reformers on one side, and the magistracy and breweries on the other. The agent and rent collector for Hanbury's brewery in Bethnal Green was Joseph Merceron. He was also a magistrate, Commissioner of Sewers, commissioner under the property tax, commissioner of the assessed taxes, treasurer of the parish, trustee of the schools, and treasurer to the road-trust.[44] Merceron had the Bethnal Green publicans in his hand, and controlled much of the licensing business. Not only was Merceron accused of cooking the parish books, but of re-licensing known disorderly houses that he either owned or had an interest in. On licensing day, 16 September 1816, Merceron was one of a small group of magistrates who re-licensed a number of public houses that had been the object of complaint by magistrates, churchwardens and overseers, and local inhabitants. The Rose and Crown, Newcastle Arms, Seven Stars, Blue Anchor, and Crown and Thistle amongst others, 'were the resort of the most dissolute persons, men and women; that their indecencies were of such a nature as to disgust and shock persons who were passing the streets; and that there were frequent riots and disturbances occasioned by the confluence of such dissolute persons'.[45] The case of Merceron is an extreme example of parochial conflict and brewery monopoly. Yet this case, and other similar ones overwhelmingly shaped the debate of the 1816 and 1817 select committees. Here, the committees believed, were conflicting interests. On the one hand the moral reformers, magistrates and local residents who were very much aware of the reputations of their parishes, and particularly the streets within those parishes—and consequently saw the control and closure of the disorderly and flash-houses as the key to the cleansing of the streets. On other hand the breweries, such as Hanbury and Truman's, and Barclay and Perkin's, who along with financially motivated and venal magistrates, encouraged disorder for pecuniary reward.

Consequently, the prevalence of so-called flash-houses in London was an issue of some concern to the Police Select Committees—however, there wasn't always consensus on exactly what they were, where they were, and how many existed. The magistrate, J. T. B. Beaumont, drew a direct relationship between the existence of flash-houses and the existing law, which he argued, 'gives to certain individuals in their several localities the power of setting up or putting down such houses, subject to no other control than that of their own private wills and unsearchable motives'.[46] The chairman of the 1817 committee, Henry Grey Bennet professed there to be 'above 200 regular flash-houses in the metropolis, all known to the police officers, which they frequent, many of which are open all night'. According to Bennet his information came from 'a list, which, though it professes to contain more precise information than what perhaps any one is able to give, yet, as its authenticity is undoubted...I think the Committee may not be unwilling to know the estimate that has been formed of the extent of this evil'.[47] The list that Bennet describes probably refers to the hand-written notebook held at the Public Record Office, titled, 'A List of Houses of Resort for Thieves of every Description' from *c.* 1815.[48] This is certainly contemporary with the select committees, and gives much the same information alluded to by Bennet. It lists sixty-six flash-houses—a number rather less than Bennet's 200.[49] Many of the locations alluded to earlier can be found in this material. Monmouth Street in Seven Dials, George Street or Dyott Street, Buckeridge Street and Broad Street in St Giles, Wentworth Street, Petticoat Lane, Winfell Street and Rosemary Lane in Whitechapel; Brick Lane, Wheeler Street, and Skinner Street in Spitalfields; and Duck Lane and Pye Street in Westminster, were well represented. Though these were streets overwhelmingly characterised by poverty, they were not main thoroughfares—what we might call the new consumer streets of London. Thus, Joseph Kinder, one of the churchwarden's of Aldgate, told the 1817 Police Committee that, 'those houses which have been named, are houses in the back streets, and alleys and places; they are not in the public streets'.[50] However, while such covert streets and alleys were typical, other major roads also featured: Oxford Street, Tottenham Court Road, the Strand, Grays Inn Lane, and Kingsland Road for instance.

The flash-houses that crowded these streets were host to a variety of activities. Many had private rooms reserved for gambling, for example the Black Hell in Winfell Street, had a 'Convenience backwards for gambling'.[51] Some had backrooms or cellars devoted to sparring, or to the cock and hen clubs where young men and women could meet for dancing and other activities described as 'Diabolical'.[52] Some of the houses were described as having some sort of escape route at the back of the building leading into the street or another building, such as the Wheatsheaf in Tothill Street Westminster where 'there is an escape at the back of the House two ways'.[53] A number of landlords were said to permit what was known as ramps, or the robbery of unwary strangers, and were themselves described as receivers of stolen goods.[54] At the Jews Harp, on Marylebone Park, the landlord William Ames frequently received complaints, 'from strangers in his house and tea-gardens who have lost their seals[55] and which he affects to treat very seriously'.[56] One of the most notorious flash-houses was the Rose in Rose Street off Long Acre. The landlord was a man named Kelly who apparently kept up a trade in stolen handkerchiefs and watches with the help of his daughter and another girl. In 1816, Nathaniel Conant was confronted with the re-licensing of the Rose, despite being described as the subject of 'repeated complaints of outrages…and riot, and the most profligate scenes of debauchery and vice'.[57] Laker, the landlord of the Cock in Angel Alley, Bishopsgate, apparently, 'considered as one of the most desperate houses', fenced watches and bank notes from pocket books. Similarly at the Rose in Lumber Court, off Monmouth Street in Seven Dials, a 'respectable' man was robbed of his watch and then turned into the street, 'a complaint was lodged against the house the next day, and Barnett [the landlord] taken into custody, but on stating before the magistrate that he knew nothing of the circumstance and never encouraged any such characters in his house, he was discharged'.[58]

If the complicity of landlords in the robberies that took place in and around such public houses was an issue for concern, the complicity between the police and the landlords and other patrons was mentioned in the case of nearly every house. At the Cart and Horses, opposite Meux's Brewhouse in St Giles, 'The Officers go in and out…know the practices, often participate, know who is wanted at the Office, but never take them'. The King's Head, at the top of Tottenham Court Road, was also said to be a regular haunt of the officers:

The officers come here, take the man they want, when they ask him if he has got money, if he has, the matter is compromised with the officers by giving him a handsome sum...at other times when an officer comes in and the landlord knows who he wants and the man is there the landlord slips a Bottle of Spirits or a handsome hand-kerchief into his Pocket and off he walks.[59]

The image of the officers drinking with the landlords, colluding with thieves, turning a blind eye, recurs frequently in these accounts, clearly reflecting the prevalent concerns about the vulnerability of the unre-formed police. In 1816 police corruption was particularly topical. The arrest and trial of a Bow Street officer, George Vaughan, who was accused of planning a series of robberies, and then arresting his accomplices, known as the 'blood money scandal', had made yet another dent in the reputation of London's police.[60] However, the police were not the only ones charged with connivance at crime. If more indirectly, the brewers and distillers were also seen as propagating profligacy. Kelly, the landlord of the Rose in Long Acre was said to be supplied by a distiller who was involved in fencing. More opaque was the case of the Roebuck in James Street, off Oxford Street. This was a house with a backroom, 'where Flash and other obscene songs are sung...in this Room there are then perhaps 20 Girls some only 12 or 13 years of age or younger, and 30 or 40 young men, particularly Apprentices and Gentlemen's Servants'.[61] Such 'respectable' young men would be made 'intoxicated' and 'insensible' and consequently lose their money. Upon complaints about the house the land-lord, Barker, denied any knowledge:

the landlord is the greater gainer as he not only gets *his share* in the booty, but the greater part of the money is spent in his House, and were he not so to *stall off* (that is, stand by) these practices, he would lose the principal and most lucrative custom of his House, as *this* goes into the value of his lease of the premises, and if a *Brewers House*, he loses his credit *there too*.[62]

In conclusion, it is clear that at the heart of the debates I have described is the fear of an immoral and ungovernable class. Whilst they could be contained in their flash-houses and disorderly houses, or at a distance in their mean streets, they perpetually threatened to spill over into the more public streets of London. Thus behind this story are the fears and anxieties of the middling and respectable classes, those other inhabitants of the London streets. However, the 'underworld', whether real or imagined, was not a self-sustaining entity. While it may have suited contemporaries to construct these areas as underworlds, as otherworlds, the truth is that squalid streets backed onto respectable addresses and both the low and the middling sort lived together in an uneasy congruence. What this meant was a continuing concern with the streets and since people often had to live and work next to the lodging-houses and public-houses that characterised certain streets there was perhaps unsurprisingly no lack of interest in schemes to clear up such areas.[63] Yet these maps of mentalities can tell us a number of things besides. First, they can tell us about the tensions inherent in the offices of law-enforcement in London prior to the establishment of the Metropolitan Police, and the multi-layered systems of negotiation which the police had recourse to, and at times, abused. Second, they can tell us about local politics and parochial and vestry conflicts. Here we see the quarrels and grudges of the local magistracy, parish officers, residents and manufacturers, who struggled to impose some sense of locality upon their neighbourhoods. Finally, they tell us about the street-life of poor Londoners. While the flash-houses were described by the respectable classes and elite commentators as 'dens of iniquity', it is difficult not to imagine that the drinking, the gambling, the fiddlers and dancing, the sparring and the sex were all valued and enjoyable parts of working-class street life in early nineteenth-century London.

11. Socialist Infidels and Messengers of Light
Street Preaching and Debate in
Mid-Nineteenth-Century London
Anna Davin

Working long ago on 1880s London socialists, I was struck by the importance of 'open-air work'. It was their chief means of recruiting, both through the speeches and discussion, and through sales of literature, for instance the Social Democratic Federation (SDF) weekly *Justice*. At the 1885 SDF conference it was claimed that through open-air work 'the truths of socialism' were 'being placed before at least 10,000 persons every week in London alone'.[1] Whenever a new branch was planned the first step was to start speaking on a local street corner or in a park or waste ground. Established branches provided regular speakers at their local pitches and sometimes also at larger ones. Large demonstrations occurred when the authorities tried to curtail such activities, as for instance at Dodd Street, Stepney, in 1885,[2] or Bell Street, Marylebone in 1886; and threats to speaking pitches from the enclosure and regulation of commons also evoked protest.

Nor were the socialists the only 'stump orators': street speaking was happening all over London. It was the obvious resource for those with something to say, whether as members of some political or religious group whose line they wanted to plug, or as individuals with questions, causes, obsessions, grievances or the simple urge to speak. A nineteen-year-old shop assistant in 1887 grew incensed about his work:

> he got his courage suddenly to go, carrying a soap box, from his governor's shop, up to St Pancras Arches, where he made a violent but broken speech about the conditions in his shop and the living-in.
>
> The following Sunday he went in the opposite direction to the SDF [Social Democratic Federation] to seek advice, and Mr John Burns

kindly helped him to make a crowd-gathering speech, which taught William George all he needed to commence real business.[3]

Outdoor debate was not an invention of the 1880s, of course. In the middle decades of the century it was a significant form of intellectual activity for numbers of people, especially in London's poorest quarters and in parks to which the poor had access. The audiences were mixed, but men predominated and it is not clear how far women joined in.[4] Speakers were mostly men, though with occasional women like the Owenite Emma Martin. The debates centred on politics, philosophy and religion: Owenite and Chartist speakers denounced the iniquities of the classes and the hypocrisy of the church; while embattled missionaries declared the truths of gospel and temperance.[5] This chapter focuses on that mid nineteenth-century clash and its place in London's political, cultural and spatial history.

London in the 1840s and '50s was still comparatively compact. Open country was within easy reach: fields and expanses of waste or common where Londoners took the air on fine Sundays furnished regular meeting-places such as Highbury Fields, Hackney Downs, Mile-End Waste, Kennington Common, Peckham Rye, Shepherd's Bush, Paddington Green and many others.

As the rural fringes were pushed outward by urban expansion, these spaces were continually being lost, to brickfields first, then to villas and terraced streets, factories, markets, or the railway juggernaut. Stations and streets had consumed Pancras Fields by 1855.[6] In Hackney, Bonner's Fields gave way to housing, though the new Victoria Park (1845) was also a local forum. Copenhagen Fields, long popular for weekend recreation besides being used for demonstrations and debate, was lost when the City Corporation acquired it in 1852 for the new Metropolitan Cattle Market (1855).

As the working population of London swelled, the importance of outdoor discussion increased. Halls often refused bookings for speakers with unorthodox opinions, and alternative venues (such as the Owenite Rotunda, the John Street Institute, or the Halls of Science) were insufficient and mostly short-lived.[7] Outside sites were free both of charge and censorship, and moreover might attract passers-by with no connection to clubs or societies.

The outdoor speakers were not silenced as the city swallowed up their fields. Urban expansion itself furnished new sites, like disused plots of ground awaiting development, or the arches of railway viaducts. Any urban space might take on the functions of park and common. The labyrinth of courts and alleys which still constituted central London had its clearings, like Clerkenwell Green, Lincoln's Inn Fields, Tower Hill or Smithfield, all regular speaking places. Street corner and court were used as outdoor clubs in the evening or on weekends by locals passing the time together; 'idle loungers' to some, to others a challenge. Missionaries would home in on them with tracts and try to engage them in argument.[8] Dr Barnardo, in the 1860s training to be a medical missionary, would join in discussions both on Mile End Waste, where crowds gathered in the long summer evenings 'listening to and disputing upon all manner of subjects— political, social and religious', and also in quieter spots off Commercial Road, with some 'small crowd of street-corner debaters'.[9]

Most crowded districts, especially in the east and the south, had certain streets, usually arteries, which on Saturday evenings and Sundays combined the functions of market, fair, park, club and parade; and these, like Lambeth New Cut, or the 'boulevards of the east' (Whitechapel Road, Mile-End Road, Commercial road),[10] furnished street orators with ready audiences. The crowds which thronged them, escaping cramped back-street homes to pass leisure hours sauntering among blazing lights and heady food smells, were high-spirited and cheerful. Saturday night, when people might have money in their pockets even after paying the week's rent and redeeming pawn pledges, was for shopping and strolling. Sunday brought a sense of release. They could forget the anxieties of the week and enjoy themselves, jostling unhurried from one point of interest to another, now stopping to inspect a coster's display and appreciate good patter, or to watch a hard bargain concluded; now to greet friends or chaff members of the other sex; now to listen to the pitch of cheapjack or quack;[11] now to watch a Punch and Judy show or a display of miraculous acrobatic skill, or to listen to singer, fiddler or German band—and now to join the crowd around an earnest speaker on barrow, step or rickety chair.[12]

Free time was often spent more agreeably out than in, and streets and parks were crowded with strollers. In 1850s Camberwell 'cheapjacks held the street corners on Saturday nights; and preachers of sorts…on Sunday afternoons and evenings'; all had 'the knack of attracting attention'.[13] Speakers in fact had varying levels of skill, as J. Ewing Ritchie conveyed in one of his sketches of London life, 'Sunday at the Obelisk'—a street space where several ways met, at the south end of Blackfriars Road (now a traffic roundabout). Ritchie compared it to the Athenian Pynx, where the populace met for political discussion, though his account is disapproving. He describes the 'crowds to whom Sunday was no Sunday in a religious sense, to whom it was a mere day of animal rest', the coffee shops 'full of working men reading newspapers', a busy 'easy shaving shop', the costermongers' lavish wares, the artists ready to take a 'likeness' 'at sixpence a head', the 'vendors of cheap prints', then goes on:

> Women were bringing their husbands' dinners, children were flocking about in shoals, and sots were yawning and gossiping, waiting for one o'clock and their beer. You ask, was no effort made to get this mass under the influence of religious teaching? Oh yes; all the morning there was a service of some kind or other at the Obelisk. As soon as one man had finished, another had commenced; and at times one man was preaching on one side and another on another. The first man I heard evidently was a working man; and if to preach all that is required were fluency and a loud voice, evidently he would have done an immense amount of good: but he was too fluent to be clear and correct…[He] had got all the stereotyped phrases, such as 'the natural man', etc., which can only be understood by persons accustomed to religious society, and therefore I did not wonder when I found he had but some twenty or thirty to hear him. To him succeeded… two men in seedy black, with dirty white chokers and cadaverous faces, whose portraits were I to give, you would tell me I was drawing a caricature… I do think it is a mistake to send out such… there are but too many disposed to sneer at and ridicule religion even when it is placed before them in its most attractive form…
>
> [Next] a host of men very earnest in discussion attracted my attention. A teetotaller was hard at work, not repeating a set of phrases parrot-like which he had learnt by heart, but discussing teetotalism, with a crowd evidently well ready to go into the whole subject. Short and sharp question and answer were flying fast, and all seemed very

good tempered... he had more success than the preachers, who seemed to make no impression whatever.[14]

Evangelical preachers were particularly attracted to these markets. The throngs that passed them were by definition Sabbath-breakers, and could not but benefit from hearing the Word of God, however briefly.

The power of the word

At the Obelisk, as at the Brill, in Lambeth New Cut, Club Row, Whitechapel Road and other market forums, the audience consisted not only of strollers and passers-by ready for diversion, but also of regulars, keenly interested in what was being said and enthusiastic for discussion. Topical issues and basic principles were thrashed out in discussion which ranged from the rights of man to the price of meat, from the oppression of the poor to the blessings of temperance and the advantages of emigration. The audience, participant or not, appreciated the thrust and parry of debate, relished forceful speakers and enjoyed the argument for its own sake; they also took seriously what was said and might be convinced by it into changing their views. Some of those present might be 'searching for the truth': dissatisfied with conventional assumptions and seeking something to replace them. They would shop around, sampling the ideas of different propagandists and testing them in argument, till they found a position or a theory which satisfied them.

An eminent example of the influence of these discussions, unusual in being well documented, is that of Charles Bradlaugh (1833–91), son of a Hackney solicitor's clerk, and later the radical and secularist MP for Northampton. His Sunday-school teacher, eager to show off a bright pupil's talents, pressed him to scriptural study. The young Bradlaugh applied himself assiduously; then puzzled by discrepancies took them to the teacher, who angrily—but prematurely—denounced him to his parents as an atheist. According to Hypatia Bradlaugh Bonner in her life of her father, 'horrified at being called an Atheist and forbidden his Sunday school, [he] naturally shrank from going to church'. He went to Bonner's Fields, 'in those days a great place for open-air meetings'.

Discussions on every possible subject were held; on the week evenings the topics were mostly political, but on Sundays theological or anti-theological discourses were as much to the fore as politics. In consequence of my father's own theological difficulties he was naturally attracted to a particular group where such points were discussed with great energy Sunday after Sunday. After listening a little, he was roused to defence of his Bible and his Church, and finding his tongue, joined in on behalf of orthodox Christianity.[15]

The freethinkers in this group were followers of Richard Carlile (1790–1843) who spoke regularly at Bonner's Fields and Victoria Park, as well as in their Bethnal Green hall at Warner Place; and the young Bradlaugh, so far from reclaiming them, was himself converted. He was particularly moved by James Savage, 'a man of considerable learning, a cool and calm reasoner, and a deliberate speaker whose speech on occasion was full of biting sarcasms'; after Savage's discourse on 'The Inspiration of the Bible' Bradlaugh admitted himself 'convinced by the superior logic of his antagonist' and abandoned his defence of orthodoxy.[16] By July 1850 he had joined the freethinkers. A writer in the lively dissenting newspaper, the *British Banner*,[17] picked Bradlaugh out for ridicule:

> The stump orator for the real scoffing party is an overgrown boy of seventeen, with such an uninformed mind, that it is really amusing to see him sometimes stammering and spluttering on his ignorant eloquence, making the most ludicrous mistakes, making all history to suit his private convenience, and often calling yea nay and nay yea, when it will suit his purpose. He is styled by the frequenters of the park as the 'baby'; and I believe he is listened to very often more from real curiosity as to what one so young will say, than from any love the working men have to his scoffings.[18]

Hypatia Bradlaugh drily observed that this first press notice of her father was 'an introductory specimen of the accuracy, justice and generosity, of which he was later to receive so many striking examples from the English press generally and the London and Christian press in particular'.

Many Christians feared the freethinkers. George Lansbury (1859–1940) recalled how his 'mother was terrified lest my brother and I should ever go near these meetings'—so they did.

> Not much harm was done us, because most of the talk centred around the questions, 'Who was Cain's wife?' 'How old the world was?', and abstruse questions connected with the Virgin birth and other irrelevant questions so far as boys of our age were concerned...
>
> When mother discovered we had been listening to these evil ones she would take us to a small Primitive Methodist chapel in Bonner Lane, where we received the message of Hell Fire and Brimstone and a general warning of what was in store for us if we listened to the wicked men on Bonner Fields.[19]

(The path Lansbury eventually followed was that of Christian socialism.)

'Infidels'—the hostile term for secularists and atheists—were a political as well as a religious threat, associated with the growth of the city and working class and identified with sedition. They were diabolical emissaries conspiring to infect the masses and to plunge London into a morass of iniquity. That they were intelligent and eager for knowledge made them all the more dangerous. A London City Missionary in 1855 reported his alarm about the spread of infidelity in workshops and factories and especially among shoemakers and tailors:

> There are forty-eight places in London where infidelity, under various names and forms, is systematically taught in lectures made purposely interesting [!], and calculated, while they improve the intellect, to deprave the heart.

He noticed too that 'a strong political bias' was invariably associated with working men's infidelity, 'one strongly against the existing form of government, bitterly opposed to the Established Church, and distinctly revolutionary'.[20] Prosecution for blasphemy could still follow the publication and sale of attacks on Christianity in the 1840s.[21] Open-air secularist speeches, however, do not seem to have been subjected to legal harassment for their content.

Challenging the infidel

One Christian response to the menace of infidel orators was to try meet-
ing them on their own ground. Methodists were traditionally the only
Christians who regularly preached outdoors. But in 1848 a writer signing
himself 'Country Parson' published an open letter calling for 'Authorized
Street Preaching…as a Remedy for our Social Evils', and headed with the
text: 'Thou hast taught in our streets' (Luke 12:26). He commented that
Christ had sent the Apostles out 'into the highways and hedges, lanes and
streets' to preach the gospel, but contemporary preachers had retreated
within consecrated walls. 'We are blind watchmen, dumb dogs', while 'the
Chartist and infidel lecturer… [disseminate] theories which tend to over-
throw all social order and prevent the growth of any religious belief'.[22]

His alarm was shared. In the summer of 1850 correspondents to the
British Banner repeatedly called attention to 'enemies to truth' 'sowing the
seeds of infidelity in the minds of the thousands… at such places as
Smithfield, Kennington-common and Bonner's-fields'.[23] At Smithfield the
Reverend W. Ferguson had seen 'nine or ten congregations', but only one
Christian preacher—'and he gave them a somewhat strong dose of
Antinomianism'.

One man had an old book from which he attempted to convince his
hearers that the Prophets were a set of drunkards. Another… said,
'if you wish to have heaven for ready money, or hell made easy, you
have but to go to one of the chapels and pay your money'. A fourth
said,—'I am a Christian and a Red Republican. My religion is this—
fill the stomach first and the soul afterwards'. This young man drew
from his pocket what he called the first number of the 'Red
Republican newspaper', and expounded passages of it to the people…
One man told his party that he was inspired, 'as a proof', said he,
'that God has inspired me, I call upon him to strike me dead and to
send me at once to hell if I am not inspired'. He paused… and
continued silent for about a minute, and then exclaimed, 'You see I
am inspired, for God has not struck me down dead!' The fellow was
evidently insane, but he had his hearers and admirers. A highly
respectable female had her group of listeners to whom she delivered
a very severe message bearing on their conduct to their wives.[24]

In the next issue 'D.J.E.' added that he had been 'pained and sickened' at Smithfield of a Sabbath evening by the 'ribald jests and blasphemous language' of 'quack theologians, mere talkers for the sake of talking and controversialists for the sake of controversy'. But Victoria Park, he warned, was still worse: 'another place of resort' where 'more vanity and thought-lessness, and foul infidelity, congregate, than any public spot in London'.

> On a fine Sabbath-day, thousands of people are sauntering there in sinful idleness, and become willing listeners to the harangues of the chartist, the socialist, the infidel and the scoffer. It is the place where all who wish to utter aloud their blasphemous sentiments may do so with impunity:—old and young meet there to spend the time in friv-olous conversation, to gloat over past crimes, or to make appointments for fresh iniquity... The first time I visited the park was on a fine Sabbath morning in May... Thousands of people were there—some sauntering about reading the *Weekly Dispatch*, or that choice organ of democracy, *Reynold's Weekly Newspaper*. In ten or twelve companies of, I should think, about 500 each, were assembled together the people, all engaged in listening to their peculiar favourite.[25]

Subsequent letters put forward the claims of Bonner's Fields, 'noted resort not only of free-thinkers, but even more of free-speakers', where 'male and female, believer and sceptic, hoary-headed age, and beardless youth' revelled in the liberty of speech while zealots proclaimed 'the ignorant self-conceit of the antinomian', total abstinence, 'fanaticism with its dreams and visions' (and an apostle 'in the form of a half-lunatic woman'), and 'infidelity in all its grades, from Socinianism down to wild and rampant atheism'. Style and audience varied:

> The fields are dotted with coteries and larger companies, some engaged in worship, some listening to a set discourse, some wrangling in a debate, accompanied with shoutings, hissings and cheerings, and some in calm and profitable discussion.[26]

The moral these writers drew was that 'able, zealous and spiritual minded men' should 'go out in the strength of the Most High against the enemies of Christianity', so that 'souls may be benefited and God glorified'.[27] They called for 'ministers, students and other gentlemen' 'to preach occasionally out of doors, and from house to house, to the masses in London who never attend any place of worship', and for 'expounders of the truth' to confront the infidels openly and refute their arguments'.[28]

In fact religion was not undefended, even in the streets and other popular gathering places. Individuals sometimes challenged the infidel speakers or testified to their own Christian beliefs. Speakers came from local missions. And the Christian Instruction Society (founded by nonconformists in 1825 to evangelize the London poor) in 1850 held services, weather permitting, every evening and on the Sabbath, not only on Bonner's Fields and Kennington Common, but at Paddington, Somers Town, Bagnigge Wells, Caledonia Fields, Hoxton Market, Bethnal Green, Bermondsey, Deptford Lower Road, Borough Road, Field Lane, Walworth Road, Camberwell Green, and Blackheath. But they were dependent on volunteers. (The experiment of employing the Reverend T. W. Taylor for three months during the previous summer had proved 'a great expense on the society'.)[29] The London City Mission, a non-denominational society founded in 1835, had a much firmer financial basis, but some of its members disapproved of 'publicly disputing with professed haters of Christianity'.[30]

Anglicans did not generally favour open-air preaching: it was tainted with Methodist revivalism and emotional excess; its practitioners seen as uneducated ranters, eccentric and unorthodox, not only laymen but beyond the steadying influence of the Church. As 'Country Parson' explained:

> One reason why we have probably shrunk from it has been that, because always resorted to by our opponents as their most powerful engine of attack, it has come to be regarded by us as the very property and badge of schism… The office of the itinerant preacher has been so shorn of its honour of late, through the extravagances and mere fury of enthusiasm in many of the Methodists… that all confidence and credit are withdrawn.[31]

The low-church evangelical counter to this was that conventional practice left unsatisfied the 'great yearning for religious truth' to be found amongst working men, who given the chance 'would listen attentively and respectfully' but now felt neglected.[32] To defend religion against secularist attack was essential, for although the hardened infidel was unlikely to be convinced, 'much mischief may be warded off from the simple and ignorant'.[33]

Such calls for action were reinforced by missionary experience. The Lambeth City Missionary in 1853, for instance, reported being driven outside for an audience one Sunday when his congregation numbered only two. After he took his stand outside 'about forty men and women gathered around'. He 'gave them an address to which they listened attentively. After this the meetings began to increase'.[34]

Calls for missionary activity were reinforced by the 1851 Religious Census of England and Wales, whose report, published in 1853, showed that on the day of the census less than half the population had attended any place of worship. The percentage attending was lower in the cities and lowest of all in working-class boroughs.[35] In Bethnal Green and Tower Hamlets attendance was particularly low, and whether the explanation was infidelity or ignorance and apathy there was cause for concern. The census also confirmed that a new anxiety already being expressed in the religious press, about Mormons, was well founded.[36] The energetic Mormon mission in England throughout the 1840s, based on outdoor preaching and distribution of tracts, had won them some 18,000 converts, according to the census.[37]

So respectable evangelicals including some members of the Church of England at last overcame their prejudice against open-air work: the Open-Air Mission was established in 1853, and in 1854 the Committee of the London City Mission announced its decision to allow and even encourage outdoor preaching by its missionaries.

But even if outdoor addresses were now permitted, there was still anxiety about the pitched battles of the open-air forum and their results. The London City Mission's 'Instructions to Missionaries' in 1858 enjoined them to 'avoid all unnecessary controversy upon religious subjects...Carefully avoid all topics of an irritating tendency... [and] studiously avoid entering upon subjects of a political nature'.[38]

A good reason for caution was that it took confidence and debating skills to contend with the experienced infidel orators. A missionary who 'engaged in opposing infidelity at Kings Cross' during the summer of 1859 reported with real pride his victory over one 'Robinson, the champion of infidelity', who had listed contradictions in the Bible and 'averred that no man could meet him'.

> I felt my spirit stirred in me and at once commenced exposing his sophistry and ignorance. He met me five Sundays following and then would meet me no more. He has not been to Kings Cross on a Sunday afternoon since.[39]

James Hillocks, writing in 1865 about the 'atheists, deists, secularists and so forth [who] claim the attention of the public in the streets and open places of London', cautioned in almost paranoid terms against infidels who looked out for weak preachers and would 'gloat over personal victory'.

> See that strongly-built man, muffled up as if afraid lest he should catch cold. His hair is gray and somewhat long; but his face and words do not permit of the qualifying term 'reverend' which his age and aspect might otherwise suggest. I saw him first at King's Cross, but he goes all over London, at every preaching station—now at the 'Brill', then at Paddington Green, then back on Tower Hill. He moves about from group to group, watching his opportunity and biding his time… Where the preacher evinces a weakness or want of guardedness, there this cunning prowler is sure to place himself. When his opportunity arrives, he draws himself up with apparent kindness and an expressed anxiety to '*learn* something'. It is soon evident that he has turned…to a point of infidelity to which he has devoted his attention… When it so happens that the preacher has not reflected upon that theme, or is unequal to the occasion, this enemy to gospel truth and real happiness triumphs at the expense of all that is sacred.[40]

Preachers were often warned to avoid direct confrontation lest the wily infidel twist their words and pierce gaps in their knowledge. The famous preacher Charles Spurgeon, after listing twelve necessary qualities for open-air preachers, cautioned his students not only to be unfailingly courteous and good tempered but to keep to the subject and never be drawn into side issues, and 'if it be a real sceptic who is assailing you… to shun debate… for your business is not to argue but to proclaim the gospel'.[41]

Nevertheless R. W. Vanderkiste, London City Missionary for Clerkenwell from 1845, who often went to Victoria Park 'to reason with the infidels', instructed a promising convert 'to argue with all the Infidels he can meet'. At the same time he observed that 'the Asiatic-like vehemence of his manner and gesture, common to the gipsy tribe, marks my poor friend really an orator'—thus flagging stump oratory as alien and 'other' even as he recommended it.[42]

Some saw the lecture and debating clubs as the more serious threat; but these raised similar problems. One missionary wrote in 1856 that he had been 'exerting myself quietly to prevent the young and inexperienced from entering the Infidels' Lecture Hall, where their poison is retailed'.[43] A bolder spirit used to attend infidel discussion classes in Marylebone (one in the coffee room in the John Street Literary Institution, one in the Westmoreland Arms clubroom, and one in a dancing room in the New Road).

> These debating classes are the hotbeds of Infidelity. A great many young men are brought together under unfavourable circumstances. Working men who rise to defend the Bible too frequently have zeal without knowledge, and in consequence do more damage than Infidels themselves… I go when I am not expected, and endeavour to follow the speaker who exerts the greatest influence over the audience.[44]

Whether from lack of confidence or institutional support, then, or because they thought their resources best deployed in outflanking rather than in confrontation, the missionaries' common policy was to work on the infidels' potential audience, to win over the vast numbers of 'unconscious secularists' of whom the census-takers had written. During the 1860s and 1870s they concentrated increasingly on work within local communities rather than at the larger forums. Open-air meetings were an integral part of their regular activity, but they were held more in courts and at street corners, where they served the double function of confirming the group solidarity of those involved and attracting new recruits.

In such locations they were less likely to be competing with other speakers, but they still needed to lure and hold their audience. Spurgeon's advice to his students included helpful tips: choose a good spot, not facing into sun or wind; use music and light to attract people and chair or kerb to give you some height; deploy illustrations and anecdotes to keep people's attention; expect interruptions ('Cut it short old boy'), and meet them with quick-witted response or repartee.[45] Similar lessons are implied in a fictionalised but part-autobiographical description of a gospel group's efforts on 'the Waste', Frank Bullen's *Apostles of the South-East* (1901). A small portable harmonium and hymn on the Waste soon gathered a crowd, then someone read a Bible chapter ('a mistake... it is a peculiarity of open air audiences that you must not read to them') and everyone drifted away, then with another hymn the audience was recovered.[46]

Regulation

Paradoxically, gospel and anti-gospel shared an interest in defending their right to speak. Charles Spurgeon suggested that express provision should be made for preaching:

> Before all open spaces are utterly swept away by the ever-swelling tide of mortar and brick, it would be a wise policy to secure Gospel Fields, or God's acre-for-the-living, or whatever you may please to call open spaces for free gospel preaching.[47]

But the spaces they shared were at risk not only from being built over, but from enclosure and regulation. In market streets there was already tension between rate-paying owners of businesses on the one hand and on the other stallholders, performers, quacks and preachers and the street crowds. For the ratepayers, street orators counted as a nuisance. Similarly, villa residents or gentry resented the democratic invasion of neighbouring waste or common on Sundays. One strategy was to get the commons enclosed and policed. It was sometimes successful, despite opposition—from less 'respectable' locals, defending their rights, from the Commons Preservation Society, or even from sympathetic officials like Benjamin Scott, Chamberlain of the City of London, who understood that park and common met different needs. In 1868 he gave evidence about the crowds of people who 'invaded' Epping Forest on fine October Sundays.

I made it a point to mingle and converse with many parties of them, and I found that it was the wildness and the openness of the Forest which brought them out. They carried their provisions in handkerchiefs, and they partook of them under the trees, without the interference of anybody to find fault with them, which of course is the case in the parks.[48]

Kennington Common, a long-established forum with a tradition both of mass meetings and of regular debate, is a case in point.[49] Earlier Methodist giants like George Whitefield and John Wesley had preached there to congregations estimated at forty thousand;[50] while in 1843, it is said, some 8,000 took the pledge there after hearing the temperance orator Father Mathew;[51] and in 1848 it was the scene of a massive Chartist demonstration. The London City Missionary for Stockwell took for granted the presence of debaters there, though unhappy at some of their views. As he stopped to distribute tracts one evening, going from one discussion group to another, his attention was caught by an infidel and a Christian in dispute. He asked an onlooker who the blasphemer was, and reported with satisfaction the response 'He's an emissary of the devil'.[52] (It is typical of this genre that the possibility of irony is not entertained.)

In 1853 'certain local gentry', after 'a long and arduous fight', succeeded in getting the common enclosed and turned into a 'public' park, with regulations considerably restricting its public use, especially as a forum. The London City Mission reported complacently:

The enclosure and planting of Kennington-common, now called Kennington Park, within the last two or three years, has tended to improve the standing of the locality and has in various ways had its beneficial effects on the neighbourhood, among which has been the putting down of infidel lecturers and nuisances of various descriptions, moral no less than physical, which the Common had attracted to itself.[53]

'An amalgamation of the plain geometrical and the English styles' was adopted; the whole park was ringed with railings, and (like the new Battersea Park) it was policed by park keepers.

The result seems to have been the migration of its old patrons (speakers included) to spaces without restrictions, such as Clapham Common, whose local gentry began in turn to call for enclosure. Before the Select Committee on the Preservation of Parks and Commons for Public Use, in 1865, Robert Hudson Esq. was asked 'as an old inhabitant' whether the numbers attending the common had increased from year to year, and replied:

> Decidedly so, especially since Battersea Park and Kennington Park have been formed. The class of people who used to congregate there are now shut out and come to Clapham Common; Battersea Park has eight or ten policemen from the Woods and Forests.[54]

Mr Benjamin Field, also of Clapham Common, made a similar point as to the 'annoyance' from 'the congregating of the classes of people who used to meet on Kennington Common and Battersea Fields'.[55]

Similar consequences were observed in Marylebone after an attempt at 'ejecting the howlers, ranters and shakers from the Parks', as a writer to *The Times* put it in 1863.[56] The *Marylebone Mercury* reported that 'street preachers both polemical and political are everywhere found disturbing the public peace', and followed with a familiar rant against their language ('both offensive and mischievous'); their theories (plausible but destructive); their use of the Scriptures ('misapplied and not infrequently misquoted texts'); and their 'torrents of blasphemous absurdities'.

> Men occasionally stand up and address a few temperate remarks to a ring of bystanders, but they form not a tenth of the whole class whose ignorance and self-assurance seem as stupendous as their lungs are stentorian.[57]

Although the Metropolitan Board of Works made sporadic attempts to put down public speaking in the parks and commons over which it gradually gained control, the right to speak was always defended. Repression was unlikely to succeed in the larger parks, especially where—as in Victoria Park or Hyde Park—the tradition was firmly established and people expected orators as much as Sunday bands as part of their holiday entertainment. If regulation of such parks meant displacement of the noisy orators into the streets, it was not the answer.

The hostile attentions of authority continued to be limited, not only by resistance, but also, first, by the liberal view that free speech was morally right and even strategically desirable, as it provided a safety valve for popular resentments; and, second, by the difficulty of framing regulations which would not also prevent the gospel being preached outside. The police would sometimes use charges of obstruction to harass those whom they thought particularly pernicious, but their case was not legally strong. They refused requests from maddened householders to interfere with noisy street services, and prosecution was only really effective against speakers without the resources and solidarity of a group behind them. In 1884–5 a fight over the right to use a dockland cul-de-sac (Dodd Street, Stepney) on Sunday mornings was eventually won by the SDF because they pulled in massive support, especially from the Radical Clubs of the metropolis.[58]

Street speaking remained a regular political form in London as in other cities and towns for the nineteenth and much of the twentieth century; and speeches at regular pitches remained a central activity for any organization, political or religious, seeking to mobilise popular support. The right to outdoor discussion continued to be hotly defended, along with the spaces where it took place. Such contestation was part of a broader struggle over the uses of public space, comparable for example with the conflict between local costermongers and customers on the one hand and on the other municipal authorities wanting to clear street stalls from thoroughfares into side streets and to control them through a system of licences.

Nowadays the political practice is best known in the debased form of the show at Speakers' Corner in Hyde Park, with the soap-box speakers often treated as cranks, to be jeered at rather than argued with. The old-style street-corner harangue and discussion (surely preferable to the passive, limited reception of selected 'news' on TV and in newspapers) can still be found, however. It survives in neighbourhoods where the streets are still used for sauntering and socialising, and in communities politicised by their specific experience and status, as among Kurds, Turks and Greeks in Green Lanes or South Asians in Bethnal Green. It can also be heard where racists and fascists attempt to whip up support, as at 'Spouters' Corner' in Wood Green. Street spaces are still contested, too, for instance where demonstrators and police clash over the route of a protest march, or the instant occupations and street parties of the Reclaim the Streets movement.

But more effective than regulation or resistance, alas, is the way that streets have been taken over by motor traffic. Street orators depended on lung power and articulation to make themselves heard, or later they might use bull-horns and similar help. But they did not have to speak over the sound of endless traffic or of blaring music, nor were they pushed off the road on to crowded pavements by cars, vans, lorries, motor-bikes and buses. Moreover their audience was local. It was local people who heard and argued with (or ignored) them, whether they came specially or paused when their interest was caught. The great thing about street debate was that it was immediate. The issues under debate might be global or local, general or specific, religious or political, but whatever the speakers' agenda, those who joined in would be airing the concerns of the neighbourhood and community as well. Motorists do not stop to see what's being discussed. They do not add their local tuppenceworth. They are always by definition on their way somewhere else. Open-air debate loses out; so do local voices. So too does the potential for broader political participation and democracy. Will the internet be a substitute?

12. Music in the Air

Noise, Performers and the Contest over the Streets of the Mid-Nineteenth-Century Metropolis

Brenda Assael

This chapter focuses on the subjectivity of noise and emerging bourgeois notions of civility and civilised behaviour in the streets of the mid-nineteenth-century metropolis.[1] In doing so, it isolates a moment in time, 1864, when the campaign against street performers launched by Charles Babbage, the professor, inventor, mathematician and scientist, culminated in parliamentary regulation. Babbage was particularly set against organ grinders or 'organ pests', as he called them, who played on their 'instruments of torture' outside his Marylebone home where he and his paid assistants worked.[2] Not all Londoners felt the way Babbage did: many smiled at the man's monomania and sympathised with the plight of the performer who aimed to make a living from the streets.[3] To be sure, the streets were key sites for performance in this capital city known for its vibrant theatrical activity. In the 1850s and 60s, which saw the rapid expansion of the music hall, circus and variety theatre, Londoners became accustomed to observing spectacles in a host of quarters throughout the metropolis, including the streets.[4] So too were the city's inhabitants traditionally accustomed to hearing music there during festival times such as the Lord Mayor's Day in the City.[5] When these sounds accumulated with others in the daily life of the modern metropolis that boundary between the 'everyday' and festival naturally broke down and became indistinguishable. In doing so, these sounds contributed to a rich world of 'carnivalesque' that daily penetrated the streets of mid-nineteenth century London, challenging and confronting bourgeois ideas of civility, industry and reason with the reality of 'excess' in the form of 'rough music' that begot laughter and crowds.[6] Street performers, in their attempt at making merry, deflected attention away from the seriousness of daily life but paradoxically cast profound questions over who owned the streets in middle-class residential areas like Babbage's. Although they acted as a 'safety valve' for urban disorder, street musicians became the target of an anti-nuisance campaign which divided the community and individuals within it. The debate over noise engendered two competing and contradictory notions of liberty: first, the right not be distracted from one's toils, as argued by Babbage; and second, the people's right to be amused and by extension, the musicians' right to earn his daily bread, as argued by Babbage's critics.[7] Ultimately, the problem underscoring the controversy centred on discovering the real purpose of the streets in the mid-nineteenth-century metropolis.

Babbage's campaign against street musicians had a history and grew from a long catalogue of grievances experienced in the preceding years. In this respect, the morning of 29 November 1859 was like many others. At 10:30 am on that day, disturbed by music that emanated from outside his study window, Babbage rose from his chair and observed 'a brass band playing immediately opposite my residence.'

> I went out and desired each of the four performers in succession to go away…[But] they did not cease [and] each continued to sound and play upon 'musical instruments' after being so required to depart…[8]

In this instance, Babbage was forced to fall back on the law of 1839 which enabled constables to order street musicians away from residences 'on account of the Illness of any Inmate of such House, or for other reasonable Cause.'[9] In practice, this meant that the onus was on him to find a constable in order to register his complaint. Even then, the officer could do nothing except report the incident to his sergeant and 'not…take any further steps without instructions from his superior officers', as Richard Mayne of the Home Office stated in a police order of 1859 which clarified the existing statute.[10] In a private response, he informed Babbage of his reluctance to extend the law any further because 'there is a very strong feeling by many persons against the enforcement of the law', further adding that he 'received many angry remonstrances against the interference of the police.'[11] Not only was this an issue about police interference, it also related in some measure to the debate over 'fair play' before and after 1843 when theatrical licensing underwent major reform.[12]

Even in those cases which got as far as the magistrates court, no coherent pattern for putting the law into practice existed as 'some magistrates decided one way and some another. Law enforcers could not agree as to what was a 'reasonable cause'.[13] One newspaper columnist for the *Marylebone Mercury* pointed out that the local police court where Babbage took his complaints was notorious for its inconsistent rulings. The reason for this was that 'there are two magistrates [there]…one of whom deals with the merits of each case, with a partial leaning…in favour of personal liberty; the other, unfortunately, has a bias against street musicians'. In keeping with many law enforcers, the writer assumed that personal liberty equated with a universal right to enjoy innocent amusements in the street, not Babbage's bourgeois claim to the right to quiet outside (and by extension, inside) his house.[14] In a word, people needed 'fancy' (to use Charles Dickens' earlier construction) defined by freedom, spontaneity, enchantment and relief from life's daily grind—a condition for which Babbage clearly had little sympathy.[15] As the columnist cynically pointed out, once the professor became aware of the leanings of the magistrates, 'he had almost invariably chosen days for the hearing of summonses' when the strict magistrate sat, as in one instance in 1858 when he brought an Italian organ grinder to court on charges of playing outside his house even 'after being requested to desist.' The magistrate then fined the performer twenty shillings or fourteen days imprisonment and furthermore told the man that if he committed the same offence, the next penalty would be more severe.[16]

While the above case met with a positive result for Babbage, it represented only the thin edge of an unresolved wedge. In a letter to the MP, Michael Bass (Liberal-Derby), Babbage calculated the number of musical disruptions he experienced over the course of 90 days in 1860: '9 brass bands, 96 organs, and 60 "others" including [organ grinders with] monkeys'.[17] He informed Bass that 'one-fourth of his time was consumed by the hindrances occasioned by street bands, and that in the course of a few days he was interrupted 182 times.'[18] Bass, the grandson of William Bass, the brewer, believed in free-trade principles. Despite his Liberal leanings and 'concern for the welfare of the working classes', he could see no contradiction between Liberal notions of individual liberty, as evidenced in J.S. Mill's writings, and Babbage's right to silence.[19] Speaking before the House of Commons about how bad this public nuisance had become, Bass pointed to Babbage's complaint but, despite or because of the professor's reputation, was met with 'a laugh' from his fellow MPs.[20] Yet, this was no joke for Babbage who found that the law, when it operated, was too little and too late. He told Mayne and Bass that usually after summoning a constable to his street (and in the process being met with the derision of 'a crowd of children, boys, women, and men [who stood] insulting, shouting and hooting [at him]'), the musicians disappeared—only to come back again when there was no threat of a lurking constable.[21] In cases when these players were caught, they 'frequently... [gave] false names and addresses', and if their faces were painted, as was the case with black-faced minstrels, he complained, 'it is [even more] difficult to identify them.'[22] More commonly, when constables could not be found householders had no other recourse but to bribe the musicians, thereby unintentionally encouraging them to come back. One angry resident of Moorgate Street informed Bass that the problem with this strategy of paying musicians to go away was that 'if I begin to pay [now], I must continue it' since the musician will return for this 'alm'.[23] Another householder calling himself, 'Paterfamilias', concurred in an editorial letter to *The Times*: that since it 'has become common 'knowledge that I object to street music [and pay out] 2s/6d...twice a-week...our street [has become] a favorite *rendez[-]vous* for all manner of discordant vagabonds.'[24] Others apparently adopted more aggressive tactics for removal: in another letter to the editor, 'SBA', spoke of a friend who 'resides in a quiet neighbourhood' and vigorously employed 'a hydropult [which] direct[ed] a stream of water so as to check the advance of the enemy.'[25]

The solution, said 'Paterfamilias', did not involve marching into all the neighbourhoods in London in order to evict the musician, just some. 'It seems to me', he said, 'that were the police instructed not to interfere with street music in localities where nobody objects to its presence, but always to remove it where a single householder requires the [officers] to do so, the evil would be effectively met.'[26] An important class distinction underscored his argument: in neighbourhoods like his own, the members of 'German boy band[s]', the worst nuisance of all, he claimed, 'attempt a different tune at the same time on a damaged wind instrument' and present themselves beneath 'open dining-room windows, where dinner parties are going on.' While this is 'surely intolerable' here, in another neighbourhood it might be desirable, he said.[27] The problem was intensified 'in summer, when the windows are open', remarked Albert Smith, the journalist, who noted the presence of these musicians in areas where 'we happen to live'.[28] [see illustration 19] Yet, as the French essayist, Alphonse Esquiros pointed out, their appearance pointed to the metropolis's rich pageant: 'As London serves as the gathering place for all the peoples and races of the earth, the street music reflects that cosmopolitan character'.[29]

Importantly, discussions about the musicians's breaching conventional bourgeois codes of conduct were never detached from the subject of their national or racial origins. In

19. 'Music in the Streets', Albert Richard Smith

fact, it was said, their lack of civility and their vulgar music was owed to their foreignness. The 'marking' of these street musicians as foreign furthermore had the effect of essentialising and racialising them as a group. Referring to them as a 'tribe', the miscellaneous writer, Charles Manby Smith, noted that the 'one thing [that] is remarkable [about them is that] they are all, with the exception of a small savour of Irishmen, foreigners'.[30] 'Take a turn anywhere in the suburbs' of the metropolis, the *City Press* instructed, 'and you shall soon see by what process a group of filthy Germans—as filthy in speech and looks—levy blackmail upon quiet loving householders.'[31] Furthermore, the discord they caused was said to degrade common sensibility, rendering them more animal than human: 'The instruments are thrust under their arms and they begin to sing—pardon the word, we mean howl; yes, they howl like so many apes and baboons escaped from the zoological gardens'.[32] Sometimes sung in a foreign tongue, one contemprary, the Rev. H. R. Haweis, said that these melodies often recalled memories of the musician's native land and 'as far as we can make out, they are as simple as they are plaintive, and consist mainly in constant repition of "Yow, yow, aie! yagger, yow, yow".'[33] Their crude music reportedly matched the crude sounds that emerged from their mouths when they spoke. Babbage noted the 'very few words of English with which [the musician] is acquainted—usually the most insulting and disgusting in our language'.[34] In cases where they knew the language, it was said that they frequently attempted to disguise their understanding in order to avoid orders to 'move on'. More often, they spoke no English at all. Babbage added that so many 'are natives of Italy, chiefly from the mountainous district, whose language is a rude *patios* [and] are entirely unacquainted with any other.'[35] Any analogy between Garibaldi's Liberal cause and the musician's liberty was lost on Babbage. Besides this linguistic barrier, what worried Babbage was the size of this population: 'there are above a thousand of these foreigners usually in London employed in tormenting the natives', an estimate that is consistent with Henry Mayhew's findings a decade earlier.[36] However great their concentration in the metropolis, these 'prowlers' were by no means only present there. They had counterparts in other parts of the country, such as Broadstairs, where Dickens complained (rather problematically given his sympathy for 'fancy')[37] of the 'most excruciating' organs, fiddles, bells, music boxes and voices; Ramsgate where Mrs Carlyle voiced her discontent over 'a brass band [which] plays all through our breakfast and repeats the performance often during the day'; Southport and Dover as Hawthorne and Thackeray wrote.[38]

'Disorderly', 'rude', and 'numerous': a critical public associated these characteristics with this class of street performer. From here, it was only a short step towards the view that they also represented the criminal classes, infusing the city streets with 'danger' and moral degradation, especially in areas such as Saffron Hill where 'sanitary officers frequently meet with cases of overcrowded dwellings of most dangerous character.' In his revelations about an 'organ grinding colony' in Eyre-place, near Holborn, during the summer of 1864 one sanitary official discovered as many as fourteen organ grinders sleeping in a single room 'and not content with that, beds were made up on the staircases.' Besides being visually repellant, Dr Gibbon, a medical officer, also 'found th[eir] stench unbearable, and he had in consequence [of his visit to this residence] an attack of low fever for a week afterwards.'[39] Seen as contributing to the underworld of violence and filth, street musicians appeared as a tangible threat to the health of the metropolis. Moreover, their entry into middle-class neighbourhoods posed a further threat to the well-being of its citizens.

Yet, what complicated the situation—and to be sure Babbage's world—was that not all middle-class residents felt the same way about street music. One observer queried in the *Marylebone Mercury*, 'what has Mr Babbage…[that] cantankerous, selfish old man…ever done that he should have the right to dictate to his neighbours?'[40] George Sala wondered why Babbage did not 'pursue his mathematical calculations in a study at the back of his house' and noted that whenever he encountered the problem he went 'to the Reading-room of the British Museum, or…out for a stroll.'[41] That 'the few must always suffer for the enjoyment of the many' was a Liberal axiom worth remembering, he added.[42] However, in middle-class neighbourhoods, the problem that existed was not between 'the few' and 'the many' but between individual neighbours, as various accounts from 1864 demonstrated. In one instance, in June, Mr Rodwell, a clergyman, told his local magistrate in Canonbury that his neighbour, Mrs Hallé, the wife of a merchant in the city, paid an organ grinder, Mr Valentine, to play outside her home despite his earlier protests. Not only did she ignore his request but her husband became so enraged by a letter of complaint from Rodwell that he, Mr Hallé, 'rushed into [Rodwell's] house and behaved in a very improper manner'.[43] Despite her husband's status in the City and their residence in one of 'those squares… of London which are inhabited by a certain class of civic people', *Punch* blasted the Hallés whose recent behaviour betrayed their *real* class origins: Mrs Hallé is a 'bouceable woman, of tawdry exterior and violent deportment whose husband, as well as herself, has connexions in Houndsditch'.[44] The facts surrounding the case turned into fictions related to the Hallés' status in the satirical press, a kind of public humiliation that was aimed at discouraging community disloyalty in the future.

In another instance, in August (after the law changed) Mr Sykes, a householder in the vicinity of Regent Street paid an organ grinder to perform outside his home—at least until the man was interrupted by Mr Robert M.

Rew, a chemist. At the Marleborough Street police court, where Rew took his complaint, he 'wished to state that, as the dispenser...of medicine...great responsibility was placed on [him], and [he] required quietude.' This was a case between 'two persons of equally respectable but...different feelings' the magistrate said.[45] As the respectables divided in their opinion over music, their role-playing demonstrated how the part of the civic-minded neighbour could be interpreted differently.[46] In yet another case that had long-term legal implications, in November, in Pimlico, Dr Synnot, who claimed to suffer from an illness, repeatedly asked his neighbour's wife, Mrs Gustavus Koenig, to cease employing an Italian organ grinder to play outside her house since the noise infiltrated into his own house and assailed his nerves. On one occasion, however, after he made repeated requests to this effect, he saw her open her window and encourage the man to keep playing largely because, it was said in court, she wished to amuse her children.[47] The subjectivity of noise thereby became apparent: what was noise to some was, to others, innocent music.[48] The contentious issue of taste (which crossed the class divide) played a crucial role in vilifying or condoning it. While the decisions of the magistrates over these cases will be discussed in the next section, it will suffice to say here that the musician acted as a wedge between neighbours whose notions of 'music' varied considerably. In such cases, feelings of community and solidarity disintegrated when taste became impossible to negotiate. Yet, in a different way communities—from Marylebone to Pimlico to Canonbury—were linked in a larger storyline about the contest between individual liberty and 'street nuisances'.[49] Within each district, factions persisted and their disputes were played-out formally in the pages of local newspapers and the police court and informally, in the street itself, where feuding neighbours lost their tempers.

Another dimension to these cases was space determined by the interaction between the public and the private: the struggle between the two meant that the streets were contested sites of community interaction.[50] By traversing from the public street to the private residence, music overrode the partition separating the public and private—or in this case the partition between the pavement, on the one hand, and the study or dining room or chemist's shop, on the other. Many commentators argued that this was the hazard of urban living. In this way, street music was no different from any other interruption, notably 'Mr Bass's beer and his drays do more harm [by loudly passing through the streets] in a month than all the itinerant musicians ever have or ever will do'.[51] So too did the costermonger's '[shrill] cries...of "a stra-a-a-wberry"...which are ear-piercing and...so hideously uncouth...[They are] far worse than street music.'[52] Emerging from these cases was the key problem: who owned the streets? Writing to *The Times* on the subject, one man calling himself 'an old lawyer' suggested that '[e]very public round or street belongs to the Sovereign', and that this ought to define the way in which public space was negotiated. The 'spatial logic' of the street made it necessary to move, not linger. He thus added that 'the interest of each individual is limited to a right of passing and repassing over such highway, and he is no more entitled to use it for business or amusement than he is to build upon it...*a fortiori*, a band of musicians has no *locus standi* on the ground.'[53] Yet the experiences of Babbage before unsympathetic police court magistrates pointed to a different view; and the police orders distributed by Richard Mayne in 1859 reinforced the notion of a more permissive society and certainly reflect more accurately the reality of London's noisy streets.[54]

Mayne's reluctance to grant the police more powers than it already possessed was reinforced by public opinion. One observer agreed with the stance taken by the *Daily Telegraph* that 'we would rather hear the little evils that we have than see them set right at the mere will and discretion of a constable.'[55] A corresponding issue, as Mayne's 1859 police order stated, was that innocent amusements should not be interfered with, suggesting the extent to which a 'moral economy' based on 'fair play' conditioned the police's involvement in the lives of residents.[56] Underpinning this concern were two key assumptions: first, it was the working classes who enjoyed such amusements; and second, any legal restriction against street musicians would act against the interests of the lower classes. The public outcry peaked in the summer of 1864 when Bass's bill was introduced before the House of Commons. The bill described the existing law of 1839 as insufficient for the protection of householders from annoyance by street musicians. What Bass proposed 'was to give the police power to arrest musicians who, upon receiving notice, refused to go away.' Under the existing statute the police could do nothing without a warrant.[57] '*Punch* I see advocates it after a fashion' wrote R. Welby to Babbage on 30 May, referring to an illustration that (not without irony) praised the brewer's grandson for his campaign to expel the 'foreign ruffian and his barrel-organ' from Britain's shores once and for all.[58] [illustration 20]. Rather than serving the interests of justice, other observers said that this proposal did the reverse: 'We are not in the habit of railing against the rich as tyrants and oppressors of the poor' said the *Marylebone Mercury*, 'but this looks like a very tyrannical measure at the expense of the only class that enjoys street music.'[59] Seen from such a standpoint, this was a matter of high culture clashing directly with low culture, thereby challenging 'crude' and 'unrefined' taste. One 'Englishwoman' wrote to the *Daily Telegraph*, lamenting that 'these men of education and refined musical taste who would deprive us of the (to my uncultivated mind) beautiful street music, cannot understand anything about our wants.' Regarding her own case, she added that:

> I am at work at home the whole weary year round, sometimes unable to leave the house for weeks together except to go to Church on Sundays, and I am passionately fond of music. I read in the columns of the *Daily Telegraph* most glowing accounts of operas, concerts, and musical festivals where such sweet melody is provided for by the rich—such harmony as I may not hope to hear in this world.[60]

As the *Marylebone Mercury* pointed out, 'what we call discordant sounds, are exquisite melody to the unfortunate little scraps of humanity who regard an organ as an *al fresco* opera.'[61] In addition to the Rev. Haweis' earlier point about the folkish origins of these tunes, Sala added that some were arias taken from famous operas like 'La Traviata' or 'Il Travatore', often sung by Italians 'six times over'. And Germans with hand-organs were known to perform 'music by Handle [sic]'.[62] Esquiros asked his readers 'not [to be] too severe towards what the English call…street minstrelsy…[since] it is accessible to all, and costs nothing—it is the opera, the concert of the poor man.'[63] Yet, the fracture within even middle-class opinion towards these musicians contradicted the assumption that only the lower classes enjoyed this music. This furthermore pointed to deep cracks in the unstable foundation constituting bourgeois notions of civility and civilised behaviour in the metropolis. In an important way, Bass's bill and the furor surrounding it were a product of conflicting ideas of what the streets were for—within bourgeois areas such as Babbage's, not in lower-class precincts that eluded the professor and his friends. Thus, Bass's bill was not a bourgeois exercise in the social control of the lower orders as some observers thought and argued; rather, it was inspired by bourgeois residents in the metropolis who wished to discipline their own middle-class neighbours.[64]

Not all MPs saw it this way, however. During the second reading of Bass's bill, many of the views articulated by the public regarding the rights of the many over the few were re-employed. Thomas Hankey (Liberal-Peterborough) said that Bass's bill threatened 'to interfere…with a large class of persons, and those the poorest of the community.' 'Why', he asked, 'should they seek to interfere with the amusements of the lower orders?'[65] In agreement, Chancellor of the Exchequer, W. E. Gladstone, said that the bill represented 'an unwarrantable interference'.[66] In discussions of the Parliamentary Committee on Street Music in the summer of 1864, Bass corrected this erroneous notion that his bill would interfere with the poor's pleasures: 'what had poor people to do in Belgrave and Eaton Squares where the nuisance existed?'[67] James Clay (Ref.-Hull) clarified that 'by the bill, street music would be only removed from that part of the town where it was not wanted to that part where… the people were anxious to enjoy it'.[68] Looked at in this light, the measure was far from a tyrannical effort at suppressing the amusements of the poor and instead represented an attempt at protecting the rights of the propertied who desired silence—in their own neighbourhoods. A petition followed, signed by aggrieved residents who gathered at homes such as Mr Harvey Lewis' of 24 Grosvenor Street for meetings designed to streamline support of the bill.[69] This campaign gained new legitimacy once Bass received letters from between '300 and 400 of the first musicians of the day' as well as from eminent *literati*, including Charles Dickens, Wilkie Collins, Alfred Tennyson and Thomas Carlyle who 'offered…their hearty thanks' to him in an open letter that appeared in his well-timed book, *Street Music in the Metropolis: Correspondence and Observations on the Existing Law and Proposed Amendments* (1864).[70]

Dismissing the 'little volume', Mr A. S. Ayrton (Liberal-Tower Hamlets) thought that Mr Bass had gone too far: '[w]hat possible right could a man have to regulate every kind of noise which was within ear-shot? The public street was no more the property of a man than was the house of his neighbour.'[71] He thought that the only right a gentleman might have to remove

THREE CHEERS FOR BASS AND HIS BARREL OF BEER, AND OUT WITH THE FOREIGN RUFFIAN AND HIS BARREL-ORGAN!

20. 'Three Cheers for Bass and his Barrel', *Punch*, vol. 46 (1864), p.222

a street musician was if he performed 'in front of any such [gentleman's] house', rather than 'near' it.[72] Whatever the views of such reluctant politicians on the subject, the bill passed in its third reading in the House in late July of 1864 by a clear majority of 31 votes.[73] Ultimately, the Members 'merely [wished] to give effect to the existing law' of 1839.[74] The new law thus clarified the earlier statute, restricting street performance by explaining that a 'reasonable cause' for asking a musician to depart could not only be 'on account of illness', as the previous statute stated, but also 'on account of the interruption of the ordinary occupations or pursuits of any inmate of such house'. It also imposed new penalties: if the musician refused to depart, the constable could take him into custody (rather than just issue a summons as under the previous statute). Furthermore, the player could be fined up to forty shillings 'or, in the discretion of the magistrate...may be imprisoned for any time not more than three days.'[75]

Thus, what was at issue with the introduction of Bass's bill and its eventual passage was that the fundamental rights of the individual challenged preconceived Liberal notions of *laissez-faire*. Bass, a Liberal, privileged the views of some discontented, 'cantankerous' individuals, such as Babbage, over what Ayrton, Hankey, Gladstone and other Liberal MPs feared might be unnecessary state intervention.[76] The complicated question of 'when is the state justified in restricting the liberty of its citizens' was foregrounded in this debate, and two competing notions of liberty emerged from the contest over the streets: first, the right of a householder to quiet; and second, the right of another householder to enjoy music outside his home, in his own patch of the residential street. In this crucial period of change in Liberal principles and leadership on the cusp of Palmerston's death and Gladstone's rise to the party's leadership, this fracture had larger implications.

Such a story is not complete without some mention of the roving musician's lot after the passage of the 1864 law on street music. One may only speculate about its effectiveness since the information about prosecutions is fragmentary.[77] The cases already mentioned of householders bringing charges against street musicians who were employed by their neighbours were remarkably successful in the period after the passage of Bass's bill. Nonetheless, even without the new law, the plaintiff could have been satisfied by the magistrates' enforcement of the 1839 Act. In all instances, an inmate of the residence was alleged to be ill or dying with the exception of plaintiff Mr Rew, the chemist, whose case was decided in his favour because he was said to be engaged in a trade that 'was [of] great responsibility.'[78] Dr Synnot won his case in November 1864 after it was decided that 'he suffer[ed] under indisposition.' The magistrate added that 'it was disgraceful and unchristainlike to annoy a neighbour in this way.'[79] Despite earlier claims about the inconsistency of the Marylebone police court magistrates, both Mr Yardley and Mr Mansfield ruled in the same manner when presented with similar cases after July of 1864. For instance, Mr George Fox told Mr Mansfield that Francis Novara, an organ grinder, persisted in playing outside his house, despite his pleas, further adding that, 'I have an illness in my house. I have had two doctors attending my child…who is suffering from the arteries at the seat of the brain.' The magistrate stated that 'this is a case in which the law must be enforced.'[80] Similarly a month later, Mr Yardley decided in favour of Mr Lumley, a retired army officer, who suffered 'a dangerous illness' after the man claimed that he was seriously disrupted by Joseph Casali's organ playing.

During the hearing, it was said that the prisoner continued to play despite pleas from Mr Lumley's servant that he should depart. The organist's reason for lingering was that 'some person next door made motions for him to continue' and when he was confronted by a constable 'the prisoner…pushed [him] away and threw himself onto the pavement.'[81] Given the fragmentary nature of the evidence, it can only be speculated that the wider effect that the new statute had was that, rather than eliminating musicians from London's streets, it encouraged magistrates to take some local householders' complaints seriously, particularly when an illness was reported. The operative word here is 'some' since Babbage's experience was different. In a private letter of 19 August 1868, he spoke of an incident outside his house 'last Friday [involving]…an Italian organ grinder' who 'was not taken into custody' when he alerted a constable to the matter:

> I have since applied to the police court magistrate and from him, *I got no*…no assistance. This nuisance has continued to increase during the last twenty years and has destroyed many years of my intellectual working power.[82]

One of Babbage's allies estimated in early 1869 that there were '1200 wretched dupes of Italian "padrones" who [continue to] creep about from early morn till late at night with their accursed organs', adding that the situation was hardly helped by the late Richard Mayne's persistent reluctance to act on the problem.[83] After years spent in the public eye as the object of derision, Babbage claimed that his personal safety was now at risk: 'A few weeks since a bolt of… iron was flung at one of my windows in my library [but fortunately did not hit me].' Furthermore, he added, 'several of my most intimate friends have cautioned me to be on my guard against moving about in the streets of London after dusk lest I should become the victim of some personal attack.'[84] But far from feeling defeated, he said, 'I am determined to put a stop to a practice disgraceful to a civilised nation', a mission that lasted only until 1871 when he died.[85] Civilisation had multiple meanings which for Babbage denoted quiet, respectable, intellectual pursuits; for the magistrates, these meanings merged with notions of liberty as they favoured, in some cases, the rights of the musician and his patrons over the aggrieved householder.[86] That 'every man has a right to annoy his neighbour is deeply rooted in a certain class of minds' remarked Lord Stanley, the Foreign Secretary, in a letter to Babbage.[87]

The 'rough music' that found its niche in the residential streets of nineteenth-century London raised important questions about the rights of individuals and the nature of community. Charles Babbage's campaign challenged his neighbours' rights to patronise those itinerant musicians who roamed his—and other middle class—neighbourhoods. His efforts at reaping justice from police magistrates, in his fight for silence, were often disappointed by justices who believed in the innocent amusements of the people, as well as the rights of private individuals to hear music on the pavement outside their homes. Not only were Babbage's eyes fixed resentfully on his neighbours, but they were also fixed on the street musician himself, whose discordant sounds were conflated with his foreign ways. London's civility was thereby compromised by this foreigner's presence. Or so some householders thought. These views escalated during the summer of 1864 and fuelled a parliamentary campaign against street noise which culminated in Bass's bill that was brought before the House in May. The debate surrounding it raised important questions concerning who owned the streets. At what point was state interference in the affairs of the individual acceptable? If music were legislated, what would be next? And if not, what would happen to civility in London's communities? From these questions arose the difficult problem of how to negotiate taste which was contested between middle class residents and MPs alike. Those with seemingly 'refined' sensibilities won the day. Yet, efforts by some middle-class residents to reclaim their streets after the passage of the Act of 1864 were arguably limited by magistrates' reluctance to interfere, except in extreme cases such as sickness, with the affairs of the individual. Even when the new law was enforced, it only gave householders control over the area immediately outside their doors. Elsewhere, in places that constituted the backdrop of this analysis, such as Whitechapel and Waterloo, music was free to resonate in the daily bustle of street life, mixing (as it did) among the crowd and whetting its appetite for 'festivity', 'excess', even 'exoticism'. The streets of the metropolis, like the music halls, circuses, and theatres, remained key sites for urban spectacle and thus contributed to the dynamism underpinning London's civilisation and citizenship in the mid-nineteenth century.

13. Observing London Street-Life
G. A. Sala and A. J. Munby
Rick Allen

This chapter offers an outline sketch of London street-life observation over the period covered by this book, with comparative case-studies of G.A. Sala and A.J. Munby to test and substantiate its generalisations.[1] These writers were acquaintances and contemporaries (both born 1828), but very different in social background, cultural milieu, temperament, and the genres of documentary writing in which they worked. Despite these differences, Sala and Munby recognizably belong to the genus of London flaneur. This roving observer of street life is generally distinguishable in motivation and attitude from the socially critical investigator of urban low life; at times, however, he does resemble (and even masquerades as) the latter type. Indeed, this resemblance is one of the factors tending to differentiate street-life observation in London from flanerie in its native Parisian habitat.

Since neither Sala nor Munby is a particularly well-known figure today, here are a few biographical facts, some of the most significant of which were kept secret from their contemporaries. Sala was born out of wedlock[2] to a mother who had come from Demarara to pursue a singing and acting career in London. This career brought her some flattering social connections but not much money; the nearest the family came to a settled abode was in the Quadrant, the adjunct of Regent Street condemned to demolition in the late 1840s as a disreputable haunt of gamblers and prostitutes. The Salas took up residence there in 1841 after a spell in France. This upbringing, in which the boy's formal education was at best sporadic, provided strong inducements to a career of bohemian flanerie, and Sala responded accordingly. Nevertheless, he became a prolific and eventually famous journalist, initially as the most prominent of 'Dickens's Young

Men' on the staff of *Household Words*, and then from the late 1850s with a variety of organs including the newly launched *Daily Telegraph*. His best-known work, *Twice Round the Clock*, was serialized in 1859 in *The Welcome Guest*, to be shortly followed by the even more ambitious-sounding *The Streets of the World*. Both these commissions show that Sala had acquired a reputation as a special authority on streets, especially London's—a reputation nurtured from his very first contribution to *Household Words* in 1851.

Munby on the other hand was the eldest son of a well-to-do solicitor, a leading citizen in York. Having been educated at Cambridge and the Inns of Court, he lived in the Temple for most of his working life as a civil servant with the Church Commission. He eventually reached a high position, but the only real attraction of the job was the extraordinary amount of free time it allowed him. Some of this leisure was given to the composition and publication of poetry and to membership of high cultural circles in Victorian London. But Munby is now primarily remembered for his secret life as husband of a servant-of-all-work and as inveterate collector of information about working women encountered in the London streets and many other places, a life copiously documented in private diaries not released to the world until forty years after his death. And despite Derek Hudson's excellent biography-cum-anthology,[3] the bulk of the diary still remains unpublished except on microfilm.[4] In contrast to Sala, Munby frequently declared a preference for rural to urban surroundings, but Hudson rightly notes that 'Munby the diarist...was at his best in London'.[5]

Two observations regarding the world of London became commonplaces near the beginning of our period and remained so to its end. The first is the phenomenon of a rushing tide of people too preoccupied by their personal business to notice anything or anyone around them. This was satirically commented on by Tom Brown as early as 1700:

the citizens...are always in motion and activity....They are equally incapable both of attention and patience, and...don't allow themselves time either to hear or see; but, like moles, work in the dark and undermine one another.[6]

Such remarks might seem equally applicable to any large industrial-commercial city, but numerous eighteenth- and nineteenth-century visitors, especially from abroad, testified to a unique intensity of frenzied purpose and self-absorption in London's street-crowds.[7]

Robert Mudie, a Scottish journalist working in the English capital in the 1820s, contrasted London in this respect with 'even the largest of our provincial places', where

> there are always individuals loitering in particular streets or particular corners…: in London, however, there is no such thing—the crowd sweeps along like a torrent;…it will bear you along whether you will or not. You meet with no yawning idler,…no peeping inquisitor into your private history….No doubt there are idlers…; but they form no feature of London, they come not abroad into the streets, and they neither arrest the steps nor disturb the thoughts of those busy crowds which are everywhere reeling around you.[8]

Though this was the received view, Mudie exaggerated, as had Brown and many others, the difficulties of strolling down London's main streets. By the mid-eighteenth century this metropolis had become the first great Mecca of modern consumerism, a reputation sustained by glittering shop-window displays in, for example, the Strand and (from the 1760s) Oxford Street; these could only be appreciated in a state of wide-eyed leisure. Brilliantly lit by the standards of the day, the large glass-fronted shops had an appeal comparable to that of the Paris arcades in the following century. Furthermore, the received view depended on the witness of people who, according to Mudie, had no discernible presence in the streets, people (such as Mudie himself!) who were not busy in the conventional sense. Much of the personal testimony to both the general character and the particularities of London street-life in the eighteenth and nineteenth centuries comes from inquisitive idlers (or pseudo-idlers)—in a word, flaneurs. The archetype of this tradition is 'Mr Spectator', the eponymous persona assumed by both Addison and Steele in their papers for the famous journal launched in 1711.

As regards the literary tradition of street-observation the archetypal paper is that by Steele known as 'The hours of London' (11 August, 1712), which begins with a classic statement about the satisfactions of discreetly observing the busy world with disinterested curiosity:

> It is an inexpressible pleasure to know a little of the world, and be
> of no character or significancy in it. To be ever unconcerned, and
> ever looking on new objects with an endless curiosity, is a delight
> known only to those who are turned for speculation. Nay, they who
> enjoy it, must value things only as they are the objects of specula-
> tion, without drawing any worldly advantage to themselves from
> them, but just as they are what contribute to their amusement, or the
> improvement of the mind.[9]

Steele uses the word 'speculation' in the original sense of 'the exercise of
the faculty of sight, the act of spectatorship'. A decade or so earlier, Ned
Ward's *The London Spy*, as its title suggests, similarly indulged in detached
scrutiny of the metropolitan scene, but more frankly as an idle pastime
without any pretence to highmindedness. Here, the business of the preoccupied crowd is more likely to be pleasure than work, as in the amusing
account of the lord mayor's show in chapter 12, where the narrator and
his companion find the rowdy spectators a far more diverting spectacle than
the official pageant.[10] A similar focus in the treatment of popular assemblies is displayed in the writings of both Sala and, more especially, Munby,
who also attends the lord mayor's show as well as, for example, the Derby
and volunteer reviews in the early 1860s: 'I as usual came chiefly to see
the spectators' (28 March, 1864).[11]

Another typical element of 'The hours of London' and *The London Spy*
is the constantly changing street-scene they record, in terms of both time
and location. As the narrator of the first remarks, '[t]he hours of the day
and night are taken up, in the cities of London and Westminster, by people
as different from each other as those who are born in different centuries.'[12]
A hundred and fifty years later Sala had essentially the same aspect of a
hugely enlarged London in mind when he referred to it as 'this monstrous
amalgam of microcosms…haunted by classes of people as peculiar as the
localities they affect, and who are seldom to be found anywhere else'.[13]
This brings us to the second perennial commonplace, enunciated in the
alternative title of a mid-eighteenth-century anonymous work: *Low Life:
Or, One Half the World Knows Not How the Other Half Live*.[14] In the preface to

Twice Round the Clock Sala acknowledged this little squib, whose vignettes of disreputable London life are likewise arranged in twenty-four hourly sections, to be the source for the shaping idea of his own book. Its appeal to Sala, author of a popular serialized study of William Hogarth, doubtless partly lay in its fulsome dedication 'to the ingenious and ingenuous Mr Hogarth'. Hogarth's *The Four Times of Day* was itself influential in the urbanization of the 'times of day' genre of literary and graphic art, while much of the power of such series as *The Harlot's Progress* and *The Rake's Progress* derived from their ironic juxtapositions of high and low life and their exposure of the narrow boundaries between the two. The 'one half' proposition was uttered in *Low Life* in satirically teasing vein, whereas a tone of moral indignation was more characteristic of Victorian usage—though as flaneurs, Munby and even Sala (especially after he was beyond Dickens' direct supervision) adopt this tone only occasionally. But all those issuing this dictum were claiming a breadth of social knowledge denied the vast majority living lives of circumscribed routine and narrow horizons both physically and mentally. We can also often sense in such cases a relish in having acquired *secret* information which the possessor might or might not choose to divulge. The voyeuristic pleasures of acquiring it were very similar to those of discreet observation testified to in Steele's *Spectator* article. There was, though, the additional gratification of an *explorer's* exclusive knowledge, especially by the nineteenth century, when the easterly reaches of the expanding city were frequently referred to as '*terra incognita*'—as in the introduction to Sala's early essay into such exploration, 'Down Whitechapel way':

> I will take a walk 'down Whitechapel way'. How many thousands of us have lived for years—for a third part of our lives, probably, in London—and have never been down the Whitechapel Road? I declare that there are not half-a-dozen persons in the circle of my acquaintance who can tell me where Bethnal Green is. As to Ratcliff Highway, Shadwell, Poplar, Limehouse, and Rotherhithe, they are entirely *terrae incognitae* to shoals of born-and-bred Londoners.[16]

We might assume that a moral criticism of middle-class Londoners' social ignorance is here implied (Dickens would have made it explicit), but the flaneur-narrator in this essay largely maintains a detached pose of anthropological curiosity. *Terra incognita* is almost literal here rather than ironic.

London by then being twice the size of Paris, a comprehensive knowledge of 'this monstrous amalgam of microcosms' would certainly involve a more vigorous kind of perambulation than we would normally attribute to an idler or to a Parisian flaneur. Moreover, because the main thoroughfares were perceived to be so inimical to idling, those wishing to walk more casually in London would naturally be induced to go off the beaten track, and there was plenty of scope for this: 'In this great city,' Munby writes (20 March 1864), 'a man can arrange his walks according to his mood: for picturesqueness and freedom, there is nothing like an East End ramble'.[16] The other option was to stroll down the main streets at times of day, or better, night, when they became defamiliarized. Both Sala and Munby were keen noctambulists, not only by personal taste but because of influential precedent, in Sala's case from Ward to Dickens, in Munby's from Pepys to De Quincey.

In our period there were numerous near-synonyms for idling in its ambulatory sense, including strolling, loitering, loafing, lounging, sauntering; and for more extended pedestrian activity, rambling, wandering, and roving. (We should also note that '*taking* a walk', as in the quotation from Sala's 'Down Whitechapel way' above, has always signified a leisure activity.) Several of these words, in a puritan, industrializing society valuing hard work and ordered, purposeful routines, tended to gather disreputable associations, especially in an urban context. Loitering, with or without intent, was (and is) decidedly suspect, and lounging only slightly less so. It's no accident that street-walking became the main and not very euphemistic euphemism for prostitution; loiterers and loungers were often perceived to be its main clients. Such dubious connotations might explain why, despite all these near-synonyms, some English writers felt the need to import another one— flanerie, the act or disposition of a flaneur—in the mid-nineteenth century. However, this borrowing also fulfilled more positive semantic functions.

First, flanerie, unlike any English-language counterpart, takes place in a specifically urban setting. Second, by connotation it combines strolling with *looking* more clearly than any pre-existing term. The arcades being glamorous shopping malls, flanerie was particularly associated with window-shopping, or with surveying crowds of window-shoppers. These associations are foregrounded in one of the earliest usages of 'flaneur' in

English prose, in an essay by Sala punningly entitled 'Arcadia' (1853). It's on *London's* shopping arcades, and Sala writes in an obviously fraternal spirit of the 'legendary *flaneurs* or…street-pacers, driven in wet weather from the much-sauntered-over boulevards, [for whom] were devised the unrivalled galleries and passages which are the delight of Paris, the admiration of strangers….Beneath those glass roofs literary and artistic reputations have been won and lost.'[17] This brings us to the third distinctive connotation of flanerie—that it was strolling observation to be put to literary or artistic use, for example in the form of the *physiologies* (sketches of social or occupational types) popular in early nineteenth-century Paris. This sense carries over into ninetenth-century English too, and in 1863 we find Munby applying the term to himself, in response to the disappointing sales of one of his volumes of poetry: 'one…forgets oneself if possible in the light studies of the flaneur—if a flaneur can be supposed to care about milk-women, or about the comparative coarseness of servant maids' hands'.[18]

Modern literary-cultural studies have embraced the idea of the flaneur with greater enthusiasm, under the prime influence of Walter Benjamin, whose brilliantly suggestive writings on second empire Paris give centrality to the role of the flaneur. The poet and essayist Charles Baudelaire was Benjamin's ideal type in this role by virtue of his fluctuating moods and contradictory attitudes, both engaged with and detached from modern urban humanity, its concerns and its commodities, at one moment plunging into the crowd or empathising with the human refuse on the street, and at the next standing aloof with patrician disdain.[19] The renewed focus on street-life observation prompted by Benjamin's studies was subsequently intensified under the influence of another Parisian-based theorist, Michel Foucault, especially his ideas of disciplinary surveillance and the voyeuristic gaze. These have fed into now extensive feminist studies of women and street culture, including debates about whether it was possible to be a flaneuse in the nineteenth-century city.[20]

We have already seen ways in which both Sala and Munby consciously identified with the role of flaneur; the Benjamin-cum-Baudelaire model suggests other affinities. Benjamin's memorable remark that the flaneur 'goes botanizing on the asphalt'[21] perfectly applies to Munby, even in its ambiguity. Does he mean that the flaneur is a collector of unusual, rare specimens or that he is a taxonomist, classifying the various types of the urban populace? As regards much of the female half of that populace Munby does both, collecting data on both idiosyncratic cases and occupational types, and he is particularly interested in hybrid forms and in borderline cases not easy to locate in the established class structure. Munby's second anthologist, Michael Hiley, cites the example of a seventeen-year-old girl called Louisa Stapleton encountered on Westminster Bridge, 26 April, 1862:

> I passed a girl whom it was not easy to classify….A strange cross between a milliner and a field-wench: she must be a mechanic of some kind. I went up to her: 'May I ask, what is your trade?' 'I'm a brush-drawer by trade, Sir,' said the girl frankly: 'but I work at a laundry now: what with the machines, a respectable girl cant get a living at the brush-drawing.[22]

This entry goes on to supply precise data on the personal economic effects of mechanization in the brush-making industry—Mayhew-like documentation of a London-centred trade that Mayhew never covered. Stapleton was a genuine and revealing case of de-skilling in later-nineteenth-century London, a case which came to light as a result of Munby's acute eye for the atypical.

Sala, on the other hand, mostly settles for peopling his urban scenes with established generic types. *His* greatest strength is in identifying and characterizing different kinds of streets and distinctive districts of the city. The character of some streets he describes is such that even so thoroughly journalistic a writer as Sala must employ symbolic pseudonyms to refer to them, as in his account of the street at the heart of the art-forgery business, 'Travels in Cawdor Street'[23] and in that of 'a den of robbers', 'Gibbet Street'.[24] Nevertheless, he provides enough topographical clues for the reader to be able to locate both these cases with some precision, and in the case of 'Cawdor Street' to identify it as Great Compton Street. Among many examples of the characterization of London neighbourhoods, 'Jack Alive in London'[25] does this in vitalizing fashion for the dockland areas, 'Perfidious Patmos'[26] for an inner-city area predominantly populated (especially since 1848) by political refugees from the Continent and cartographically defined with Sala's customary exactitude:

> The Patmos of London I may describe as an island bounded by four

squares; on the north by that of Soho, on the south by that of Leicester, on the east by the quadrangle of Lincoln's Inn Fields (for the purlieus of Long Acre and Seven Dials are all Patmos), and on the west by Golden Square.[27]

Building on earlier work of this kind (though with a self-indulgent discursiveness absent from the best of it), *Twice Round the Clock* sets out to evoke the distinctive local identity of a substantial proportion of districts of the metropolis as a whole.

Munby's readiness to adopt the role of private investigator, not scrupling to exploit his class superiority in extracting the information he seeks, is undeniably voyeuristic in Foucault's sense, and seems illustrative of the close link Benjamin posits between the flaneur and the detective in the nineteenth-century city.[28] On the other hand, Munby was also 'a man of the crowd'[29] to a greater extent than has been generally recognised, plunging in Baudelairean fashion (i.e., discreetly) into the multitude. Munby joined crowds not only on the lookout for individual specimens but because he was sympathetically disposed towards popular culture and sensitive to nuances of group behaviour—so long as it did not challenge hierarchical norms. Derby Day, 20 May 1863, and Garibaldi's visit to London, 11 April, 1864 offer moving examples of such imaginative sympathy. On Derby Day, as on many other such occasions, Munby found solace from personal depression in a collectivity to which he himself did not really belong:

> A damp grey morning: but soon after ten a hope (delusive like other hopes) of fine weather appeared, and I determined to go to the *Derby*: not to see the race, but to see those who go to see it, and to observe the humours of the course…Moreover, I was in a moody and despondent condition: and a race course or other suchlike place is to me the best resort at such times. Not that I am pleased at all by its pleasures, but that the study of them and of those who are pleased by them calls out one's power of observation and one's love of reverie into a set of subjects other & better than one's self…Whether the awe be divine or devilish, the unanimous enthusiasm of fifty thousand human beings, the thunder of their voices and the swaying to and fro, is in a high sense awful: *is* perhaps the most tremendous expression of an

unseen force that one can conceive of, except a storm at sea.[30]

The subdual of self ('an ego athirst for the non-ego', as 'The Painter of modern life' has it)[31] through a blend of observation and reverie sounds thoroughly Baudelairean, yet Munby had no knowledge of Baudelaire's writings.[32]

Again like Baudelaire and like Thomas de Quincey (the London scenes of whose *Confessions of an English Opium-Eater* profoundly influenced Baudelaire as well as Munby), this London diarist-flaneur has a poignant sense of fleeting and elusive connections in the large anonymous city; subsequent meetings with or glimpses of those encountered by chance are therefore cherished and memorialized. Hiley reprints Munby's report of a second sighting of a young dustwoman with whom he had had one of his embarrassing misunderstandings at the photographer's (22 March 1862); eleven months later (20 February 1863), he saw her running wildly through the crowds across Westminster Bridge.[33] Exactly a year before this, Munby recorded a more substantial but still fortuitous reunion with one Louisa Hamilton-Finney, a *soi-disant* fallen woman of genteel origins who had recounted her poignant but romantic autobiography to him on a Hyde Park bench (14 June 1861).[34] When they bumped into one another again in a Coventry Street restaurant she updated her story (she was happier and better-off now, married but separated, and working as an artist's model): 'upon learning the interesting and impressive denouement of her romance, I put her into a cab and sent her home to Chelsea' (21 February 1862).[35] In reality Ms Hamilton-Finney's life-story had reached no clear denouement; her future was as uncertain as ever. But for Munby, the sense of auspicious connection and continuity which the chance reunion provided, in an urban world governed by forces of impersonality and contingency, was of sufficient value in itself. Partly for the same reason he meticulously recorded every sighting of the numerous London milkwomen whom he individualized with appropriate invented names; half-fantasised as *rus-in-urbe* figures they also alleviated his pastoral longings.

In Baudelaire's essay, 'The painter of *modern* life', the graphic artist Constantin Guys ('M.G.'), is heroized on account of his search 'for that indefinable something we may be allowed to call modernity'.[36] The author of *Tableaux Parisiens* and *Le spleen de Paris* was essentially the poet of urban modernity: for him, Paris and modernity were virtually synonymous.[37]

On the other hand, Munby's record of the modern city is in very English fashion imbued with nostalgia for an older world. This is not only apparent in his introduction of *rus in urbe* motifs whenever possible, but in a sentimental enthusiasm for the survival of folk customs and ceremonies such as 'Kiss-in-the-Ring',[38] in patronage of the city's best antiquarian bookshops, and in conscientious descriptions and inventories of old buildings facing demolition.[39] Yet his reverence for the past is perhaps most eloquently expressed in understated tribute to Pepys, a decided urbanite and man of contemporary affairs, together with that other great diarist of late-seventeenth-century London, John Evelyn. This comes as the climax to a day of characteristic flanerie in the city's riverside districts now full of modern industry but, for this observer, with potent literary-historical associations and aesthetic appeal as well:

Beyond Bermondsey, I passed through Horsleydown,...and so up into the Lower Deptford Road, by which Evelyn went to Saye's Court and Pepys to the dockyards. The streets end at Blue Anchor Lane, up which I turned, and passed under the S.Eastern railway into a land of market gardens, dotted with small cottages....It was now four o'clock, and twilight, and the moon was rising [in] a clear blue sky. I turned back, and went down several old side streets into Rotherhithe, with a view of reaching the Thames Tunnel. Large wharves and warehouses lined the narrow streets, but all was quiet and old....

A man and some boys were hanging about; and we discoursed of mudlarking.

...[A]fter the great fire in June, all the women and girls of the neighbourhood turned out with the boys and men, to gather the fat which floated in vast cakes down the river....For days and weeks it went on....Four feet is the average depth of the mud but at these times many women & girls waded up to their necks in mud and water....Some too went up the great sewers hereabouts for the same purpose; and two or three girls fell overhead into the deep slush at the mouths of these drains, which were just below us....

Finding there was a ferry here...I went down the steps and along a causeway, and crossed the river in the boat. The moon shone on the broad water; forests of shipping on either hand, and dark old riverside houses; and stillness almost perfect everywhere. I landed too on classic ground—at Wapping Old Stairs. From whence I made my way by the London and Katherine Docks to Tower hill. Then up through Crutched Friars and Hart St, where Pepys lived and where his parish church St Olave's still stands. I stopped awhile to realise, if possible, his days… (14 December 1861).[40]

At the centre of this passage we encounter interesting material of the kind for which Munby is best known—contemporary history of working women doing dirty jobs. However, there can be doubt that the emotional heart of this journal entry lies elsewhere—in Munby's imaginative evocation of late-seventeenth-century London. Indeed, even the topical story of salvaging floating fat from the river is indirectly related to Munby's elective affinities with Pepys and Evelyn. The 'great fire' referred to was the Tooley Street fire in June 1861, which Munby witnessed and described with vivid fullness in his diary.[41] This fire was immediately recognised to have been the largest and most destructive in London since the Great Fire of 1666; it seems certain that in penning so unusually elaborate a description of a current disaster Munby was seeking to emulate those celebrated accounts by Pepys and Evelyn of the 1666 fire. And this in turn may partly account for these predecessors being in the forefront of his mind on the atmospheric walk of 14 December.

Sala's work seems to present a sharp tonal and ideological contrast to Munby's. In the first place he repeatedly proclaims a preference for urban to rural surroundings; the opening of 'Down Whitechapel way', a veritable manifesto for London flanerie, may again serve as illustration:

'Sir', said Samuel Johnson to the Scotch gentleman—'sir, let us take a walk down Fleet Street.' If I had not a thousand other reasons to love and revere the memory of the great and good old doctor, I should still love and revere it for his preference of Fleet Street to the fields—of streets generally to sylvan shades—of the hum of men and the rattling of wheels to the chirp of the cricket or the song of the skylark. It may be prejudice, or an unpoetic mind, or so on; but I am of the streets, streety.[42]

Even here, though, there is more than a hint of a reverence as strong as Munby's for distinguished predecessors in the field (or rather the street), and as we shall see, most of the remainder of this opening paragraph celebrates the atmospheric appeal of some of London's most historic locations. However, Sala also gives many of his essays in *Household Words* a radical gloss which we hardly ever encounter in Munby's writing. This is particularly the case with pieces written in 'one-half-not-knowing-the-other' vein, often set in hours of darkness with a noctambulist narrator. Indeed, the title of his first collection of essays culled from *Household Words* is *Gaslight and daylight*, and one of these pieces is actually called 'The secrets of the gas'—thus bringing together four properties Benjamin associates with flanerie: noctambulism, gaslight, secrecy, and detective work:

> As I walk about the streets by night, endless and always suggestive intercommunings take place between me and the trusty, silent, ever-watchful gas, whose secrets I know....He who will bend himself to listen to, and avail himself, of the secrets of the gas, may walk through London streets proud in the consciousness of being an Inspector—in the great police force of philosophy—and of carrying a perpetual bull's-eye in his belt....Not a bolt or bar, not a lock or fastening, not a houseless night-wanderer, not a homeless dog, shall escape that searching ray of light which the gas shall lend him, to see and to know.[43]

The essay's staple (and overworked) conceit is not a very convincing one: the claim that 'the gas has its secrets, and I happen to know them' is not in fact borne out, since several enumerated—such as the cause and circumstances of death in the case of corpses now at the bottom of the river—are not within human ken. Furthermore, as shown in the passage quoted above, there is a much stronger sense of elation than of moral purpose in the possession of secret power. As often in Sala's *Household Words* pieces, however, the popular philosophic note on which the essay ends is the characteristically Dickensian one of *nihil humanum a me alienum pute* (I regard nothing human as alien to me):

> So, from where the town begins to where it ends; from the twinkling

lights of Putney and Kew, to the marshy flats below Deptford; the gas shines through the still night, and is the repository of secrets known to *few*, but which all who *choose* to make the gas their friend, may *read*, to the softening of their hearts, perhaps, even as they run.[44]

The essay with which Sala gained entry to *Household Words* in the first place, 'The key of the street',[45] has similar components, but this account of a night spent as one of the homeless on the London streets is too crudely an exercise in role-play to be really effective. Much more convincing in every way is 'Houseless and hungry',[46] reporting a visit to a night shelter in the Barbican, and perhaps the immediate inspiration of Luke Fildes's famous drawing with the same name, first published in *The Graphic* (4 December 1869): 'I made my way to an open doorway, whence issued a stream of light; and before which were ranged, in a widish semi-circle, a crowd of cowering creatures, men, women and children, who were patiently awaiting their turn of entrance.'[47] Prior to this, Sala characteristically offers an epitome of the district through which he has had to pass in search of the shelter:

> The whole neighbourhood is pervaded with a miasma of grinding, unwholesome, sullen, and often vicious poverty. Everything is cheap and nasty; and the sellers seem as poor as the buyers….Chandlers' shops, marine stores, pawn-shops, and public houses, occur over and over again in sickening repetition. There is a frowsy blight on the window-panes and the gas-lamps….The air is tainted with exhalations from rank tobacco, stale herrings, old clothes, and workshops of noxious trades.[48]

This essay is very different in tone from those more perfunctorily invoking liberal-humanitarian principles. From beginning to end 'Houseless and hungry' resonates with a grim indignation that such things as this reporter has seen and heard of destitution and starvation should be commonplace occurrences in London's streets, and even more that such shameful actualities should be unknown to, or questioned by, so many in more comfortable circumstances. He alludes to two 'friends', Pragmos and Sharplynx, who hold that in modern society destitution can only be self-inflicted or feigned, and that therefore cheap (and luxurious?) night shelters necessarily do more harm than good. Sala's account of his visit to the House of Poverty in Playhouse Yard, off Whitecross Street, is written in refutation of these widely held attitudes:

> Everything was...of the simplest and roughest nature; yet everything seemed to me to answer admirably the purpose for which it was designed....I believe I have sufficient knowledge of the street-world to tell a professional beggar from a starving man; but I declare I saw no face that night passing the hatchbut in which I could read: Ragged and Tired—Dead Beat—Utterly Destitute—Houseless and Hungry.[49]

Sala may well have been influenced here by a passage in Mayhew's *London Labour and the London Poor* on the same subject,[50] especially since he follows Mayhew in employing the 'There but for the grace of God go I' motif while surveying the scene from an elevated viewpoint:

> Looking down upon this solemn, silent, awful scene made you shudder; made you question by what right you were standing up, warm, prosperous, well-fed, well-clad, with these destitute creatures, your brothers and sisters...? But for the absence of marble floors and tanks, the place might be some kennel for hounds; but for the rags and the eyes, these might be sheep in the pens in Smithfield Market.[51]

But more unusually, Sala's essay also questions his own role as voyeuristic journalist in such a place:

> The eyes are upon you, you know, gazing sternly, moodily, reproachfully. You feel almost as if you were an intruder. You are not the doctor to heal, the priest to console, the Lady Bountiful to relieve. What right have you to be there, taking stock of human miseries, and jotting down sighs and tears in your notebook?[52]

This might be taken as just another rhetorical set-piece, but it stands in sharp contrast to Munby's failure ever to question the legitimacy of *his* intrusions into the lives of the women he engaged in conversation. But as noted earlier, Munby was not writing for publication. Sala, it seems, had a penchant for pornography and worse in his private life,[53] but in print he not infrequently gestured *against* voyeurism. On this occasion it comes across as more than a gesture, and this is because it is in keeping with the tone and spirit of the whole essay. The sustained note of sober, socially critical engagement is, as I've said, unusual in Sala's writing, and makes 'Houseless and hungry' more akin to the work of Dickens and Mayhew at its most critically sombre. However, this also means that it is *not* a piece of literary flanerie.

Sala shows less sympathy for the poor in his post-Dickensian work. This shift may be part of an effort to shed his bohemian image, a bid for respectability and conventionality. However, it seems just as likely that Sala was reverting to a position inculcated by his earliest influences and experience—by an upbringing in shabby and indeed sham gentility, uncomfortably close to poverty and crime. In his portrait of Regent Street in *Twice Round the Clock*, he recalls his first acquaintance with it at the age of four, when he witnessed a trade-union demonstration there in the company of a nurse: 'She said…that they were half a million in number, and I recollect her portending, in a grave low voice, that there would be riots that night….[L]ong after, whenever I saw a crowd, I used to ask whether there would be any riots that night.'[54] An equally strong sense of the collective working class as an unpleasant threat emerges in the article on 'Drury Lane' in his 'Streets of the world' series. It is not only the street's most disreputable denizens who are severely dealt with: 'the vilest scum of London's dangerous classes who, hands on haunches, pipe in mouth, oath and ribaldry always on lip, leer and fleer, and scoff and blaspheme'; he is equally dismissive of 'the vast amount of non-criminal rags and wretchedness trenching on the extreme confines of turpitude.'[55] But these distasteful elements having been summarily dispatched, the tone completely alters in an expanded recapitulation of the affectionate allusion to this particular street in the introduction to 'Down Whitechapel way': 'Drury Lane I affect especially, past and present—the Maypole, Nell Gwynn, and the Earls of Craven, dividing my interest with Vinegar Yard, the costermongers, the pawnbrokers, and the stage-door of the theatre round the corner.'[56] The later article enlarges on this with a loving invocation of the bohemian atmosphere of the local theatres and a celebration, Dickensian in its vitality, of the writer's childhood memories of characterful shops and businesses in the street's westerly environs:

There are loquacious barbers, who sell walking-sticks, keep poll-
parrots, and make a grand show in their little sanctums with wood-
cuts cut from the illustrated papers, stuck all over the walls, among
the razors and pomatum pots. There are pie shops, the cynosure of
hungry boys, who stand before them with longing eyes, watering
mouths, and fingers nervously twitching in their too often vacuous
pockets….Ah! the delight of those pie shops! the savoury smelling
muttons, the unapproachable kidneys! the fruit tarts, with a delicate
rime of powdered sugar on their crusts, and little streaks of crimson
tears oozing down their sides.[57]

Indulgent remembrance of things past begins much earlier in Sala's work,
for example in 'Things departed',[58] where the twenty-four-year-old author
adopts the persona of a man twice his age to recall changes in the city
since 1822. The note of nostalgia becomes increasingly pronounced from
Twice Round the Clock onwards. That book opens in Billingsgate Market at
four o' clock in the morning, and we might expect Sala to grab our attention immediately with an eye-witness account of this lively scene. When
such an account is eventually offered it is much briefer than the preceding discursive passage of literary-historical allusion—to the poetry of
Thomson and Wordsworth, and more particularly to the 'jovial, brutal,
vulgar, graphic' prose of Ned Ward in *The London Spy*, one of Sala's chief
models for the 'round-the-clock' design.[59]
Thus, I would suggest that London flaneurs were more adventurous than
their Parisian cousins, more inclined to ramble than to stroll. On the other
hand, they were less zealously the chroniclers of modernity: even though
primarily a record of the contemporary urban scene, their perceptions were
strongly shaped and coloured by conscious participation in the city's long
tradition of street-life observation. More precisely, one should refer to
traditions in the plural, since as we have seen Munby and Sala take inspiration from different predecessors representing distinct strands and genres
of urban writing. The city of London was already complex and modern
enough in the early eighteenth century to call forth the 'endless curiosity'
of one of the principal progenitors of London flanerie, Mr Spectator.
Victorian flaneurs could readily identify with fore-ramblers whose urban
experience had in certain essential ways been similar to their own.

Notes

Place of publication is London, unless otherwise stated.

Introduction
Tim Hitchcock and Heather Shore

1 BL, Add. MS, 27,828, 'Place Papers. Vol. xl: Manners and Morals', fol. 7–8.
2 *The Diary of John Evelyn*, cited in Stephen Inwood, *A History of London*, 1998, p.243.
3 William Stow, *Remarks on London*, 1722, p.4.
4 Richard Steele, 'The Hours of London', *The Spectator*, no. 455, 11 August 1712.
5 Henry Fielding, *An Inquiry into the Causes of the Late Encrease of Robbers, etc, With some Proposals for Remedying this Growing Evil*, 1751, pp.142–3.
6 Pierce Egan, *Life in London Or, The Day and Night Scenes of Jerry Hawthorn, Esq., and His Elegant Friend Corinthian Tom, Accompanied by Bob Logic, the Oxonian, in Their Rambles and Sprees through the Metropolis*, 1821. For a discussion of Egan and other similar literature see John Marriott and Masaie Matsumura, eds, *The Metropolitan Poor: Semi-Factual Accounts, 1795–1910*, 6 vols., 1999, particularly vol.1.
7 Gustave Doré and Blanchard Jerrold, *London, A Pilgramage*, 1872, passim.
8 Daniel Defoe, *The Great Law of Subordination Consider'd*, 1724, p.125.

1. At Shakespear's-Head, Over-Against Catharine-Street in the Strand
Cynthia Wall

1 William Stow, *Remarks on London*, 1722, sig. A5.
2 Edward Soja, *Postmodern Geographies: The Reassertion of Space in Critical Social Theory*, 1989, p.84.
3 For more on pre-Fire attitudes toward London, see my *Literary and Cultural Spaces of Restoration London*, Cambridge, 1998, ch.1.
4 Wenceslaus Hollar, *A Map or Grovndplot of the Citty of London, and the Suburbs thereof...by which is Exactly Demonstrated the Present Condition Thereof, since the Last Sad Accident of Fire*, 1666.
5 See *Literary and Cultural Spaces*, chs.2, 3.
6 *The Mercury*, no.21, 15–19 August 1667 (my emphasis).
7 Stow, *Remarks*, sig. A4.
8 *A Book of the Names of All Parishes, Market Towns, Villages, Hamblets and Smallest Places, in England and Wales. Alphabetically Set Down, as they be in Every Shire. With the Names of the Hundreds in Which They Are and How Many Towns There are in Every Hundred*, 1677.
9 A.F. Johnson, *One Hundred Title-Pages, 1500–1800*, 1928, p.v. See also Henry Lemoine, *Typographical Antiquities: Origin and History of the Art of Printing, Foreign and Domestic...from*

the *Infancy of Printing, to the End of the Eighteenth Century, Extracted from the Best Authorities, by a Late Bibliopolist*, 2nd edition, corrected and enlarged by T. A. of the Inner Temple, esq., 1813: In earlier productions 'The name of the printer, place of his residence, &c. &c. were either wholly neglected, or put at the end of the book, with some pious ejaculation, or doxology. The date was likewise omitted, or involved in some crampt circumstantial period', p.xxviii.

10 Theodore Low De Vinne, *The Practice of Typography; a Treatise on Title-Pages*, New York, 1904, p.36 (my emphasis).

11 See chapter four in this collection, for example; see also Lawrence Manley, *Literature and Culture in Early Modern London*, Cambridge, 1995, ch.2; Richard Sennett, *Flesh and Stone: The Body and the City in Western Civilization*, New York, 1994, ch.8.

12 See also Alfred W. Pollard, *Last Words on the History of the Title-Page*, 1891; Grolier Club, *Catalogue of Original and Early Editions of some of the Poetical and Prose Works of English Writers from Wither to Prior*, New York, 1905; Stanley Morison, *The Typographic Book, 1450–1935; A Study of Fine Typography Through Five Centuries*, 1963; Stanley Morison, *The Art of the Printer*, 1925; Bella Landauer, *Printers' Mottoes*, New York, 1926; A.F. Johnson, *A Catalogue of Engraved and Etched English Title-Pages Down to the Death of William Faithorne*, 1934; Theodore Low De Vinne, *Title-Pages as Seen by a Printer*, New York, 1901; R.V. Tooley, *Title-Pages from 16th to 19th Century*, 1975; A. Edward Newton, *The Format of the English Novel*, Cleveland, 1928.

13 De Vinne, *The Practice of Typography*, p.viii.

14 Joseph Moxon, *Mechanick Exercises: or, The Doctrine of Handy Works*, 1683, vol.2, numb. XV, sect. XXII, 'The Compositers Trade', p.222.

15 Another contributing factor to this topographical specificity may be that from the mid sixteenth century, the Stationers' Company required printers to work in London. Other European printers did not have similar requirements for urban practice.

16 Nathaniel Crouch, *Historical Remarques and Observations of the Ancient and Present State of London*, 1681, p.114.

17 Stow, *Remarks*, sig. A4.

18 *New Remarks of London: Or, a Survey of the Cities of London and Westminster…Collected by the Company of Parish-Clerks*, 1732, p.vii.

19 Edward Copeland, 'Remapping London: *Clarissa* and the Woman in the Window', in Margaret Anne Doody and Peter Sabor (eds), *Samuel Richardson, Tercentenary Essays*, Cambridge, 1989.

20 Frances Burney, *Evelina*, 1778, ed., Kristina Straub, Bedford Cultural Editions , Boston, 1997.

21 Burney, *Evelina*, p.213.

22 Burney, *Evelina*, p.212.

23 Burney, *Evelina*, pp.237–8.

24 Burney, *Evelina*, p.239.

25 Frances Burney, *Cecilia*, 1782, eds, Peter Sabor and Margaret Anne Doody, Oxford, 1988.

26 Burney, *Cecilia*, p.897.

27 Daniel Defoe, *Moll Flanders*, 1722, ed., G.A. Starr, Oxford, 1971, p.192.

28 Burney, *Cecilia*, p.901.

29 James Boswell, *Boswell's London Journal 1762–1763*, ed. Frederick A. Pottle, New York, 1950, p.153.

30 *Boswell's London Journal*, p.47.

31 *Boswell's London Journal*, p.232.

32 *London Journal*, pp.255–6, 10 May 1763.

33 *Boswell's London Journal*, pp.272–3, 4 June 1763.
34 *Boswell's London Journal*, p.273.
35 Burney, *Diary & Letters of Madame D'Arblay*, ed. Charlotte Barrett, 1904, vol.1, pp.61–2.
36 Stow, *Remarks*, sig. A5.

2. The Polite Town
Lawrence E. Klein
Earlier versions of this paper were presented at the Bay Area Eighteenth-Century Studies Group, Berkeley, California, and the Early Modern British History Seminar at the Huntington Library, San Marino, California. For the first of those opportunities, I would like to thank David Lieberman and David Brewer, and, for the second, Barbara Donagan.

 1 John Gay, *The Present State of Wit, in a Letter to a Friend in the Country*, 1711, p.5. The date and place appear on p.22.
 2 Gay, *Present State of Wit*, pp.7, 23. Gay's effort here to distance himself from his previous journalistic endeavour was a step in his self-transformation from a provincial draper's apprentice into a polite man of letters: politeness was, among other things, a program of self-fashioning. See David Nokes, *John Gay: A Profession of Friendship*, Oxford, 1995, pp.51–92.
 3 This is a significant point in light of the whiggish tendency in scholarship to see developments in the history of the press as ineluctable steps toward democracy. See the critique of this tendency in Joad Raymond, *The Invention of the Newspaper: English Newsbooks, 1641–1649*, Oxford, 1996, pp.3–6.
 4 Gay, *Present State of Wit*, p.14.
 5 Peter Borsay, *The English Urban Renaissance: Culture and Society in the Provincial Town, 1660–1770*, Oxford, 1989, especially pp.257–83. On London as a 'blueprint' for the provincial towns, see pp.286–7.
 6 Quoted in Amanda Vickery, *The Gentleman's Daughter: Women's Lives in Georgian England*, New Haven and London, 1998, p.172.
 7 William Matthews, ed., *The Diary of Dudley Ryder, 1715–1716*, 1939, p.38—entry for 18 June 1715.
 8 For instance, James Boswell, *Boswell's London Journal 1762–1763*, ed. Frederick A. Pottle, New York, 1950, pp.129–30, entry for 8 January 1763: 'Mrs. Gould and Mrs. Douglas and I went in the Colonel [Gould]'s chariot to the Haymarket. As we drove along and spoke good English, I was full of rich imaginations of London, ideas suggested by the Spectator and such as I could not explain to most people, but which I strongly feel and am ravished with. My blood glows and my mind is agitated with felicity'.
 9 Lawrence Manley, *Literature and Culture in Early Modern London*, Cambridge, 1995, pp.481–530, especially 483–6; Martin Butler, *Theatre and Crisis, 1632–1642*, Cambridge, 1984, pp.100–80. On the wider social and ideological change underpinning the appearance of the Town, Anna Bryson, *From Courtesy to Civility: Changing Codes of Conduct in Early Modern England*, Oxford, 1998.
10 Felicity Heal and Clive Holmes, *The Gentry in England and Wales*, 1994, pp.311–17; James Rosenheim, *The Emergence of a Ruling Order: English Landed Society, 1650–1750*, London and New York, 1998, pp.215–52; Susan Whyman, *Sociability and Power in Late-Stuart England: The Cultural Worlds of the Verneys 1660-1720*, Oxford, 1999, pp.87–109.
11 Peter Earle, *The Making of the English Middle Class: Business, Society and Family Life in London 1660–1730*, 1989, pp.269–301, 327–37 (though Earle's references to middle-class 'gentility' are scattered throughout the book).
12 The most comprehensive account of the geographical expansion and spatial organi-

sation of London in the seventeenth century is still Norman Brett-James, *The Growth of Stuart London*, 1935; also, Lawrence Stone, 'The Residential Development of the West End of London in the Seventeenth Century', in Barbara C. Malament, ed., *After the Reformation: Essays in Honor of J. H. Hexter*, Philadelphia, 1980, and John Summerson, *Georgian London*, 1945.

13 Brian Cowan, 'The Social Life of Coffee: Commercial Culture and Metropolitan Society in Early Modern England, 1600–1720', Ph.D. thesis, Princeton University, 2000, pp.116–66, 255–403; Steve Pincus, '"Coffee Politicians Does Create": Coffeehouses and Restoration Political Culture', *Journal of Modern History*, 67, 1995, pp.807–34; Lawrence E. Klein, 'Coffeehouse Civility, 1660–1714: An Aspect of Post-Courtly Culture in England', *Huntington Library Quarterly*, 59, 1996, pp.31–51.

14 Richard W. Bevis, *English Drama: Restoration and Eighteenth Century, 1660–1789*, London and New York, 1988, pp.31–6, 117–20.

15 Butler, *Theatre and Crisis*, pp.141–3.

16 See Lawrence E. Klein, 'Politeness for Plebes: Consumption and Social Identity in Early Eighteenth-Century England', in Ann Bermingham and John Brewer (eds), *The Consumption of Culture 1660–1800: Image, Object, Text*, London and New York, 1995, pp.364–5, and references cited there.

17 R. Malcolm Smuts, 'Cultural Diversity and Cultural Change at the Court of James I', in Linda Levy Peck, *The Mental World of the Jacobean Court*, Cambridge, 1991, pp.99–112, especially 103–5.

18 R.O. Bucholz, *The Augustan Court: Queen Anne and the Decline of Court Culture*, Stanford, 1993, pp.247–8.

19 Two basic accounts of the periodical press in this era are: James Sutherland, *The Restoration Newspaper and its Development*, Cambridge, 1986, and C. John Sommerville, *The News Revolution in England: Cultural Dynamics of Daily Information*, Oxford, 1996.

20 Among continuators of the *Poor Robin* tradition in the periodical genre were: *Poor Robins Publick and Private Occurances*, 1688; *The London Spy*, 1698–1700; *The English Lucian*, 1698; *The Town Spy*, 1704; and *The Comical Observator*, 1704. John Dunton's *The Night Walker*, 1698–1700, represents the seedy side of London from a non-polite albeit reformist standpoint.

21 One or more of these features are noted in: Margaret Ezell, 'The *Gentleman's Journal* and the Commercialisation of Restoration Coterie Literary Practices', *Modern Philology*, 89, 1992, pp.323–40; Kathryn Shevelow, *Women and Print Culture: The Construction of Femininity in the Early Periodical*, 1989, pp.22–57; Sommerville, *The News Revolution*, pp.109–18, 146–60.

22 On Motteux's career, Robert Newton Cunningham, *Peter Anthony Motteux, 1663–1718: A Biographical and Critical Study*, Oxford, 1933.

23 *Gentleman's Journal*, January 1692, p.1.

24 *Gentleman's Journal*, January 1692, p.52.

25 *Gentleman's Journal*, July 1693, p.217.

26 *Gentleman's Journal*, June 1692, p.2.

27 *Gentleman's Journal*, February 1693, p.61.

28 *Gentleman's Journal*, April 1693, p.131.

29 In most numbers.

30 *Gentleman's Journal*, September 1692, p.26.

31 *Gentleman's Journal*, February 1692, p.2.

32 *Gentleman's Journal*, February 1693, p.54.

33 *Gentleman's Journal*, January 1692, pp.10–11.

34 *Gentleman's Journal*, December 1693, p.23.

35 *The Diverting-Post*, 28 October 1704.
36 *Gentleman's Journal*, January 1692, p.52.
37 *Gentleman's Journal*, March 1692, p.1.
38 The transformation of London possibility registered in the *Tatler* was the result of the actual transformation of London in this period but it was also a function of London representation being taken over (in part) by gentlemen or would-be gentlemen who were not Londoners but who were participating in the new aspect of London that was undergoing rapid elaboration through the Restoration and post-1688 decades. John Gay was one example, Peter Motteux another; but so too were Richard Steele and Joseph Addison and myriad others. Joseph Addison (1672–1719) and Richard Steele (1672–1729) followed a path that paralleled, on a considerably higher level, that of Gay. Addison and Steele shared a similar background: from the lower rungs of the gentlemanly class. They had a similar trajectory that took them from the provinces to London where they built a career through connections and patronage and through public offices and through writing.
39 The *Tatler*, ed., Donald F. Bond, Oxford, 1987, II, pp.422–6 (Number 167, 4 May 1710).
40 *Tatler*, II, pp.435–8 (Number 170, 11 May 1710).
41 *Tatler*, III, pp.10–13 (Number 186, 17 June 1710).
42 *Tatler*, II, pp.418–22 (Number 166, 2 May 1710), II, pp.168–72 (Number 111, 24 December 1709), II, pp.369–73 (Number 155, 6 April 1710), II, pp.242–6 (Number 127, 31 January 1710).
43 *Tatler* II, p.10 (Number 186, 17 June 1710).
44 *Tatler*, III, pp.97–100 (Number 207, 5 August 1710).
45 *Tatler*, I, pp.326–8 (Number 46, 26 July 1709). For further discussion on the landed and the moneyed gentleman, see Lawrence E. Klein, 'Property and Politeness in the Early Eighteenth-Century Whig Moralists: the Case of the *Spectator*', in John Brewer and Susan Staves (eds), *Early Modern Conceptions of Property*, London and New York, 1995, pp.221–33.
46 *Tatler*, II, pp.348–52 (Number 151, 28 March 1710) and II, pp.410–4 (Number 164, 27 April 1710). See Richmond P. Bond, *The Tatler: the Making of a Literary Journal*, Cambridge, Massachusetts, 1971, pp.167–70.
47 Gough Square, Johnson's Court, and Bolt Court: Dorothy Marshall, *Dr. Johnson's London*, New York, 1968, p.9. Sheer Lane is shown on the very important map of 1676 by John Ogilby and William Morgan, reproduced with apparatus in Ralph Hyde, *The A to Z of Restoration London (The City of London, 1676)*, Lympne Castle, Kent, 1992, p.62. Its path is now occupied by part of the Law Courts.
48 *Tatler*, I, p.16 (Number 1, 12 April 1709).
49 Bryant Lillywhite, *London Coffee Houses*, 1963, pp.243, 500, 639–40, 655–8.
50 *Tatler*, II, pp.229–33 (Number 124, 24 January 1710).
51 On the practice and meaning of visits in gentle life, see Vickery, *The Gentleman's Daughter*, pp.195–225, and Whyman, *Sociability and Power*, pp.91–6.
52 *Tatler*, II, pp.402–5 (Number 162, 22 April 1710).
53 *Tatler*, II, p.175 (Number 112, 27 December 1709), II, pp.186–91 (Number 115, 3 January 1710), II, pp.214–5 (Number 120, 14 January 1710), II, pp.220–4 (Number 122, 19 January 1710), II, pp.288–91 (Number 137, 23 February 1710), and II, pp.310–1 (Number 142, 7 March 1710).

3. Circulation and Disorder
Mark Jenner

My thanks to audiences in Leeds, London and York, to Michael Berlin, Paul Griffiths, James

220   *The Streets of London*

Robertson and the editors for their help and particular thanks to Patricia Greene for reading drafts of this paper and for so much more. I wish to acknowledge the financial assistance of the Transport History Trust in some of the research for this chapter.

1 Tobias Smollett, *The Expedition of Humphrey Clinker*, ed., L. M. Knapp, rev., P-G. Boucé, Oxford, 1998, p.88.
2 E.g., *London and its Environs Described*, 5 vols. (1761), iii, 122–3. For their early history, S. Piggott, *Wagon, Chariot and Carriage: Symbol and Status in the History of Transport*, 1992, ch.4.
3 *The Diary of Robert Hooke 1672–1680*, ed., H. W. Robinson and W. Adams, 1935, p.227.
4 J. Taylor, *The World Runnes on Wheeles*, 1623, sig. A[2v]; S. Whyman, *Sociability and Power in Late-Stuart England: The Cultural Worlds of the Verneys, 1660–1720*, Oxford, 1999, ch.4.
5 Peter Earle, *The Making of the English Middle Class*, 1989, pp.343–4.
6 *OBSP*, 15–18 June 1718, p.4.
7 E.g., *OBSP*, 14–17 January 1714/15, pp.5–6; OBSP, 8–10 July 1719, p.4; *OBSP*, 1–4 March 1720, p.2.
8 Ralph Houlbrooke, *Death, Religion, and the Family in England 1480–1750*, Oxford, 1998, pp.285–6.
9 Carl Philip Moritz noted it was 'a great advantage of the English hackney coaches' that you paid no more to ride with a trunk and thus could save on porters' costs', *Journeys of a German in England in 1782*, trans & ed., R. Nettel, 1965, p.31.
10 On the use of hackney coaches when drunk, *OBSP*, 4–7 Dec 1734, pp.15–16. For walking, P. J. Corfield, 'Walking the City Streets: The Urban Odyssey in Eighteenth-Century England', *Journal of Urban History*, 16, 1990, 132–74
11 PRO, PC2/47 p.287; C. H. Firth & R. S. Rait, *Acts and Ordinances of the Interregnum*,1911, ii, 922–4.
12 13 & 14 Chales II c.2; 5 & 6 William & Mary c.22; 9 Anne c.23; 11 George III c.24.
13 Similar forms of regulation were introduced in other European cities, e.g., B. Causse, *Les Fiacres de Paris aux xviiᵉ et xviiiᵉ Siècles*, Paris, 1972.
14 J. F. Larkin ed., *Stuart Royal Proclamations II*, Oxford, 1983, pp.494–6.
15 Firth & Rait, *Acts and Ordinances*, ii 922–4. For their nomination, CLRO, Rep. 63 fos. 108–08v.
16 13 & 14 Charles II c.2.
17 *The Act for Repairing the High-ways and Sewers, ... and for Licensing and Regulating Hackney-Coaches ... Expires at the end of this present Session*, n.d., [1679].
18 For bequests of licenses, GL, 9171/47 fo. 21 & 9171/49 fo. 219. For leasing, PRO, E112/712/2036.
19 PRO, T1/403/15–20.
20 CLRO, Jnl. 50 fo. 369; 5 & 6 William & Mary c.22; *CSPD 1695 & Addenda 1689–95*, p.245.
21 *Reports from Committees of the House of Commons 1715–1801*, 1803, xii, 55.
22 Calculated from J. Hoppitt ed., *Failed Legislation 1660–1800*, 1997.
23 R. Sennett, *Flesh and Stone*, 1994, pp.255–71; D. Trotter, *Circulation: Defoe, Dickens and the Economies of the Novel*, Basingstoke, 1988, ch.1.
24 M. S. R. Jenner, forthcoming.
25 Ibid. Cf. N. Papayanis, *Horse-Drawn Cabs and Omnibuses in Paris: The Idea of Circulation and the Business of Public Transit*, Baton Rouge, 1996, ch.1.
26 Cf. M. Hallett, *The Spectacle of Difference: Graphic Satire in the Age of Hogarth*, New Haven and London, 1999, ch.4.
27 *The Diary of Samuel Pepys*, ed., R. Latham and W. Matthews, 1970–83, ix, 383.
28 L. Mumford, *The City in History*, Harmondsworth, 1966, p.423.

29 Mumford, *City in History*, p.424.
30 M. de Certeau, *The Practice of Everyday Life*, trans. S. F. Rendall, Berkeley, Los Angeles and London, 1984, p.96.
31 *CJ*, 13 (1699–1702), p.176; GL 4069/2 fos. 132v, 136, 139v, 143; *CJ*, 19 (1718–21), p.119; CLRO, City Sessions Papers January 1693, brief about indictment against hackney coachmen.
32 *The Poems of John Oldham*, ed., H. F. Brooks, Oxford, 1987, p.257; J. Gay, *Poetry and Prose*, ed., V. A. Dearing with C. E. Beckwith, Oxford, 1974, i, 161.
33 P. Bourdieu, *Outline of a Theory of Practice*, trans. R. Nice, Cambridge, 1977, esp. pp.93–5.
34 E.g., *The St. James Evening Post*, 1178, December 4–6, 1722.
35 E.g., *Pilkington Mayor, Jovis Decimo sexto Die Julii 1691. This Court Considering…*(1691); GL, 4069/2, fos. 180 & 229.
36 CLRO, Jnl. 45 fo. 264v.
37 *Further Reasons against increasing the number of Hackney Coaches*, 1690?; *Act of Common Council for the Better Regulation of Hackney-Coaches*, 1683, pp.2–3.
38 LMA, WJ/OC/1 fos. 6v–7.
39 *Diary of Samuel Pepys*, i 286.
40 GL, 4069/2 passim.
41 CLRO, Rep.148 pp.445 & 474–5. Cf. Rep.153 p.305; Rep. 154 pp.267–8.
42 Commissioners of Hackney Coaches, *Order, By-laws, and Ordinances, For the good Government…of the Persons Licensed to Keep and Drive Hackney-Coaches*, 1717.
43 Michel Foucault, *Discipline and Punish* (English trans., 1977).
44 CLRO, Rep.63 fo.56v; *CSPD 1654*, p.109.
45 *To the Right Hon:ble the Commons of England … The Humble Petition of the Auntient Hackney-Coachmen of London and Westminster, 1660; The Hackney Coachmens Case, Humbly offered to … Parliament*, n.d., 1692?.
46 E.g., *The Parliamentary Diary of Narcissus Luttrell 1691–1693* ed., H. Horwitz, Oxford, 1972, p.151; *The Diary of Dudley Ryder*, ed., W. Matthews, 1939, p.183.
47 For good descriptions of this, LMA, DL/C/249 fos. 168–9(bis)v.
48 Tim Meldrum, 'London Domestic Servants from Depositional Evidence' in T. Hitchcock, P. King and P. Sharpe eds, *Chronicling Poverty: the Voices and Strategies of the English Poor, 1640–1840*, Basingstoke, 1997, p.59. I shall discuss the gendering of hachney coaches and their drivers in another article.
49 David Underdown, *Start of Play: Cricket and Culture in Eighteenth-Century England*, 2000, p.86.
50 *Spectator*, ed. D. F. Bond, Oxford, 1965, iv, 267–8.
51 CLRO, Rep. 63 fos. 257–57v.
52 *The English Intelligencer*, 1, 21 July 1679.
53 J. Playford, *Vade Mecum, or the Necessary Companion*, 1680 edn, pp.162–3.
54 Cf. N. Papayanis, *The Coachmen of Nineteenth-Century Paris: Service Workers and Class Consciousness*, Baton Rouge, 1993, ch.2.
55 *Statutes of the Realm*, 1810–28, v 353.
56 *Statutes of the Realm*, ix 449; PRO, E351/1586.
57 LMA, MJ/OC/3 fo. 27.
58 *A New Review of London*, 3rd edn, 1728, p.50.
59 LMA, MJ/OC/3 fo.27.
60 LMA, MJ/OC/3 fo.27.
61 *The Book of Coach-Rates*, 1770, p.iii.
62 *The London Companion*, 1773, p.iii. See also *Bowles's New Hackney-Coach Directory*, 1786,

which listed over 50,000 fares.

63 M. Ogborn, *Spaces of Modernity: London's Geographies 1680–1780*, 1998; J. Bender, *Imagining the Penitentiary*, Chicago, 1987; J. B. Harley, 'Maps, Knowledge and Power', in D. Cosgrove and S. Daniels eds, *The Iconography of Landscape*, Cambridge, 1988.

64 See, for example, the tables of the distances between the main towns and cities in Britain issued by Daniel Paterson, assistant to the Quarter-Master-General, *A New and Accurate Description of all the ... Cross Roads in Great Britain*, 1771.

65 Ogborn, *Spaces of Modernity*, ch.5.

66 Cf. W. Behringer, 'Bausteine zu einer Geschichte der Kommunikation: Eine Sammelrezension zum Postjubiläum', *Zeitschrift für Historische Forschung*, 21, 1994, 92–112.

67 Cf. Ogborn, *Spaces of Modernity*, esp. ch.3.

68 H. Humpherus, *History of the Origin and Progress of the Company of Watermen and Lightermen*, 3 vols., 1874–86; W. M. Stern, *The Porters of London*, 1960; E. Bennett, *The Worshipful Company of Carmen of London*, 1952.

69 Cf. CLRO, Jnl.41 fo.102ff and *Rules, Directions and By-Laws, devised ... by the Court of Aldermen ... for Regulation of Hackney Coachmen*, 1654.

70 *A Strange, True and Dreadful Relation of the Devils Appearing to Thomas Cox a Hackney-Coach-Man*, 1684, p.4. Cox's fare turned out to be the devil.

71 Daniel Defoe, *The Great Law of Subordination Consider'd*, 1724, p.125.

72 Defoe, *Great Law*, pp.125–9. Cf. PRO, C6/407/19 for a Chancery case ensuing from a similar dispute.

73 E.g. PRO, E112/712/2036; LMA, AM/PI(2)/1683/53; AM/PI(2)/1694/50.

74 PRO, E351/1572. The commissioners' accounts do not list all license holders, but 41 of the 106 licensees in arrears held more than one licence.

75 GL, 33011/8 [microfilm] fo.225v. My thanks to Paul Griffiths for this reference.

76 Tim Meldrum, *Domestic Service and Gender 1660–1750: Life and Work in the London Household*, 2000, pp.174–6.

77 *Low-Life: Or One Half of the World Knows not how the Other Half Live*, 1752, p.94.

78 *A List of the 400 Hackney-Coaches Licensed ... by the Commissioners*, 1664, p.13; Whyman, *Sociability and Power*, p.60. See also Meldrum, *Domestic Service and Gender*, p.176. Cf. Papayanis, *Coachmen of Paris*, p.14

79 *List of the 400 Hackney-Coaches*, 1664.

80 *Spectator*, iv, 100.

81 M. Hellman, 'Furniture, Sociability and the Work of Leisure in Eighteenth-Century France', *Eighteenth-Century Studies*, 32, 1999, 415–45.

4. *Public Spaces, Private Disputes?*
Robert B. Shoemaker

1 Lawrence Klein, 'Gender and the Public/Private Distinction in the Eighteenth Century: Some Questions about Evidence and Analytic Procedure', *Eighteenth-Century Studies*, 29, 1995, pp.103–05.

2 Miles Ogborn, *Spaces of Modernity: London's Geographies 1680–1780*, New York and London, 1998, esp. chs.2–3; Penelope J. Corfield, 'Walking the City Streets: The Urban Odyssey in Eighteenth-Century England', *Journal of Urban History*, 16, 1990, p.154.

3 Jürgen Habermas, *The Structural Transformation of the Public Sphere*, translated by Thomas Burger, 1962; reprint edition, Cambridge Mass., 1989.

4 Nicholas Rogers, *Crowds, Culture and Politics in Georgian Britain*, Oxford, 1998, pp.274–5.

5 Rogers, *Crowds*; Kathleen Wilson, *The Sense of the People: Politics, Culture and Imperialism in England, 1715–1785*, Cambridge, 1995; Robert B. Shoemaker, 'The London "Mob"

in the Early Eighteenth Century', *Journal of British Studies*, 26, July 1987, pp.299–301.

6　Laura Gowing, *Domestic Dangers: Women, Words and Sex in Early Modern London*, Oxford, 1996, pp.98–9.

7　LMA, DL/C/239, fo. 9v; DL/C/240, fo. 48.

8　LMA, DL/C/255, fo. 186.

9　Gowing, *Domestic Dangers*, p.98.

10　LMA, DL/C/247, fo. 212.

11　LMA, DL/C/284, fo. 14.

12　LMA, DL/C/272, fo. 232; DL/C/255, fo. 362.

13　For the contrasting socio-economic characteristics of these different types of streets, see M.J. Power, 'The Social Topography of Restoration London', in A.L. Beier and Roger Finlay, eds, *London 1500–1700: The Making of the Metropolis*, 1986, pp.209–12.

14　Although published in 1720, the map was drawn up by Richard Blome in 1694, and subject to only minor amendments in 1707: John J. Morrison, 'Strype's Stow: The 1720 Edition of "A Survey of London"', *London Journal*, 3, 1977, p.47.

15　*Daily Post*, 13 November1741.

16　John Gay, *Trivia: Or, the Art of Walking the Streets of London*, 1716, Book II, lines 271–84, reprinted in *John Gay: Poetry and Prose*, ed., V.A. Dearing, Oxford, 1974, i, p.151.

17　LMA, DL/C/243, fo. 237v.

18　LMA, DL/C/270, fos 47, 49.

19　Cynthia Wall, *The Literary and Cultural Spaces of Restoration London*, Cambridge, 1998, pp.212–14.

20　LMA, DL/C/278, fo. 14.

21　The following is based primarily on an analysis of depositions in murder cases kept in the CLRO and LMA, as well as a 10 per cent sample of trials for murder reported in the *OBSP*.

22　Robert B. Shoemaker, 'Male Honour and the Decline of Public Violence in Eighteenth-Century London', *Social History*, 26, 2001, pp.199–200

23　*OBSP*, May 1761, p.202.

24　LMA, MJ/SP/May 1694, 4a.

25　*The Proceedings on the King's Commission*, December 1721, p.4.

26　CLRO, Sessions Papers May 1718, depositions concerning the death of William Bowen.

27　*Gentleman's Magazine*, 1731–86, *passim*.

28　*London Journal*, 20 November 1731.

29　*General Evening Post*, 18 May 1771.

30　Lawrence E. Klein, 'Coffeehouse Civility, 1660–1714: An Aspect of Post-Courtly Culture in England', *Huntington Library Quarterly*, 59, 1996, pp.31–59, quotation from p.32.

31　LMA, Accession 1268, deposition dated 17 May 1761.

32　Peter Borsay, '"All the Town's a Stage": Urban Ritual and Ceremony, 1660–1800', in P. Clark (ed.), *The Transformation of English Provincial Towns 1600–1800*, 1984, p.249.

33　Robert B. Shoemaker, 'Streets of Shame? The Crowd and Public Punishments in London, 1700–1820', in S. Devereaux and P. Griffiths, eds, *Punishing the English* (forthcoming); Robert B. Shoemaker, 'The Taming of the Duel: Masculinity, Honour and Ritual Violence in London, 1660–1800', *Historical Journal* (forthcoming); John Beattie, *Policing and Punishment in London, 1660–1750*, Oxford, 2001, chaps 3–5; *OBSP*, *passim*; Elaine A. Reynolds, *Before the Bobbies: The Night Watch and Police Reform in Metropolitan London, 1720–1830*, Stanford, 1998.

34　Robert B. Shoemaker, 'The Decline of Public Insult in London, 1660–1800', *Past and Present*, 169, November 2000, pp.97–131.

35 J.W. Von Archenholz, *A Picture of England: Containing a Description of the Laws, Customs, and Manners of England*, Dublin, 1791, p.211; Robert B. Shoemaker, 'The Taming of the Duel: Masculinity, Honour and Ritual Violence in London, 1660–1800', *Historical Journal* (forthcoming).

36 Shoemaker, 'Male Honour and the Decline of Public Violence'.

37 Shoemaker, 'Decline of Public Insult', pp.109–11.

38 LMA, DL/C/278, fo. 451.

39 Ogborn, *Spaces of Modernity*, p.79.

40 LMA, MJ/SR/3407, R. 218, 223, 316 (September 1781).

41 For example, see LMA, MJ/SR/3118, R. 180, 257 (September 1761); 3246, R. 463 (Sept. 1771); 3537, R. 569, 660, 1055 (September 1791).

42 Ogborn, *Spaces of Modernity*, p.113.

43 *London Evening Post*, 3 September 1761.

44 *General Evening Post*, 4 June 1771.

45 Rogers, *Crowds*, pp.170–1.

5. 'You bitches...die and be damned'
Tim Hitchcock

I would like to thank Ian O'Neill for generously supplying personal details for several of the actors in this drama.

1 See LMA, 'Middlesex Sessions Papers, Goal Delivery Roll, 9 September 1742' MJ/SR 2783, items 8, 9, 10, 60, 61. For Mary Wood, Ann Branch, Elizabeth Beaumont and Mary Hammond see *OBSP*, 9–10 September 1742, pp.47, 48, 53, 54. For Betty Eaton see *OBSP*, 13–15 October 1742, p.72. For Mary Innings see PRO, TS 11/894/3042, Treasury Solicitor's Papers, 'Rex vs. Bird'.

2 See *Select Trials for Murder, Robbery, Burglary, Rapes, Sodomy, Coining, Forgery, Pyracy and other offences and misdemeanours, at the Sessions-House in the Old-Bailey*, 1744, p.51.

3 The *Daily Post*, 22 July 1742. At some level this refers to the Reformation of Manners campaigns which punctuate eighteenth-century urban history. For literature on this see J. Innes, 'Politics and Morals: The Reformation of Manners Movement in Later Eighteenth-Century England' in E. Hellmuth, ed., *The Transformation of Political Culture: England and Germany in the Late Eighteenth Century*, Oxford, 1990; T. Isaacs, 'The Anglican Hierarchy and the Reformation of Manners, 1688–1738', *Journal of Ecclesiastical History*, 33, 3, 1982, pp.391–411; R.B. Shoemaker, 'Reforming the City: The Reformation of Manners Campaign in London, 1690–1738' in L. Davison, et al. eds, *Stilling the Grumbling Hive: The Response to Social and Economic Problems in England, 1688–1750*, Stroud, Glouc., 1992.

4 *OBSP*, 13–15 October 1742, p.70.

5 *OBSP*, 13–15 October 1742, pp.70, 72; WAC, 'St Martin in the Fields, Parish Records, Vestry Draft Minutes, 1736–1754', F2028, p.241.

6 *OBSP*, 13–15 October 1742, p.70.

7 The site is shown on a map included in George Gater and Walter H. Godfrey, *Survey of London: Trafalgar Square and Neighbourhood (The Parish of St Martin-in-the-Fields, Part III*, vol.20, 1940, plate 2.

8 Henry B. Weatley, *London Past and Present*, 1891, vol.11, p.485.

9 *OBSP*, 9–13 September 1742, p.45.

10 *OBSP*, 9–13 September 1742, pp.43–5.

11 See Tony Henderson, *Disorderly Women in Eighteenth-Century London: Prostitution and Control in the Metropolis, 1730–1830*, 1999, ch.2.

12 *OBSP*, 13–15 October 1742, p.76.

13 *OBSP*, 13–15 October 1742, p.72.

14 WAC, 'St Martin in the Fields, Workhouse Day Book, 1742–1746', F4004, p.88; see also *OBSP*, 9–13 September 1742, p.53.

15 WAC, 'St Martin in the Fields, Parish Records, Examination Books, 1741–1742', F5034, p.339.

16 *OBSP*, 9–13 September 1742, p.53.

17 The foundation stone of the Foundling Hospital was laid two months later, on 16 September 1742. See *The Universal Spectator and Weekly Journal*, 18 September, 1742.

18 For recent accounts of the experience of eighteenth-century prostitution see Henderson, *Disorderly Women*; S. Nash, 'Prostitution and Charity: The Magdalen Hospital, a Case Study', *Journal of Social History*, 17, 1974, pp.617–28; R.B. Shoemaker, 'Reforming the City'; S. Staves, 'British Seduced Maidens', *Eighteenth-Century Studies*, 14, 1980–81, pp.109–34; and Randolph Trumbach, *Sex and the Gender Revolution: Volume One, Heterosexuality and the Third Gender in Enlightenment London*, Chicago, 1998. For the development of social policy largely directed at women see D.T. Andrew, *Philanthropy and Police: London Charity in the Eighteenth Century*, Princeton, N.J., 1989; V.L. Bullough, 'Prostitution and Reform in Eighteenth-Century England' in R.P. Maccubbin, ed., *'Tis Nature's Fault': Unauthorized Sexuality during the Enlightenment*, Cambridge, 1987; T. Hitchcock, '"Unlawfully Begotten on her Body": Illegitamacy and the Parish Poor in St Lukes Chelsea' in T. Hitchcock, P. Sharp and P. King, eds, *Chronicling Poverty: The Voices and Strategies of the English Poor, 1640–1840*, 1996; A. Wilson, 'Illegitimacy and Its Implications in Mid-Eighteenth-Century London: The Evidence of the Foundling Hospital', *Continuity and Change*, 4, 1, 1989, pp.103–64.

19 *OBSP*, 9–13 September 1742, p.48.

20 For pregnancy and crime see J. Hurl, '"She being bigg with child is likely to miscarry": Pregnant Victims Prosecuting Assault in Westminster 1685–1720', *London Journal*, 24, 2, 199, pp.18–33.

21 *OBSP*, 9–13 September 1742, p.48.

22 *OBSP*, 9–13 September 1742, p.46.

23 WAC, 'St Martin in the Fields, Parish Records, Vestry Draft Minutes, 1736–54', F2028, pp.237–49.

24 *OBSP*, 13–15 October 1742, p.70.

25 *Select Trials*, 1744, p.51

26 *OBSP*, 9–13 September 1742, p.44.

27 *OBSP*, 13–15 October 1742, p.72.

28 *OBSP*, 9–13 September 1742, p.48.

29 *OBSP*, 13–15 October 1742, p.76.

30 WAC, 'St Martin in the Fields, Parish Records, Workhouse Day Book, 1742–1746', F4004, p.66.

31 'An Act for the Better Regulating the Nightly Watch and Beadles within the parish of St Martin in the Fields', 9 George II c.8, WAC, 'St Martin in the Fields, Parish Records, Vestry Draft Minutes, 1736–54', F2028, pp.1–5. See also *The Case of the Dean and Chapter of Westminster, with Respect to the Bill for Regulating the Nightly Watch: Now Depending in Parliament*, c.1720.

32 The most comprehensive account of the politics and evolution of parochial government in Westminster in this period remains Sidney and Beatrice Webb, *English Local Government, Vol.1: The Parish and the County*, 1906, reprinted 1963, pp.227–62. For a recent account of the evolution of the watch see Elaine Reynolds, *Before the Bobbies: The Night Watch and Police Reform in Metropolitan London, 1720–1830*, 1998. On crime and social policy see also J.M. Beattie, *Crime and the Courts in England, 1660–1800*, Oxford, 1986; Davison, et al, *Stilling,*

ch.2–5; C. Emsley, *The English Police: A Political and Social History*, 1991; Norma Landau, *The Justices of the Peace, 1679–1760*, Berkeley CA, 1984; P. Linebaugh, *The London Hanged: Crime and Civil Society in the Eighteenth Century*, 1991; R. Paley, 'Thief-takers in London in the Age of the McDaniel Gang, c.1745–1754', in D. Hay and F. Snyder, eds, *Policing and Prosecution in Britain, 1750–1850*, Oxford, 1989; R. Paley, ed., *Justice in Eighteenth-Century Hackney: The Justicing Notebook of Henry Norris and the Hackney Petty Sessions Book*, London Record Society, 28, 1991; R.B. Shoemaker, 'The London "Mob" in the Early Eighteenth Century', *Journal of British Studies*, 26, 3, 1987, pp.273–304; R.B. Shoemaker, *Prosecution and Punishment: Petty Crime and the Law in London and Rural Middlesex, c.1660–1725*, Cambridge, 1991.

33 WAC, 'St Martin in the Fields, Parish Records, Vestry Draft Minutes, 1736–54', F2028, p.30.

34 William Bird's most likely date of baptism is 22 Oct 1705.

35 WAC, 'St Martin in the Fields, Parish Records, Workhouse Day Book, 1742–1746', F4004, p.66.

36 *OBSP*, 9–13 September 1742, p.43.

37 Lee Davison, 'Experiments in the Social Regulation of Industry: Gin Legislation, 1729–1751' in Davison, et al., *Stilling*, pp.25–48; Jessica Warner and Frank Ivis, '"Damn You, You Informing Bitch." *Vox Populi* and the Unmaking of the Gin Act of 1736', *Journal of Social History*, winter, 1999, pp.299–330.

38 Patrick Pringle, *Hue and Cry: The Birth of the British Police*, 1955, p.61.

39 Lord Justice Hardwicke removed 75 justices from the Middlesex Bench in 1738 for corruption. Landau, *Justices of the Peace*, pp.126–7.

40 *The Annals of Europe for the year 1742*, 1745, p.309.

41 *Memoirs of the Life and Times of Sir Thomas DeVeil*, 1748, p.46.

42 Pringle, *Hue and Cry*, p.64.

43 *The Letters of William Shenstone*, ed., Marjorie Williams, Oxford, 1939, p.56.

44 *The Champion; or the Evening Advertiser*, 20 July 1742.

45 *London Evening-Post* 15–17 July 1742. The same advertisement is reproduced in *The Annals of Europe for the year 1742*, pp.307–11. DeVeil disclaimed responsibility for this publication at Bird's trial. See *OBSP*, 9–13 September 1742, p.52.

46 On general warrants see *The Law of Arrests*, 1742, p.173. See also, R.B. Shoemaker, *Prosecution and Punishment*, pp.263–5. They were eventually declared illegal after their use against John Wilkes later in the century.

47 At his first trial Bird claimed that the advertisement purposely made him 'appear to be as cruel a dog as ever lived'. *OBSP*, 9–13 September 1742, p.52.

48 *London Evening Post*, 20–22 July 1742.

49 *OBSP*, 9–13 September 1742, p.55; *OBSP*, 13–15 October 1742, p.77.

50 *Letters of William Shenstone*, p.56.

51 *OBSP*, 9–13 September 1742, p.42.

52 *London Evening Post*, 9–11 September 1742.

53 *Rayners London Morning Advertiser*, 15 September 1742.

54 *London Evening Post*, 14–16 October 1742.

55 See PRO, High Court of Admiralty, Criminal Records, HCA 1 20, part 1, item 9. 'Indictment of Barnett Bond, for the murder of William Bird, 26 April 1744'; *Gentleman's Magazine*, vol.xii, November 1742, p.600.

56 WAC, 'St Martin in the Fields, Parish Records, Examinations Book, 1750–51', F5041, p.117.

57 See *Gentleman's Magazine*, vol.17, December 1747, p.563. Posthumously, DeVeil published a guide to the role of Justice of the Peace. Thomas DeVeil, *Observations on the Practice*

of a Justice of the Peace, 1747.

58 WAC, 'St Martin in the Fields, Parish Records, Vestry Draft Minutes, 1736–54', F2028, pp.274, 281.

59 WAC, 'St Martin in the Fields, Parish Records, Watch Rates. Collectors Book, 1735–1757', F2676, pp.153, 183, 241, 271, 273, 299, 323, 327, 351, 355, 381, 485.

60 WAC, 'St Martin in the Fields, Parish Records, Watch Rates. Collectors Book, 1735–1757', F2676, pp.125–7.

61 See above ftn 32.

62 The rambunctious character of the Westminster electorate is a commonplace of eighteenth-century political history. See for example J.A. Hone, *For the Cause of Truth: Radicalism in London, 1796–1821*, Oxford, 1982.

6. 'Every lane teems with instruction, and every alley is big with erudition' Lisa Forman Cody

I wish to thank Amy Lyford, Charlotte Eyerman, and Bill Forman for their especially helpful suggestions.

1 *The Connoisseur*, no. 86, 18 September 1755, pp.517–22, 518.

2 Jürgen Habermas, *The Structural Transformation of the Public Sphere*, trans. Thomas Burger, Cambridge, Massachusetts, 1989; John Brewer, *The Pleasures of the Imagination*, New York, 1997.

3 Doris Jones-Baker, 'The Graffiti of Folk Motifs in Cotswold Churches', *Folklore*, 92, 1981, pp.160–7, quote on p.161.

4 *Spectator*, no. 220, 12 November 1711; Serge Ramond, 'When people talked to stones (Musée des Graffiti Historiques, Verneuil-en-Halatte, France)', *Museum International*, 47, January-March 1995, pp.46–9.

5 *A Hellish Murder Committed by a French Midwife*, 1688, p.22.

6 Helen H. Tanzer, *The Common People of Pompeii: A Study of the Graffiti*, Baltimore, 1939, pp.83–9; Aaron Sheon, 'The Discovery of Graffiti', *Art Journal*, 36, 1976, pp.16–22; Susan Sontag, 'The Pleasure of the Image', *Art in America*, 75, November 1987, pp.122–31; Helen Levitt, *In the Street: Chalk Drawings and Messages, New York City, 1938–1948*, Durham, NC, 1987.

7 Ronald Paulson, *Hogarth. Art and Politics, 1750–1764*, New Brunswick, 1993, III, pp.123–4.

8 John Brand, *Observations on Popular Antiquities*, 1888, pp.547–8.

9 *The Connoisseur*, p.518.

10 Many thanks to Tim Hitchcock for this reference; newspaper clipping (circa 1773) in BL, Add. MS 27,825, Place Papers, vol.37, fo. 118.

11 *The Merry-Thought: Or, the Glass-Window and Bog-House Miscellany*, part 1, 1731; reprinted Los Angeles, 1982, introduced by George R. Guffey, p.16.

12 The first part included ninety-five examples of graffiti; eighteen were from London. The following three parts included 265 examples, fifty-six of which came from London. I have not included examples from toast glasses.

13 *The Merry-Thought*, part 1, p.14.

14 Joseph Addison, *Tatler*, ed. Donald F. Bond, Oxford, 1987, no. 224 (10 September 1710), III, pp.166–71; Paulson, 'The sign painters' exhibition of 1762', in *Hogarth Art and Politics, 1750–1764*, III, pp.336–61.

15 *A Collection of Epigrams*, 1727, no. 382, quoted in George R. Guffey's introduction to *The Merry-Thought*, part 1, p.v.

16 *The Merry-Thought*, part 3, p.4.

17 Habermas, *Public*, p.33; on women's presence in coffeehouses, see Steve Pincus, '"Coffee Politicians does Create": Coffeehouses and Restoration Political Culture', *Journal of Modern History*, 67, 1995, pp.807–34.

18 *[The Loyal Protestant]; The Domestick Intelligence*, no. 67, 20–24 February 1680.

19 PRO, KB 33/6/5, July 1795.

20 Philip Gosse, *Dr. Viper: The Querulous Life of Philip Thicknesse*, 1952, p.278 for a copy of the handbill.

21 *Connoisseur*, p.521.

22 *The Merry-Thought*, part 3, pp.17–18.

23 Reginald L. Hine, 'Church Graffiti', *The Transactions of the St Paul's Ecclesiological Society*, 8, 1921, pp.207–13, p.210.

24 *[The Loyal Protestant]; The Domestick Intelligence*, no.39, 18 November 1679.

25 *Cambridge Chronicle*, 21 May 1770; *Leeds Mercury*, 28 March 1769, quoted in John Brewer, *Party Ideology and Popular Politics at the Accession of George III*, Cambridge, 1976, p.153.

26 John Brewer, 'The Number 45: A Wilkite Political Symbol', in Stephen Baxter, ed., *England's Rise to Greatness*, Berkeley, 1983, pp.349–80, 355.

27 *Wilkes's Jests, or the Patriot Wit*, 1770, pp.28–9.

28 Henry Bunbury, 'Newmarket a shot at a mark', c. 1770, British Museum Catalogue of Satires, no. 4717.

29 Diana Donald, *The Age of Caricature*, New Haven, 1996, pp.149, 234, fn. 60; Kevin Gilmartin, *Print Politics*, Cambridge, 1996, p.69.

30 John Brewer, 'Commercialization and Politics', in Neil McKendrick, John Brewer, and J. H. Plumb, eds, *The Birth of a Consumer Society*, Bloomington, 1982, pp.197–263.

31 Donald, *Age*, p.149.

32 *The Times*, 16 May 1788, p.3b.

33 Karen Farrington, *History of Punishment and Torture* (London, 2000), p.159. My thanks to Jason Lippenberger for sharing this reference.

34 'On trains, Her Majesty is allowed to smoke in the lavatories, although not cigars or pipes', *The Times*, 21 April 1999.

35 For typical examples, *The Times*, 9 Noember. 1787; 15 August 1789.

36 Katie Trumpener, *Bardic Nationalism*, Princeton, 1997.

37 *Journal de Fouilles*, 18 October 1765; *The Edinburgh Review*, October 1859, reprinted in *Littel's Living Age*, Boston, Massachusetts, October-December 1859, pp.643–57, 646–7.

38 *Journal de Fouilles*, 18 October 1765; *The Edinburgh Review*, October 1859, reprinted in *Littel's Living Age*, Boston, Massachusetts, October-December 1859, p.649.

39 'The Graffiti of London', *Punch, Or the London Charivari*, 29 October 1859, pp.174–5.

7. *Illegitimacy, Sexual Relations and Location in Metropolitan London, 1735–85* John Black

1 James Boswell, *Boswell's London Journal, 1762–3*, Frederick A. Pottle, ed., New York, 1950, p.262.

2 See L. Stone, *Family, Sex and Marriage in England, 1500–1800*, 1977; R. Trumbach, *Sex and the Gender Revolution, vol.1: Heterosexuality and the Third Gender in Enlightenment London*, Chicago, 1998; P. Carter, 'James Boswell's Manliness', in M. Cohen and T. Hitchcock, eds, *English Masculinities, 1660–1800*, 1999, pp.111–30.

3 See *Boswell's London Journal*, pp.49–50, 119, 137–40, 227, 231, 237, 240–1, 255, 262, 263–4, 272–3, 280, 300, 304, 332.

4 For the cultural, demographic and socio-economic dynamics of illegitimacy in eighteenth-century England , see P. Laslett, K. Oosterveen and R. M. Smith, eds, *Bastardy and its*

*Comparative History: Studies in the History of Illegitimacy and Marital Nonconformism in Britain, France, Germany, Sweden, North America, Jamaica and Japan,*1980; R. Adair, *Courtship, Illegitimacy and Marriage in Early Modern England,* Manchester, 1996; P. Laslett, *Family Life and Illicit Love in Earlier Generations,* Cambridge, 1977; A. Wilson, 'Illegitimacy and its Implications in Mid-Eighteenth-Century London: The Evidence of the Foundling Hospital', *Continuity and Change,* 4, 1989, pp.103–64; G. Wyatt, 'Bastardy and Prenuptial Pregnancy in a Cheshire Town during the Eighteenth Century', *Local Population Studies,* 49, 1992, pp.121–50; E. Shorter, *The Making of the Modern Family,* 1977; N. Rogers, 'Carnal Knowledge: Illegitimacy in Eighteenth-Century Westminster' *Journal of Social History,* 23, 1989, pp.355–75.

5 WAC, 'St Clement Danes Settlement and Bastardy Examination Books, 1738–87', B1168–1187. These books are subsequently referred to in abbreviated format as St Clement's SBEB.

6 WAC, 'St Mary-le-Strand Bastardy Examination Books, 1739–1802', G1015–1016. These books are subsequently referred to in abbreviated format as St Mary's BEB.

7 GL, 'St Botolph Aldgate Pauper Examination Books, 1742–61', Reference Numbers MS 2676 Vols. 1–3. These books are subsequently referred to in abbreviated format as St Botolph's PEB.

8 LMA, 'St Leonard Shoreditch Settlement and Bastardy Examination Books, July 1758––March 1792', P91/LEN/1200–1211. These books are subsequently referred to in abbreviated format as St Leonard's SBEB.

9 LMA, 'St Luke's Chelsea Settlement and Bastardy Examination Books, 1733–66', P74/LUK/121–122. These books are subsequently referred to in abbreviated format as St Luke's SBEB

10 For a more in-depth description of the bastardy statements and the socio-legal context in which they were created see T. Hitchcock and J. Black, eds, *Chelsea Settlement and Bastardy Examinations, 1733–66,* London Record Society, vol.33, 1999, pp.vii–xxi.

11 For a more detailed analysis of illegitimacy as encapsulated in metropolitan bastardy statements, see John Black, 'Illegitimacy and the Urban Poor in London, 1740–1830', PhD thesis, University of London, 1999.

12 For profiles of these five London parishes, see M.D. George, *London Life in the Eighteenth Century,* 1965 edn; L.D. Schwarz, *London in the Age of Industrialisation: Entrepreneurs, Labour Force and Living Conditions, 1700–1850,* Cambridge, 1992; W. Gaunt, *Chelsea,* 1954; R. Porter, *London, A Social History,* 1994; T. Faulkner, *A Historical & Topographical Description of Chelsea and its Environs,* 1810; R.G. Clark, *Chelsea Today,* 1991; T. Holmes, *Chelsea,* 1972.

13 WAC, St Clement's SBEB, B1183, fo.73.

14 LMA, St Luke's SBEB, P74/LUK/121, 06/12/1739.

15 LMA. St Luke's SBEB, P74/LUK/121, 17/03/1741.

16 WAC, St Clement's SBEB, B1185, fo.239.

17 Quotation in E.J. Burford, *Wits, Wenchers and Wantons, London's Low Life: Covent Garden in the Eighteenth Century,* 1986, p.117

18 WAC, St Clement's SBEB, B1170, fo.79.

19 For the historiography of seduction in the eighteenth century, see R. Rousel, *The Conversation of the Sexes: Seduction and Equality in Selected Seventeenth- and Eighteenth-Century Texts,* New York, 1986; A. E. Simpson, 'Vulnerability and the Age of Female Consent: Legal Innovation and its Effect on Prosecutors for Rape in Eighteenth-Century London', in G.S. Rousseau and R. Porter (eds), *Sexual Underworlds of the Enlightenment,* Manchester, 1987, pp.181–205; Susan Staves, 'British Seduced Maids', *British Journal for Eighteenth-Century Studies,* 14, 1980, pp.109–34.; W.A. Speck, 'The Harlot's Progress in Eighteenth-Century England', *British Journal for Eighteenth-Century Studies,* 3, 1980, pp.127–39.; R.

Trumbach, 'Sex, Gender and Sexual Identity in Modern Culture: Male Sodomy and Female Prostitution in Enlightenment London', *Journal of the History of Sexuality*, vol.2, no.2, 1991, pp.186–203.

20 WAC, St Mary's BEB, G1016, fo.105.

21 Boswell himself fathered an illegitimate child by a domestic servant. See Stone, *Family Sex and Marriage*, p.354; for more examples see Trumbach, *Sex and the Gender Revolution*, Vol.1, passim.

22 See T. Henderson, *Disorderly Women in Eighteenth-Century London: Prostitution and Control in the Metropolis, 1730–1830*, 1999, pp.33, 45–6, 58, 142–7; George, *London Life*, pp.294–5; P. Clark, *The English Alehouse: A Social History, 1200–1830*, 1983, pp.187, 235–6, 310–11, 322–3.

23 *Boswell's London Journal*, pp.263–4.

24 WAC, St Clement's SBEB, B1189, fo.187.

25 WAC, St Clement's SBEB, B1185, fo.280.

26 Burford, *Wits, Wenchers and Wantons*, pp.91–3

27 Burford, *Wits, Wenchers and Wantons*, passim.

28 For an example of misogyny and the sexual eploitation of women in the urban inn, tavern and alehouse, see T. Hitchcock, 'Sociability and Misogyny in the Life of John Cannon, 1684–1743', in T. Hitchcock and M. Cohen, eds, *English Masculinities, 1660–1800*, 1999, pp.25–43. For specific examples in London, see A. Clark, *The Struggle for the Breeches: Gender and the Making of the British Working Class*, London, 1995.

29 LMA, St Leonard's SBEB, P91/LEN/1200, 14/05/1762.

30 See Henederson, *Disorderly Women*, pp.33–5, 61, 101, 147; George, *London Life*, pp.54, 97–8, 126–7; Clark, *The English Alehouse*, p.322.

31 WAC, St Clement's SBEB, B1187, fo.147 & fo.153.

32 See Henderson, *Disorderly Women*, pp.33–5.

33 WAC, St Mary's BEB, G1015, fo.480.

34 WAC, St Mary's BEB, G1015, fo.71.

35 WAC, St Mary's BEB, G1015, fo.189.

36 WAC, St Clement's SBEB, B1185, fo.320.

37 For adultery and representations of adultery in the early modern period, see Martin Ingram, *Church Courts, Sex and Marriage in England, 1570–1640*, Cambridge, 1987; Susan Dwyer Amussen, *An Ordered Society: Gender and Class in Early Modern England*, Oxford, 1988; Laura Gowing, *Domestic Dangers: Women, Words and Sex in Early Modern London*, Oxford, 1996. For adultery in the eighteenth century, see Donna T. Andrews, '"Adultery à la Mode": Privilege, the Law and Attitudes to Adultery, 1770–1809', *History*, 82, 1997, pp.5–23; L. Stone, *Road to Divorce: A History of the Making and Breaking of Marriage in England*, Oxford and New York, 1995; L. Stone, *Uncertain Unions & Broken Lives*, Oxford, 1995; Katherine Binhammer, 'The Sex Panic of the 1790s', *Journal of the History of Sexuality*, 6, 1996, pp.409–34; D. D. Turner, 'Representations of Adultery in England, c.1660–c.1740: A Study of Changing Perceptions of Marital Infidelity in Conduct Literature, Drama, Trial Publications and the records of the Court of Arches', D. Phil. Thesis, Oxford University, 1998.

38 WAC, St Clement's SBEB, B1171, fo.77 & fo.82.

39 WAC, St Clement's SBEB, B1184, fo.659.

40 LMA, St Luke's SBEB, P74/LUK/122, fo.173.

41 For sexual violence and rape, see A.Clark, *Women's Silence, Men's Violence: Sexual Assault in England, 1770–1845*, 1987; Simpson, 'Vulnerability and the Age of Female Consent; R. Porter 'Rape—Does it have a Historical Meaning?', in S. Tomasseli and R. Porter (eds), *Rape: An Historical and Cultural Enquiry*, Oxford, 1986, pp.216–36; A. Clark, 'Humanity or Justice? Wifebeating and the Law in the Eighteenth and Nineteenth

Centuries', in C. Smart, ed., *Regulating Womenhood: Historical Writings on Marriage, Motherhood and Sexuality*, 1992, pp.187–206; Trumbach, 'Sex, Gender and Sexual Identity.

42 WAC, St Clement's SBEB, B1168, fo.218–19.

43 WAC, St Mary's BEB, G1015, fo.135.

44 For female servants and marriage, see Bridget Hill, *Servants: English Domestics in the Eighteenth Century*, Oxford, 1996, pp.57, 108–10, 147–8, 174, 178, 202–5, 209–13.

45 See John R. Gillis, *For Better, For Worse: British Marriages, 1600 to the Present*, New York, 1985, p.168.

46 WAC, St Clement's SBEB, B1189, fo.197.

47 LMA, St Luke's SBEB, P74/LUK//122, fo. 8.

48 WAC, St Clement's SBEB, B1185, fo.45.

8. The Spatiality of the Poor in Eighteenth-Century London
John Marriott

1 J. Spranger, *A Proposal or Plan for an Act of Parliament for the Better Paving, Cleansing, and Lighting of the Streets, Lanes, Courts and Alleys ... Within the Several Parishes of the City and Liberty of Westminster*, 1754.

2 C.L. Kingsford, *John Stow: A Survey of London. Reprinted from the Text of 1603*, Oxford, 1971, p.xlii.

3 J. Strype, *Stow's Survey of London*, 1720, Book III, p.71.

4 M. Ogborn, *Spaces of Modernity: London's Geographies, 1680–1780*, New York, 1998, pp.30–1.

5 J. Entick, *A New and Accurate History and Survey of London, Westminster and Southwark, and Places Adjacent*, 1766.

6 Entick, *Survey of London*, p.132.

7 Spranger, Proposal Preface. See also chapter two in this volume.

8 M. Byrd, *London Transformed: Images of the City in the Eighteenth Century*, New Haven, 1978, pp.12–13.

9 P. Rogers, *Hacks and Dunces: Pope, Swift and Grub Street*, 1972, pp.2–9.

10 Ogborn, *Spaces of Modernity*; R. Sennett, *The Fall of Public Man*, 1986.

11 C. Morris, *Observations on the Past Growth and Present State of the City of London*, 1751, p.1.

12 J. Agnew, 'Coming Up for Air: Consumer Culture in Historical Perspective', in J. Brewer and R. Porter, eds, *Consumption and the World of Goods*, 1993, p.24; N. McKendrick, 'The Consumer Revolution of Eighteenth-Century England', in N. McKendrick, J. Brewer, and J. Plumb, eds, *The Birth of Consumer Society: The Commercialisation of Eighteenth-Century England*, Bloomington, 1982.

13 A.L. Beier, *Masterless Men: The Vagrancy Problem in England, 1560–1640*, 1985.

14 N. Rogers, 'Policing the Poor in Eighteenth–Century London: The Vagrancy Laws and their Administration', *Histoire Sociale—Social History*, 24, 1991, pp.127–47.

15 Beier, *Masterless Men*, p.132.

16 Rogers, 'Policing the Poor', p.128.

17 MD, *A Present Remedy for the Poor*, 1700, p.3.

18 M.D. George, *London Life in the Eighteenth Century*, 1966 edn, remains the best account, even though published originally in 1925.

19 Anon, *The Vices of the Cities of London and Westminster*, Dublin, 1751, pp.17–18.

20 The eighteenth-century classification of the poor derived from the Elizabethan poor law. There were three groups— aged and impotent, children, and persons able but unemployed. This classification, however, was inflected by the age-old distinction between the deserving and undeserving poor which governed much of the thinking

around the implementation of the poor laws. Vagrants, on the other hand, were classed by the eighteenth-century vagrancy laws into the idle and disorderly, rogues and vagabonds, and incorrigible rogues. Such imprecision was open to abuse, particularly by local officials attempting to avoid undue expenditure and rid the parish of vagrancy.

21   Pat Rogers contends that the public imagination in every age marks out a particular crime, and that of the eighteenth century was theft (*The Augustan Age*),1974.

22   The undue attention given to female beggars has to be seen also as part of the gendering of metropolitan streets that occurred in the eighteenth century. In a study of fictional imagery, Elizabeth Kubek ('Women's Participation in the Urban Culture of Early Modern London', in A. Bermingham and J. Brewer, eds, *The Consumption of Culture, 1600–1800*, 1995) has shown how the narrative mapping of London increasingly subjected its transgressive spaces to the male gaze, thereby confining women as objects with neither self-knowledge nor place. Women were also subject to more intense forms of surveillance and control through the machinery of the law (see chapter six in this volume).

23   Rogers, 'Policing the Poor', pp.133–6. Note, however, that many charged with petty theft would not have found their way to the formal courts.

24   L. Manley, *Literature and Culture in Early Modern London*, Cambridge, 1995, p.356.

25   I explore this in more detail in J.W. Marriott ed., *Unknown London: Early Modernist Visions of the Metropolis 1815–45*, 6 vols, 2000.

26   *The Country Gentleman's Vade-Mecum*, 1699.

27   Among the earlier versions were *A Trip Through the Town*, 1735; Anon, *A Trip from St James to the Royal Exchange*, 1744, and *The Tricks of the Town Laid Open*, 1747. The last I have been able to find was *Sinks of London Laid Open*, 1848. By this time it was apparent that a new urban literature attendant on the 'age of inquiry' had rendered this genre obsolete.

28   *A Trip Through the Town*, p.113.

29   Max Byrd suggests that images of forests and labyrinths invoked not only adventure, but also alienation and anonymity at a time when the scale and pace of metropolitan growth seemed beyond comprehension. Their popularity, however, derived from a versatility in conjuring up a range of discourses, including an antithetical unknown (no doubt with Freudian undertones), and imperial expansion. Byrd, *London Transformed*, p.25.

30   Anon, *The Foreigner's Guide*, 1729. This guide, in English and French, was designed to 'assist the curious in seeing what is most remarkable in this great City.... [S]omething of this kind [was] published a few years ago, but in every respect so imperfect that it does shame to the title it bears', p.vii.

31   The term is one used by Byrd, *London Transformed*.

32   Anon, *A Trip from St James's to the Royal Exchange*, p.12.

33   *Trip from St James's*, pp.12–13.

34   J. Gee, *Trade and Navigation of Great-Britain Considered*, 1729, pp.38–9.

35   Henry Fielding, *An Inquiry into the Causes of the Late Encrease of Robbers and related writings*, ed., M.R. Zirker, Oxford, 1988.

36   Fielding, *An Inquiry*.

37   Fielding, *An Inquiry*, p.65.

38   Fielding, *An Inquiry*, p.48.

39   Fielding, *An Inquiry*, pp.139–40.

40   Fielding, *An Inquiry*, p.116.

41   J.L. McMullan, *The Canting Crew: London's Criminal Underworld, 1550–1700*, New Jersey, 1984, p.55.

42   McMullan, *The Canting Crew*; F. McLynn, *Crime and Punishment in Eighteenth-Century*

England, 1989.

43 These should be distinguished from itinerant domestic beggars and the beggarly self-employed who were less numerous and perceived to be rather less of a problem, see T. Hitchcock, 'Begging and the Publicity of Poverty in Early Eighteenth-Century London', in Julia Merritt, ed., *Imagining Early Modern London*, Cambridge, 2001.

44 Some of these were portrayed in an outstanding collection of contemporary engravings in John Smith, *Vagabondiana*, 1817.

45 L.D. Schwarz, *London in the Age of Industrialisation: Entrepreneurs, Labour Force and Living Conditions, 1700–1850*, Cambridge, 1992, pp.90–9.

46 F.W. Chandler, *The Literature of Roguery*, 1907.

47 C. Hill, *Liberty Against the Law: Some Seventeenth-Century Controversies*, 1996.

48 C.H. Wilkinson, *The King of the Beggars: Bampfylde-Moore Carew*, Oxford, 1931.

49 Chandler, *The Literature of Roguery*, p.168.

50 L.B. Faller, *Turned to Account: The Forms and Functions of Criminal Biography in Late Seventeenth- and Early Eighteenth-Century England*, Cambridge, 1987.

51 Faller, *Turned to Account*, p.90.

52 J.W. Marriott, 'Policing the Poor: Social Inquiry and the Discovery of the Residuum', *Rising East*, 3, 1999, pp.23–47.

53 P.J. Corfield, 'Walking the City Streets: The Urban Odyssey in Eighteenth-Century England', *Journal of Urban History*, 16, 1990, pp.132–74.

54 This process is explored in my introduction to J.W. Marriott and M. Matsumura, eds, *The Metropolitan Poor: Semi-Factual Accounts, 1795–1910*, 6 vols., 1999.

9. Private Crime in Public and Private Places
Deirdre Palk

1 The latter date in each case is the year when the crimes ceased to be capital offences.

2 The views of Henry Fielding, Patrick Colquhoun, Jonas Hanway, and evidence to the *Select Committee on the State of the Police of the Metropolis*, 1816.

3 Sources for this chapter are predominantly from the *Old Bailey Sessions Papers*, and the Criminal Registers, held at the PRO (HO26). All shoplifting cases 1780–2, 1789–95, 1798–89, 1800–8, 1815–18, 1820–23. All pickpocketing cases 1780–2, 1789–95, 1798–89, 1800–8.

4 J. M. Beattie, *Crime and the Courts In England 1660–1800*, Oxford, 1986, pp.178–81; C. Emsley, *Crime and Society in England 1750–1900*, Harlow, 1987, pp.20–1.

5 Private larceny in a shop as a crime was deprived of benefit of clergy in 1699 by 10 & 11 William 3 c.23.

6 For discussion of development of shops in London, see J. Rule, *Albion's People - English Society 1714–1815*, Harlow, 1992, pp.76–80; C. Walsh, 'Shop Design and the Display of Goods in Eighteenth-Century London', *Journal of Design History*, 8, 1995, pp.157–76; L. Weatherill, 'Consumer Behaviour and Social Status in England, 1650–1750, *Continuity and Change*, 2, 1996, pp.191–216.

7 William Hawkins, *A Treatise on the Pleas of the Crown*, vol.1, 1795, p.260.

8 Sophie Van La Roche, ed., *Diary, 1786*, quoted in Rick Allen *The Moving Pageant: a Literary Sourcebook on London Street-Life 1700–1914*, 1998, pp.75–7.

9 *OBSP*, case 453, June 1802. Location not recorded in court report.

10 Pall Mall linen draper, robbed of a shawl by three women; *OBSP*, Case 3, December 1805.

11 1819 Select Committee on Capital Punishment in Felonies (585); vol.vii, p.50, evidence of the Rt. Hon, Sir A. MacDonald.

12 From figures in the *OBSP* and PRO Criminal Registers, HO26.

13 8 Elizabeth c. 4.

14 Statute preamble from Danby Pickering, *The Statutes at Large from the 2nd to 31st Year of Elizabeth*, vol.vi, Cambridge, 1764.

15 Heather Shore, *Artful Dodgers: Youth and Crime in Early Nineteenth-Century London*, Woodbridge, Suffolk, 1999, pp.58–61 for a view of the character of young pickpockets.

16 For example, *Lloyds Evening Post*, 6/8 June 1781; *London Chronicle*, 15/17 October 1782.

17 *The Gentleman's Magazine and Historical Chronicle*, 1795, vol.65, part ii, p.657.

18 1 Leach 240, recorded in Sir L. Radzinowicz, *A History of English Criminal Law and its Administration from 1750*, vol.1, appendix 2, 1956, p.663.

19 Radzinowicz, *English Criminal Law*, i., p.663.

20 Heather Shore, 'The Trouble with Boys', in Margaret L. Arnot and Cornelie Usborne, eds, *Gender and Crime in Modern Europe*, 1999, p.78.

21 Peter King, 'Female Offenders, Work and Life Cycle Change in Late Eighteenth-Century London', *Continuity and Change*, 2, 1996, pp.191–216. In 1791 and 1793 about a fifth of all women tried at the Old Bailey (two-fifths of those where a work context was established) 'involved alleged sexual transactions for money'. Bridget Hill, *Women, Work and Sexual-Politics in Eighteenth-Century England*, 1994; Tony Henderson, *Disorderly Women in Eighteenth-Century London: Prostitution and Control in the Metropolis, 1730–1830*, Harlow, 1999.

22 *OBSP*, case 133, February 1781.

23 *OBSP*, case 476, 1795.

24 *OBSP*, case 717, 1802.

25 *OBSP*, case 420, 1807.

26 *OBSP*, case 181, February1799.

27 *OBSP*, case 160, January1803.

28 For instance, *OBSP*, case 402 (Catherine Burn), April 1802, and case 575 (Catherine Forrester), September 1807.

29 *OBSP*, case 15, December 1781.

30 PRO, Criminal Register, HO26.

31 J. M. Beattie, *Crime and the Courts in England 1660–1800*, Oxford, 1986, pp.67–72 for the link between street lighting and policing.

32 *OBSP*, case 133, February 1781.

33 *OBSP*, case 433, June 1806.

34 *OBSP*, cases 640–1, October 1781.

35 *OBSP*, case 666, 1781.

36 *OBSP*, case 123, 1790.

37 *OBSP*, case 128, 1790.

38 *OBSP*, case 717, 1802.

39 *OBSP*, case 616, 1790.

40 *OBSP*, case 63, 1803.

41 *OBSP*, case 222, May 1792.

42 *OBSP*, case 324, June 1799.

43 *OBSP*, case 11, December 1802.

44 *OBSP*, case 11, December 1805; case 364, June 1799.

45 *OBSP*, cases 472 and 473, July 1805.

46 *OBSP*, case 466, June 1807.

47 *OBSP*, case 387, September 1795.

48 *OBSP*, Case 421, 1793. This adult female dexterity contrasts with the view of a boy that girls were not as dextrous as boys, 'they pull it out all of a flare', quoted in Shore,

Artful Dodgers, 1999, p.59.

49 *OBSP*, case 157, May 1782.

50 *OBSP*, case 18, December 1789.

51 *OBSP*, case 381, April 101.

52 *OBSP*, case 39, December 1798.

53 *OBSP*, case 81, January 1799.

54 The wearing of a red cloak was seen as an old-fashioned mark of poverty by Pastor Moritz in 'Travels in England' quoted in Rosamond Bayne-Powell *Travellers in Eighteenth-Century England*, 1st edn 1951, p.184. On the other hand, Jane Tozer and Sarah Levitt, *Fabric of Society: A Century of People and their Clothes 1770–1870. Essays Inspired by the Collections at Platt Hall, the Gallery of English Costume, Manchester*, Manchester, 1983, show red cloaks as a country woman's dress, out of fashion by the second decade of the nineteenth century, and only worn by the elderly. There is no suggestion that a red cloak marked out a prostitute, although the link between poverty, life-cycle distress and prostitution suggests a connection. See chapter five in this book.

55 *OBSP*, case 257. February 1808.

56 *OBSP*, case 363, July 1795.

57 *OBSP*, case 304, July 1804.

58 *OBSP*, case 17, December 1792.

59 *OBSP*, case 471, September 1804.

60 A large, and growing, literature, including: Leonore Davidoff and Catherine Hall, *Family Fortunes: Men and Women of the English Middle Class, 1750–1850*, 1987, and Leonore Davidoff, 'Regarding Some "Old Husbands' Tales": Public and Private in Feminist History', in L. Davidoff, ed., *Worlds Between: Historical Perspectives on Gender and Class*, Cambridge, 1995; Bridget Hill, *Women, Work and Sexual Politics in Eighteenth-Century England*, 1989 and 1994; Laurence E. Klein, 'Gender, Conversation and the Public Sphere in Early Eighteenth-Century England', in Judith Still and Michael Worton, eds, *Textuality and Sexuality: Reading Theories and Practices*, Manchester and New York, 1993, pp.100–15; idem, 'Gender and the Public/Private Distinction in the Eighteenth Century; Some Questions about Evidence and Analytic Procedure', *Eighteenth-Century Studies*, 29, 1, 1995; Dena Goodman 'Public Sphere and Private Life: Towards a Synthesis of Current Historiographic Approaches to the Old Regime', *History and Theory*, vol.31, no.1, 1992; Amanda Vickery 'Golden Age to Separate Spheres? A Review of the Categories and Chronology of English Women's History', *The Historical Journal*, 32, 2, 1993; and the introduction to her *The Gentleman's Daughter: Women's Lives in Georgian England*, New Haven and London, 1998; John Brewer, 'This, That and the Other: Social and Private in the Seventeenth and Eighteenth Centuries', in Dario Castiglione and Lesley Sharpe, eds, *Shifting the Boundaries: Transformations of the Language of Public and Private in the Eighteenth Century*, Exeter, 1995; Hannah Barker and Elaine Chalus (eds), *Gender in Eighteenth-Century England: Roles, Representations and Responsibilities*, Harlow, 1997, especially their Introduction pp.1–29, and Richard Connors' chapter, 'Poor Women: The Parish and the Politics of Poverty,' pp.126–47; Robert B. Shoemaker, *Gender in English Society 1650–1850: The Emergence of Separate Spheres?*, Harlow, 1998.

61 Doreen Massey, *Space, Place and Gender*, Cambridge, 1994, p.186.

62 Beattie, *Crime and the Courts*, pp.59–72.

10. Mean Streets
Heather Shore

1 Charles Dickens, *Oliver Twist*, 1835–7, Collins edn, 1954, p.71.

2 For example see Pierce Egan, *Life in London: the Day and Night Scene*, 1822, the writings of Francis Place, and Flora Tristan's *London Journal*, 1840.

3 For example see John Dunton, *The Nightwalker: or, Evening Rambles in Search after Lewd Women*, September 1696–April 1697; Daniel Defoe, *Some Considerations Upon Street-Walkers*, 1726; idem., *Street Robberies Considered: The Reason of their Being so Frequent*, 1728. See also, Miles Ogborn, *Spaces of Modernity: London's Geographies, 1680–1780*, 1998, pp.75–115.

4 See R.B. Shoemaker, 'Reforming the City: The Reformation of Manners Campaign in London, 1690–1738', in L. Davison, et al., eds, *Stilling the Grumbling Hive: The Response to Social and Economic Problems in England, 1689–1750*, Stroud, 1992, pp.99–120. Also T.B. Isaacs, 'Moral Crime, Moral Reform, and the State in Early Eighteenth Century England: A Study of Piety and Politics', Ph.D. thesis, University of Rochester, 1979.

5 Alsatia was the term used to describe the Mint in Southwark, and seems to have been popularised through a work by Thomas Shadwell, *The Squire of Alsatia*, 1688. Rookery was a term peculiar to the nineteenth century, used by Thomas Beames in his *The Rookeries of London: Past, Present and Prospective*, 1850, but also earlier in Charles Dickens's, *Sketches by Boz*, First Series, 1836. According to Partridge, a rook was 'a swindler or thief'. Eric Partridge, *A Dictionary of the Underworld*, 1989 edition, pp.6, 576.

6 Dolly Shop refers to an illegal pawn-shop, see Partridge, *Dictionary*, pp.197.

7 See Heather Shore, 'Cross Coves, Buzzers and General Sorts of Prigs: Juvenile Crime and the Criminal "Underworld" in the Early Nineteenth Century', *British Journal of Criminology*, vol.39, no. 1, 1999, pp.10–24.

8 *Select Committee on the Police of the Metropolis*, 1816, V; *Select Committee on the Police of the Metropolis*, 1817, VII (hereafter *SCPM*). See also the earlier *Select Committee on the Nightly Watch and Police of the Metropolis*, 1812, II, and the later *SCPM*, 1818, VIII; *SCPM*, 1822, IV; *SCPM*, 1828, VI; *SCPM*, 1834, XVI; *Select Committee on Metropolitan Police Officers*, 1837, XII.

9 See Ruth Paley, '"An imperfect, inadequate and wretched system"? Policing London before Peel', *Criminal Justice History: An International Annual*, X, 1989, pp.95–130; also L. Radzinowicz, *A History of English Criminal Law, II: the Clash between Private Initiative and Public Interest in the Enforcement of the Law*, 1956.

10 *The Times*, 3 September 1817.

11 Two contemporary documents provide our knowledge of the flash-houses and disorderly houses of early nineteenth century London. The first is 'A List of Houses of Resort for Thieves of every Description' from c. 1815, the author is unknown. The second is a notebook from 1816 apparently compiled by the Recorder of London, Sir John Silvester. This includes two lists: primarily a list of 'Receivers of Stolen Property, particularly from Boys; secondly A List of Houses of resort for Thieves of every description' (clearly related to the 1815 list). PRO – HO42/146, microfilm pp.83–107, 'A List of Houses of Resort for Thieves of Every Description'; British Library, MS Egerton 3710, Sir John Silvester notebook (1816). For the provenance of the notebooks see, Donald Low, *Thieves' Kitchen: The Regency Underworld*, 1987, pp.75, 123.

12 See Shore, 'Cross Coves', pp.10–24.

13 See the commentaries on prostitution in London by Bracebridge Hemyng and John Binny in Henry Mayhew, *London Labour and the London Poor, vol.IV, Those Who Will Not Work, Comprising Prostitutes, Thieves, Swindlers and Beggars*, by several contributors, 1861–2, reprinted 1968, pp.217–20, 236–43, 356–61.

14 *SCPM*, vol.v, 1816, p.23.

15 For example see Mayhew, *London Labour and the London Poor*, vol.iv, pp.294–301, 311–16, 330–4; John Hollingshead, *Ragged London in 1861*, 1986 edn.

16 John McMullan, *The Canting Crew: London's Criminal Underworld, 1550–1700*, New Jersey,

1984, pp.53–4.

17 Beames, *Rookeries*.

18 Beames, *Rookeries*, p.63.

19 Inspector Field was Charles Field, the Chief Inspector of the Detective Department in Scotland Yard. Charles Dickens, 'On Duty with Inspector Field', *Household Words*, 14 June 1851, pp.265–70.

20 See Nicholas Rogers, 'Confronting the Crime Wave: The Debate over Social Reform and Regulation, 1749–1753', in Davison, et al, *Stilling*, pp.78–98.

21 C. Emsley, *Crime and Society in England, 1750–1900*, revised edn, 1999, p.34.

22 *SCPM*, 1816, p.33. For another point of view see *SCPM*, 1816, p.56, for comments from Robert Raynsford, the Hatton Garden Magistrate.

23 Heather Shore, *Artful Dodgers: Youth and Crime in Early Nineteenth Century London*, Woodbridge, Suffolk, 1999, particularly pp.17–34; idem., 'Cross Coves'. Also Peter King, 'The Rise of Juvenile Delinquency in England, 1780–1840', *Past and Present*, 160, 1999, pp.116–66.

24 S*CPM*, 1816, p.65.

25 F. W. B. Bullock, *Voluntary Religious Societies, 1520–1799*, St Leonards on Sea, 1963, pp.225–6; Leon Radzinowicz, *A History of English Criminal Law and its Administration from 1750: vol.III, The Reform of the Police*, 1957, pp.141–65.

26 Radzinowicz, *Reform*, p.155.

27 *SCPM*, 1817, p.387.

28 *SCPM*, 1817, pp.53–4.

29 See Rogers, 'Crime Wave', particularly, pp.78, 81, 87; Peter Linebaugh, 'The Tyburn Riot Against the Surgeons', in Douglas Hay, et al., eds, *Albion's Fatal Tree: Crime and Society in Eighteenth Century England*, 1975, pp.65–117.

30 Elaine Reynolds, *Before the Bobbies: The Night Watch and Police Reform in Metropolitan London, 1720–1830*, 1998.

31 *Select Committee...Nightly Watch*, 1812, II. For recent discussion of the night-watch see Reynolds, *Bobbies*, pp.103–24.

32 *SCPM*, 1816, p.21.

33 *SCPM*, 1816, p.48.

34 *SCPM*, 1816, p.147.

35 In the early years of the nineteenth century police reformers were trying to transfer the office of High Constable from the hands of the parish watch authorities and place it under the control of the police magistrates. Reynolds, *Bobbies*, pp.11–12, 90, 99–100.

36 *SCPM*, 1816, p.104.

37 Sidney and Beatrice Webb, *English Local Government from the Revolution to the Municipal Corporations Act: The Parish and the County*, 1906, p.571.

38 Webb, *Parish and the County*, p.570.

39 MS. Minutes, Quarter Sessions, Middlesex, 16 September 1790, quoted in Webb, *Parish and the County*, p.563.

40 M. Dorothy George, *London Life in the Eighteenth Century*, 1966 edn, p.41. See also, Peter Clark, *The English Alehouse: A Social History, 1200–1830*, 1983, particularly pp.250–72; Peter Haydon, *The English Pub: A History*, 1994.

41 John Burnett, *Liquid Pleasures: A Social History of Drinks in Modern Britain*, 1999, p.119.

42 Burnett, *Liquid Pleasures*, pp.119–20.

43 *SCPM*, 1817, vol.vii, p.61.

44 *SCPM*, 1816, vol.v, p.87. . The Merceron case is referred to throughout this volume, and was also a major subject for the 1817 *SCPM*, vol.vii. For a detailed account of Merceron's activites see the Webb's *Parish and the County*, pp.79–90.

45 *SCPM*, 1817, p.37.
46 *SCPM*, 1816, p.67.
47 *SPCM*, 1817, p.540.
48 PRO, HO42/146, microfilm, pp.83–107, 'A List of Houses of Resort for Thieves of Every Description'.
49 A comparable document from 1816 contains a list of 'houses of resort for thieves' numbering just under 300. BL, MS Egerton 3710, Sir John Silvester notebook (1816).
50 *SCPM*, 1817, p.53.
51 'Houses of Resort', p.94.
52 'Houses of Resort', pp.89–90, 94, 95–6.
53 'Houses of Resort', pp.90–1.
54 The landlord of the Black Horse public house in Tottenham Court Road, mentioned by both Henry Grey Bennet and Samuel Taunton (a Bow Street officer) in 1817, was said to have been a thief for fifteen years. *SCPM*, pp.393, 540–1. The Black Horse is also mentioned in 'List of Houses of Resort for Thieves of Every Description' appended to, MS Egerton 3710, Sir John Silvester notebook (1816), p.37.
55 A trinket containing a stone for sealing letters, worn from the fob.
56 'Houses of Resort', p.86.
57 *SCPM*, 1816, p.19.
58 'Houses of Resort', p.102.
59 'Houses of Resort', pp.89–90
60 L. Radzinowicz and R. Hood, *A History of the English Criminal Law and its Administration from 1750: vol.5, The Emergence of Penal Policy*, 1986, pp.333–46.
61 'Houses of Resort', pp.99–100.
62 'Houses of Resort', p.100.
63 See 'Proceedings of the Common Council of the City of London, in the several Mayoralties of 1814 and 1816, for clearing the Streets of Vagrants, Prostitutes, and Idle and Disorderly Persons', appendix no. 12, *SCPM*, 1816, pp.368–80. Moreover, we can trace schemes to police and clean the streets of disorderliness and sexual immorality at a number of points in the past. See Andy Croall, 'Street Disorder, Surveillance and Shame: Regulating Behaviour in the Public Spaces of the Late Victorian British Town', *Social History*, vol.24, no. 3, October, 1999, pp.250–68; Tony Henderson, *Disorderly Women in Eighteenth-Century London: Prostitution and Control in the Metropolis, 1730–1830*, 1999.

11. Socialist Infidels and Messengers of Light
Anna Davin

1 *Justice*, 5 August 1885, p.3. The same issue listed where Sunday open-air meetings were to be held, with the branches responsible: Battersea Park (Battersea); Hampstead Heath (Marylebone); Bricklayers' Arms (Walworth); Burdett Rd (Limehouse); Clerkenwell Green (Clerkenwell); Duppas Hill (Croydon); Ash Grove (Shoreditch); Hyde Park (Paddington); Regents Park (Marylebone); Stamford Hill (Tottenham); Islington Green (Clerkenwell); Tottenham (Tottenham); Victoria Park (Shoreditch).
2 See *Justice*, 15 August, 1885, for the first report of clashes with the police at Dodd Street; and subsequent issues for arrests of Socialist speakers; broadening support and growing mobilization; and crowd prevention of arrests (e.g. *Justice*, 26 September). For events at the court hearings which followed arrests on 20 September, see E.P. Thompson, *William Morris: Romantic to Revolutionary*, 1955, reprinted 1977, pp.393–8 (Morris himself was arrested after a fracas in court). The police backed off after adverse publicity and

a huge demonstration two weeks later when some 50,000 people converged in processions from different parts of East London ('60,000': *Justice*, 3 October). The New York section of the Socialist Labour Party of North America sent a message of support (*Justice*, 24 October). A similar struggle over a regular pitch at Bell Street was won in 1886, again with mobilzation of broader support including from Morris: Thompson, *Morris*, pp.399–403; and see reports in *Justice* and *Commonweal*, July-September.

3 Margaret Bondfield, *A Life's Work*, 1948, p.50. She is quoting a letter from Stewart George about his father, one of the founders of the Shop Assistants' Union.

4 For Martin, see Barbara Taylor, *Eve and The New Jerusalem: Socialism and Feminism in the Nineteenth Century*, 1983, pp.130–56. For women in radical politics at this time see also Dorothy Thompson, 'Women and Radical Politics: a Lost Dimension', in Juliet Mitchell and Ann Oakley, eds, *The Rights and Wrongs of Women*, Harmondsworth, 1976, and *The Chartists: Popular Politics in the Industrial Revolution*, Aldershot, 1986; Jutta Schwarzkopf, *Women in the Chartist Movement*, 1991; Anna Clark, *The Struggle for the Breeches: Gender and the Making of the British Working Class*, London, 1995.

5 The Chartist Ernest Jones was still addressing open-air meetings in 1857, according to W.E. Adams, with 'the old fervour and the old eloquence' but 'the pinched face' and 'threadbare garments' of poverty: *Memoirs of a Social Atom*, 1903, p.230.

6 A missionary recalled how Somers-town had previously 'consisted of open fields, with here and there a house'; and 'the Chartists held their Sunday Meetings in an open space near the bottom of the township called Pancras-fields, but now there is no spot unoccupied in the locality': *London City Mission Magazine*, October 1855, p.245. Cf. the fields in Hackney and Brixton where Spurgeon had preached 'years ago', but 'not a spare yard remains': Charles Spurgeon, *Lectures to my Students*, 2nd ser., 1877, p.86.

7 Brian Simon, *The Two Nations and the Educational Structure, 1780–1870*, 1974, pp.235–43.

8 *London City Mission Magazine*, July 1852, p.166. Cf. Spurgeon, *Lectures to My Students*, 1877, p.86: every poor neighbourhood had its 'street corners, quiet nooks and wide spaces wherein to proclaim the gospel'.

9 Syrie Louise Barnardo and James J. Marchant, *Memoirs of the Late Dr Barnardo*, 1907, pp.32, 35.

10 Walter Besant's phrase: see *All Sorts and Conditions of Men*, [1882], 1889, p.95.

11 A Workers' Theatre Movement show in 1930 included a monologue purporting to be by 'a market quack in Hackney', which evoked the tradition: see *History Workshop Journal*, 4, 1977, pp.128–9.

12 Cf. J. Ewing Ritchie, *Here and There in London*, 1859, pp.78–83; and, for a later description, Besant, *All Sorts and Conditions*, pp.94–7.

13 A. R. Bennett, *Illustrated Times*, 10 October 1868.

14 J. Ewing Ritchie, 'A Sunday at the Obelisk', *Here and There*, pp.79–81.

15 Hypatia Bradlaugh Bonner, *Charles Bradlaugh by his Daughter*, pp.8–9; cf. Adolphe Smith Headingley, *The Biography of Charles Bradlaugh*, 1880, p.19.

16 Bonner, *Charles Bradlaugh*, p.12.

17 The writer was probably the controversial Congregationalist, John Campbell (1844–71), 'the greatest religious editor of the mid-century and perhaps of the century', whose publications, especially *Christian's Penny Magazine* (1846–81) and the *British Banner* (1848–58), had 'as near to a mass audience as Victorian religion could reach'. See Josef L. Altholz, *The Religious Press in Britain, 1760–1900*, Westport CT, 1989, pp.68–9. Altholz also quotes (note 8, p.159) from Campbell's 'How to Write for Periodicals', *Christian Witness*, 1, June 1844: 'Sink rhetoric... Commence with your leading thought, and avoid irrelevant digressions... Your article at the first is four-fifths too long... Begin

by crossing out all explanatory sentences. Leave nothing but simple propositions'.

18 *British Banner*, 31 July 1850 (quoted in Bonner, *Bradlaugh*, p.20).

19 George Lansbury, *My Life*, 1928, p.28.

20 *London City Mission Magazine*, December 1855, p.297.

21 See Hypatia Bradlaugh Bonner, *Penalties upon Opinion: Or Some Records of the Laws of Heresy and Blasphemy*, 1912, pp.55–69. 'Prosecutions for blasphemy did not cease to menace the plebeian and vulgar till this side of 1900', according to Geoffrey Best, *Mid-Victorian Britain, 1851–75* [1971], 1979, p.193. See also Susan Budd, *Varieties of Unbelief: Atheists and Agnostics in English Society, 1850–1960*, 1977, pp.26–9.

22 'Country Parson', *Authorized Street Preaching Proposed as Remedy for our Social Evils in a Letter to the Archbishop*, London, 1848, p.3. Cf. Bonner's Fields, Hackney (*London City Mission Magazine*, March 1862, p.55): 'covered every Lord's day with infidel crowds, who gathered round their bold and blasphemous leaders, and weekly drank in more deadly poison than that of asps'.

23 *British Banner*, 21 August 1850.

24 *British Banner*, 24 July 1850.

25 *British Banner*, 31 July 1850.

26 *British Banner*, 14 August 1850.

27 *British Banner*, 14 August 1850. It continues: 'Shall the infidel be at his post, night after night, diligently pursuing his dark vocation of debauching character and destroying souls, and shall not the children of light with devout and sagacious zeal, be ready to neutralize his mischief, and even carry his war into the enemies' camp?'

28 *British Banner*, 24 July 1850.

29 Christian Instruction Society, Annual Report, 1850. See Donald M. Lewis, *Lighten their Darkness: the Evangelical Mission to Working-class London, 1828–1860*, New York, 1986, p.227 for a handbill jeering at missionaries paid to do open-air work for neglecting 'that plan that Christ and his Disciples acted, which was "freely ye have received—freely give"'.

30 See Lewis, *Lighten their Darkness* for a general account of the London City Mission; and pp.223–5 on the development of open-air work.

31 'Country Parson', *Authorised Street Preaching*, 1848, p.13.

32 *British Banner*, 31 July 1850 (also: 'Their constant cry is "The white chokers will not come to us"'). Accusations that the established church neglected the poor, with an implied suggestion of snobbery, were often made by low-church evangelists: see for instance 'Hesba Stretton' [Sara Smith], *Jessica's First Prayer*, 1867, esp. ch.7.

33 *British Banner*, 14 August 1850. Cf. the 'conscientious sceptics, who honestly wish that their doubts may be removed', recalled by missionary James Inches Hillocks, *My Life and Labours in London*, 1865, pp.206.

34 *London City Mission Magazine*, January 1853.

35 See Best, *Mid-Victorian Britain*, pp.196ff; K.D. Inglis, 'Patterns of Religious Worship in 1851', *Journal of Ecclesiastical History*, 11, 1960; Hugh McLeod, *Class and Religion in the Late Victorian City*, 1974.

36 Lewis, *Lighten their Darkness*, p.224.

37 Best, *Mid-Victorian Britain*, p.192, based on 1851 Religious Census.

38 Lewis, *Lighten their Darkness*, Appendix E, p.284.

39 *London City Mission Magazine*, January 1861, p.20.

40 Hillocks, *My Life and Labours*, pp.206–7.

41 Charles Spurgeon, *Lectures to my Students*, 1877, p.94. The qualities needed (pp.93–4) were: a good voice; naturalness of manner; self-possession; a good knowledge of Scripture and of common things; adaptability; good illustrative powers; zeal, prudence

and common sense; a large, loving heart; sincere belief in all he says; entire dependence on the Holy Spirit for success; a close walk with God by prayer; and a consistent walk before men by a holy life.

42 *London City Mission Magazine*, July 1852, pp.166–7. See also R. W. Vanderkiste, *Notes and Narrative of a Six Years Mission, principally among the Dens of London*, 1852.
43 *London City Mission Magazine*, May 1858, p.99.
44 *London City Mission Magazine*, 1853, p.74. The Literary Institute in John Street (the modern Whitfield Street) was an Owenite centre.
45 Spurgeon, *Lectures to My Students*, 1877, pp.259–63.
46 Frank Bullen, *Apostles of the South-east*, 1901, pp.46–9.
47 Spurgeon, *Letters to My Students*, 1877, p.62.
48 *PP* 1868–9 X, qq.257–8.
49 John James Sexby, *The Municipal Parks, Gardens and Open Spaces of London*, 1898, p.150, quotes this exchange from 'The Hypocrite', produced at Drury Lane in 1769:
Lady Lambert: Did you ever preach in public?
MawWork: I got up on Kennington Common last review day; but the boys there threw brickbats at me and pinned crackers to my tail; and I have been afraid to mount, your ladyship, ever since.
50 Ben Weinreb and Christopher Hibbert, eds, *The London Encyclopaedia*, p.422. See also Sexby, *Municipal Parks*.
51 Sexby, *Municipal Parks*, p.150.
52 *London City Mission Magazine*, 1853.
53 *London City Mission Magazine*, 21, May 1856, p.98.
54 *PP* 1865 VIII, q.3,610.
55 *PP* 1865 VIII, q.3,636.
56 *The Times*, 21 April 1863, p.9. col.6.
57 *Borough of Marylebone Mercury*, 25 April 1863, p.2.
58 For clubs, see Stan Shipley, *Club Life and Socialism in Mid-Victorian London*, History Workshop Pamphlet, Oxford, 1971.

12. Music in the Air
Brenda Assael

An earlier version of this paper was presented in December 1999 at "The Streets of London, 1660–1870" conference, as well as in February 2000 at the Charles Booth Centre for the Study of Social Investigation in the Open University. I wish to thank Rohan MacWilliam, David Eastwood and Marcus Collins for their useful comments on this piece. I also wish that I had had an opportunity to consult John M. Picker, 'The Soundproof Study: Victorian Professionals, Work Space, and Urban Noise', *Victorian Studies*, 42, 3, Spring 2000, pp.427–53, an article which appeared after I wrote this piece.

1 For a recent historical discussion of this subject, see Peter Bailey, *Popular Culture and Performance in the Victorian City*, Cambridge, 1999, ch.9
2 Charles Babbage, *A Chapter on Street Nuisances*, 1864, p.4. Babbage's home at 1 Manchester Square, near Baker Street, had workshops for his experiments and was in an area known for attracting street musicians. Babbage wrote this book in order to add steam to his campaign.
3 James Winter, *London's Teeming Streets, 1830–1914*, 1993, p.73; for a treatment on other open spaces, see H.L. Malchow, 'Public Gardens and Social Action in Late Victorian London', *Victorian Studies*, 29, 1, 1985, pp.97–124.
4 Deborah Epstein Nord, 'The City as Theatre: From Georgian to Early Victorian London', *Victorian Studies*, 31, 2, 1988, pp.159–88; Michael R. Booth, 'East End and West

End: Class and Audience in Victorian London', *Theatre Research International*, 2, 2, 1977, pp.98–103; Richard Altick, *The Shows of London*, Cambridge, MT, 1978; Murray Baumgarten, 'London, Dickens and the Theatre of Homelessness', in Debra N. Mancoff and D.J. Trela (eds), *Victorian Urban Settings: Essays on the Nineteenth Century City and its Contexts*, New York, 1996; Peter Bailey, 'Theatres of Entertainment/Spaces of Modernity: Rethinking the British Popular Stage, 1890–1914', *Nineteenth Century Theatre*, 26, 1, 1998, pp.5–24; David Harvey, *Consciousness and the Urban Experience*, Oxford, 1985; for an interesting discussion of the representation of London in the theatre, see Michael R. Booth, 'The Metropolis on Stage', in H.J. Dyos and M. Wolff, eds, *The Victorian City*, vol.1, 1973. The 1850s marked the start of the expansion of commercialised entertainment which rapidly advanced in the 1860s; for examples, see Peter Bailey, *Leisure and Class in Victorian England*, reprinted 1987, ch.7; Brenda Assael, 'The Circus and Respectable Society', Ph.D. thesis, University of Toronto, 1998, ch.1; and idem, *The Circus and Victorian Society*, (forthcoming, ch.1; on Paris during the fin-de-siècle, see Vanessa Schwartz, *Spectacular Realities: Early Mass Culture in Fin De Siecle Paris*, Berkeley, 1998, which explores urban experience and modern life through visual representation.

5 See E.P. Thompson, *Customs in Common*, 1991, pp.467–531; on festival behavior and folk culture, see Mikhail Bakhtin, *Rabelais and His World*, trans. Hélène Iswolsky, Indiana, 1984, esp. ch.1 on laughter; David Cannadine, 'The Context, Performance and Meaning of Ritual: The British Monarchy and the Invention of Tradition', in Eric Hobsbawm and Terence Ranger, eds, *The Invention of Tradition*, Cambridge, 1983; Peter Stallybrass and Allon White, *The Politics and Poetics of Transgression*, Ithaca, 1986, ch.2; J.M. Golby and A.W. Purdue, *The Civilization of the Crowd: Popular Culture in England, 1750–1900*, New York, reprinted 1985, ch.3.

6 Bakhtin, *Rabelais*, ch.3 on festive forms; see also, Natalie Zemon Davis, *Society and Culture in Early Modern France*, Stanford, reprinted 1987, ch.4.

7 See Siegmund Levarie, 'Noise', *Critical Inquiry*, 4, 1977, pp.21–31.

8 Letter from Charles Babbage to Richard Mayne, 9 November 1859, BL, Add Ms 37197, fos. 448, 468.

9 'An Act for Further Improving the Police In and Near the Metropolis', 2 & 3 Victoria c. 47, s. 57; 'Street Music (Metropolis)', *PP*, 50, 1864, 173

10 'Street Music (Metropolis)', *PP*, 50, 1864, republished police order from Richard Mayne dated, 17 December 1859.

11 Response to Babbage's letter by Richard Mayne, 21 July 1860, BL, Add Ms. 37198 fo.95.

12 See, for instance, Watson Nicholson, *The Struggle for a Free Stage in London*, Boston, 1906, reprinted New York, 1966.

13 *Hansard*, 3rd ser., c. 172 (1863) c.973.

14 'Street Music and the Liberty of the Subject', *Marylebone Mercury*, 13 August 1864, p.3.

15 As expressed in *Hard Times*, 1854. On this subject, see Philip Collins, 'Queen Mab's Chariot Among the Steam Engines: Dickens and "Fancy"', *English Studies*, 42, 1, 1961, pp.78–90; Paul Schlicke, 'Introduction' in Charles Dickens, *Hard Times*, Oxford, reprinted 1989; and Michael Slater, *An Intelligent Person's Guide to Dickens*, 1999, ch.1.

16 'Street Music and the Liberty of the Subject', *Marylebone Mercury*, 13 August 1864, p.3; 'Organ Grinder Nuisance', *The Times*, 5 June 1858, p.11.

17 Letter from Babbage to Bass, in M.T. Bass, *Street Music in the Metropolis: Correspondence and Observations on the Existing Law and Proposed Amendments*, 1864, pp.22, 19.

18 *Hansard*, 3rd ser., 172 (1863), c. pp.972–3.

19 'Michael Thomas Bass', *Dictionary of National Biography*, v.3, 1885, pp.371–2; see J.S. Mill,

'On Liberty,' in *Three Essays*, Oxford, reprinted 1984, introduction by Richard Wolheim.
20 *Hansard*, 3rd ser., 172, 1863, c.973.
21 Draft of a letter from Charles Babbage to Richard Mayne, 12 July 1860, BL, Add. Ms., 37198 ff 91, 95; Bass, passim, p.22.
22 Letter from Charles Babbage, 13 July 1863, in Bass, passim, p.19; on black-faced performers in Britain, see J.S. Bratton, 'English Ethiopians: British Audiences and Black-Faced Acts, 1835–1865', *Yearbook of English Studies*, 11, 1981, pp.127–42; George F. Rehin, 'Black-faced Minstrels in Victorian London and its Resorts: Popular Culture and its Racial Connotations As Revealed in Polite Opinion', *Journal of Popular Culture*, 15, 1, 1981, pp.19–38; Michael Pickering, 'White Skin, Black Masks: "Nigger" Minstrelsy in Victorian Britain', in J.S. Bratton, ed., *Music Hall: Performance and Style*, Milton Keynes, 1986; Douglas A. Lorimer, *Colour, Class and the Victorians*, Leicester, 1978; Simon Featherstone, 'The Blackfaced Atlantic: Interpreting British Minstrelsy', *Journal of Victorian Culture*, 3, 2, 1998, pp.234–51; and for a discussion of the meaning of the black face in terms of anthropological development, see Amanda Hodgson, 'Defining the Species: Apes, Savages and Humans in Scientific and Literary Writing of the 1860s', *Journal of Victorian Culture*, 4, 2, 1999, pp.228–51; Jonathan Schneer, *London 1900: The Imperial Metropolis*, New Haven and London, 1999, pp.97, 113.
23 Letter from James S. Kingdon, 6 June 1864 in Bass, passim, pp.15–16.
24 'To the Editor', *The Times*, 5 August 1863, p.12. An early literary depiction of this problem may be found in Henry Mayhew's one-act farce, 'The Wandering Minstrel', 1834, which confuses minstrelsy with vagrancy.
25 'To the Editor', *The Times*, 6 August 1863, p.10.
26 'To the Editor', *The Times*, 5 August 1863, p.12. On residential segregation as a sign of inhabitants' social status and recognised ways of behaving in public, see Paul Johnson, 'Conspicuous Consumption and Working-Class Culture in late Victorian and Edwardian Britain', *Transactions of the Royal Historical Society*, 5th ser., 38, 1988, esp. pp.31–4.
27 'To the Editor', *The Times*, 5 August 1863, p.12.
28 Albert Smith, 'Music in the Streets,' in idem, et. al., *Sketches of London Life and Character*, reprinted 1859, first published in 1849, pp.39–40. The desire for silence (or at least controlled sound) in the middle-class neighbourhood was consistent with contemporary drives elsewhere, as in Paris, under the rebuilding plans of Haussmann; see Richard Sennett, *The Fall of the Public Man*, New York, reprinted 1976, p.215.
29 Alphonse Esquiros, *The English At Home*, trans. Lascelles Wraxall, 1861, vol.i, pp.288–9. His description included Indians 'singing something in Hindoo' which usually conveyed a 'dull sadness...[based on their] longing for an absent country'.
30 Charles Manby Smith, *Curiosities of London Life: Or, Phases, Physiological and Social of the Great Metropolis*, 1853, p.17 see also Hodgson, passim.
31 'Street Music', *City Press*, 4 June 1864, p.4.
32 'Street Music', *City Press*, 4 June 1864, p.4.
33 The Rev. H.R. Haweis, *Music and Morals*, 1871, p.566.
34 Letter from Charles Babbage to Richard Mayne, 12 July 1860, BL, Add . Ms. 37198 fos, 91, 95.
35 Babbage, *A Chapter*, p.5. Roughly a generation later, new arguments were applied to those 'wretched' Italians who were seen to 'make a living from their children' at a time when the padrone system came to the public's attention. Some of these children took up work as street singers although they were often confused with beggars. See, for instance, 'Italian Children in England', *The Child's Guardian*, February 1890, p.13;

'Italian Beggar Children', *The Child's Guardian*, September 1891, p.103; Cf. Judith R. Walkowitz, *City of Dreadful Delight: Narratives of Sexual Danger in Late-Victorian London*, Chicago, 1992.

36 Babbage, *A Chapter*, p.5; Mayhew calculated that there were 1,000 musicians and 250 ballad singers, see Henry Mayhew, *London Labour and the London Poor*, reprinted 1861; iii, p.169; and cf. note 80 in this chapter.

37 Although Philip Collins has said that Charles Dickens defended popular amusements out of a sense of public duty, there is clear evidence of his growing ambivalence and intolerance as he aged; Cf. Philip Collins, 'Dickens and popular amusements', *Dickensian*, vol.81, 7 January 1965.

38 Cited in J.A.R. Pimlott, *The Englishman's Holiday: A Social History*, New York, 1847, reprinted 1976, pp.132–3; see also, A.W.J.G. Ord-Hume, *Barrel Organ: The Story of the Mechanical Organ and Its Repair*, 1978, ch.8.

39 'Organ-grinders' Colony', *The Times*, 24 August 1864, p.9; reprinted in *Clerkenwell Dial*, 24 August 1864, p.3; also in *Marylebone Mercury*, 27 August 1864, p.4.

40 'Street Music', *Borough of Marylebone Mercury*, 18 June 1864, p.2; a sarcastic defence of organ grinders was made in *All the Year Round*, vol.11, 11 June 1864, pp.421–4.

41 George Augustus Sala, *Twice Around the Clock; Or, The Hours of the Day and Night in London*, 1858, p.107.

42 Sala, *Twice Round the Clock*, p.107.

43 'The Organ-grinding Nuisance in Canonbury', *Clerkenwell Dial*, 4 June 1864, p.3; reprinted in *Islington Times*, 8 June 1864, p.2; cf. J.M. Rodwell's letter to M.T. Bass, 11 May 1864 in Bass, passim, p.13, in which he observes itinerant musicians in 'low' areas, like Saffron Hill, where he held the incumbency of the parish church for ten years.

44 'Organ grinding at Highbury', *Punch*, 11 June 1864, p.247.

45 'Marleborough Street—Street Music', *Daily Telegraph*, 22 August 1864, p.2.

46 Cf. Peter Bailey, '"Will the Real Bill Banks Please Stand Up?": Towards a Role Analysis of Mid-Victorian Working Class Respectability', *Journal of Social History*, 12, 3, pp.336–54.

47 'Westminster Organ-grinders and the Public', *Daily Telegraph*, 18 November 1864, p.2.

48 Bailey, *Popular Culture and Performance*, passim; Cf. James Obelkevich, 'In Search of the Listener', *Journal of the Royal Musical Association*, 114, 1, 1989, pp.102–8.

49 On the development of 'community', see Benedict Anderson, *Imagined Communities: Reflections on the Origin and Spread of Nationalism*, reprinted 1992.

50 For a recent treatment on the subject, see James Epstein, 'Spatial Practices/Democratic Vistas', *Social History*, 24, 3, October 1999, pp.294–310.

51 'Street Music and the Liberty of the Subject', *Marylebone Mercury*, 13 August 1864, p.3.

52 'Street Nuisances', *Spectator*, 11 June 1864, p.674.

53 'Street Music, notes on its illegality', *The Times*, 23 July 1863, p.9; reprinted in Babbage, *A Chapter*, pp.24–5.

54 Winter, *Teeming Streets*, passim.

55 'Street Music: To the Editor of the Daily Telegraph', *Daily Telegraph*, 12 July 1864, p.5.

56 See note13 above.

57 *Hansard*, 3rd ser., v.175 (1864), c.2118.

58 Letter from the Rev. J.S. Hall to Charles Babbage, 4 June 1864, BL Add. Ms. 37199, fo.76; *Punch*, 28 May 1864, p.222.

59 'Street Music', *Marylebone Mercury*, 13 August 1864, p.3.

60 'Street Music', *Daily Telegraph*, 7 July 1864, p.5.

61 'Street Music', *Marylebone Mercury*, 9 June 1864, p.2.

62 G.A. Sala, *Twice Round the Clock*, p.105; A.W.J.G. Ord-Hume, *Barrel Organ*, p.240, cited from *Chambers Edinburgh Journal*, summer 1852.

63 Esquiros, *English at Home*, v.i, p.287.

64 See the early literature on social control in A.P. Donajgrodzki, ed., *Social Control in Nineteenth-Century Britain*, Totawa, NJ, 1977, and Robert D. Storch, ed., *Popular Culture and Custom in Nineteenth Century England*, New York, 1982; and the influential critiques on this thesis, Gareth Stedman Jones, 'Class Expression versus Social Control: A Critique of Recent Trends in the Social History of "Leisure"', in idem, *Languages of Class: Studies in English Working Class History, 1832–1982*, Cambridge, 1983; and F.M.L. Thompson, 'Social Control in Victorian Britain', *Economic History Review*, 34, 1981, pp.189–208.

65 *Hansard*, 3rd ser., v. 175 (1864), c. 1529.

66 *Hansard*, 3rd ser., v. 175 (1864), c. 1531.

67 *Hansard*, 3rd ser., v. 176 (1864), c. 472.

68 *Hansard*, 3rd ser., v. 176 (1864), c. 473.

69 Letter from the Rev. J.S. Hall to Charles Babbage, 4 June 1864, BL Add. Ms. 37199, fo.76

70 Bass, passim, pp.41–2; cf. an anonymous tract, *Observations on the Abuse of Toleration Permitted to the Itinerants Who Prowl About the Streets of London With Machines Assuming To Be Music Played Mechanically By the Hand*, 1863.

71 *Hansard*, 3rd ser., v. 176 (1864), c. 468. In arguing his point, he also believed this to be a bill supporting masters and aimed against their servants who enjoyed minstrel singing.

72 *Hansard*, 3rd ser., v. 176 (1864), c. 470.

73 *Hansard*, 3rd ser., v. 176 (1864), c. 1074.

74 *Hansard*, 3rd ser., v. 176 (1864), c. 473.

75 27 & 28 Victoria, c.55.

76 See J.S. Mill, 'On Liberty', passim; Stefan Collini, *Public Moralists: Political Thought and Intellectual Life in Britain, 1850–1930*, Oxford, 1991; and idem, Donald Winch and J. Burrow, *That Noble Science of Politics: A Study in Nineteenth Century Intellectual History*, Cambridge, 1983, ch.4.

77 The judicial statistics for this period are silent over the issue.

78 'Marleborough Street—Street Music', *Daily Telegraph*, 22 August 1864, p.2.

79 'Westminster Organ Grinders and the Public', *Daily Telegraph*, 18 November 1864, p.2.

80 'The Organ Nuisance', *Bayswater Chronicle and Kensington and Paddington Journal*, 17 September 1864, p.4; reprinted in *Marylebone Mercury*, 17 September 1864, p.4.

81 'The Organ Grinding Nuisance', *Bayswater Chronicle and Kensington and Paddington Journal*, 29 October 1864, p.4; summarised also in the *Marylebone Mercury*, 29 October 1864, p.3.

82 Letter from Charles Babbage to Dr Hooker, 19 August 1868, BL, Add. Mss, 37199, fo. 435.

83 Letter from Charles Babbage to Richard Mayne, 7 September 1868, BL, Add. Mss, 37199, fo. 462.

84 Babbage Collection, BL, Add. Mss, 37199, fo. 435, fo. 444.

85 Letter from Charles Babbage to Dr Hooker, 19 August 1868, BL, Add. MS, 37199, fo. 435.

86 On the subject of London's citizens and evolving civilisation, see Roy Porter, *London: A Social History*, 1994.

87 Letter from Lord Stanaley to Charles Babbage, 14 September 1868, BL, Add. Mss, 37199, fo. 460.

13. *Observing London Street-Life*
Rick Allen

1   A few passages in this essay have already appeared in my article 'Munby Reappraised: The Diary of an English Flaneur', *Journal of Victorian Culture*, 5, 2, Autumn 2000, pp.260–86.

2   See P.D. Edwards, *Dickens's 'Young Men': G.A. Sala, Edmund Yates and the World of Victorian Journalism*, Aldershot, 1997, p.25.

3   Derek Hudson, *Munby Man of Two Worlds: The Life and Diary of Arthur J. Munby, 1828–1910*, 1972.

4   'Working Women in Victorian Britain, 1850–1910: the diaries and letters of Arthur J. Munby and Hannah Cullwick from Trinity College', Cambridge, 28 reels, Marlborough, 1993. Subsequent references to this edition supply the relevant reel and volume numbers.

5   Hudson, *Munby*, p.206.

6   Tom Brown, *Amusements Serious and Comical, and Other Works*, ed. A.L.Hayward, 1927, p.21. The passage is reprinted in Rick Allen, *The Moving Pageant: A Literary Sourcebook on London Street-Life, 1700–1914*, 1998, p.31.

7   See, for example, Joanna Schopenhauer, *Travel Diaries*, 1816, in *London 1066–1914: Literary Sources and Documents*, ed., Xavier Baron, II, p.158; and Heinrich Heine, *English Fragments*, 1828, in Allen, *Moving Pageant*, p.99. Both these writers compare the everyday London streets to Leipzig fair, finding the crowds in the former far more dense and frenetic.

8   Robert Mudie, *Babylon the Great*, 1825, pp.53–4.

9   Richard Steele, 'The Hours of London', *Spectator*, no.455, 11 August 1712.

10 E. Ward, *The London Spy*, 1700, this edition 1924 . The passage referred to is in Allen, *Moving Pageant*, pp.31–3.

11 Munby/Cullwick, *Working*, 5, 24.

12 *Spectator*, no.455.

13 Sala, *Twice Round the Clock*, 1859, reprinted Leicester 1971, p.165.

14 *Low Life: Or, One Half the World Knows Not how the Other Half Live*, 1752.

15 *Household Words*, 1 November 1851, IV, p.126.

16 Munby/Cullwick, *Working*, 5, 24.

17 *Household Words*, 18 June, 1853, VII, p.376.

18 Hudson, *Munby*, p.154.

19 Walter Benjamin, *Charles Baudelaire: A Lyric Poet in the Era of High Capitalism*, trans. H. Zohn, 1983, brings together three texts completed in this form in the late 1930s (though all were conceived as merely parts of the grand Arcades project): 'The Paris of the second empire in Baudelaire' (1938), 'Some motifs in Baudelaire' (1939), and 'Paris— the capital of the nineteenth century' (1935). The first English-language assembly of all the project material has recently appeared: *The Arcades Project*, trans. Howard Eiland and Kevin McLaughlin, Cambridge, Mass., 1999.

20 For Foucault's ideas referred to here, see especially *Discipline and Punish: The Birth of the Prison*, Harmondsworth, 1977, and *The History of Sexuality*, 2 vols., Harmondsworth, 1978. On women in the city, a large current topic which for reasons of space is touched on only indirectly in this essay, see, for example, Elizabeth Wilson, *The Sphinx in the City*, 1991; Judith Walkowitz, *City of Dreadful Delight: Narratives of Sexual Danger in Late-Victorian London*, 1992; Deborah E. Nord, *Walking the Victorian Streets: Women, Representation and the City*, Ithaca, 1995; Allen, *Moving Pageant*, pp.17–21 and most recently and convincingly, Lynda Nead, *Victorian Babylon: People, Streets and Images in Nineteenth-Century London*, 2000, esp. pp.67–73. For rare and revealing evidence of the routines of, and constraints upon, conventional middle-class women's walking around London in the 1870s, see

Zuzanna Schonfield, *The Precariously Privileged*, Oxford, 1987, esp. pp.44–6.

21 Benjamin, *Baudelaire*, p.36.

22 *Victorian Working Women: Portraits from Life*, 1979, p.14.

23 *Household Words*, 21 February 1852, IV, pp.517–21.

24 *Household Words*, 15 March 1856, XIII, pp.193–6.

25 *Household Words*, 6 December 1851, IV, pp.254–60.

26 *Household Words*, 12 March 1853, VII, pp.25–9.

27 *Household Words*, 12 March 1853, VII, p.26.

28 Benjamin, *Baudelaire*, pp.40–8.

29 The phrase has strongly established itself in flaneur studies because of Benjamin's discussions (pp.48–54, 128–35) of the Edgar Allan Poe short story with this title; Baudelaire, a biographer and translator of Poe, gave his most famous account of the artist as 'a man of the crowd' in 'Le Peintre de la vie moderne' (1863), tr. as 'The painter of modern life' in C. Baudelaire, *Selected Writings on Art and Literature*, trans. P.E. Charvet, Harmondsworth, 1972, pp.390–435.

30 Hudson, *Munby*, pp.162–3. The Garibaldi street-procession is partly reprinted in Hudson, *Munby*, pp.186–7.

31 Baudelaire, 'Painter', p.400.

32 See Hudson, *Munby*, p.233.

33 Hiley, *Victorian Women*, p.80.

34 Munby/Cullwick, *Working*, 2, 8.

35 Munby/Cullwick, *Working*, 2, 12.

36 Baudelaire, 'Painter', pp.402–3.

37 See Keith Tester, ed., *The Flaneur*, 1994, p.16.

38 See, for example, Hudson, *Munby*, pp.103–5.

39 For his walk around old Southwark (4 March 1869) shortly before old inns such as The Tabard were pulled down, see Hudson, *Munby*, p.267.

40 Munby/Cullwick, *Working*, 2, 11.

41 Hudson, *Munby*, pp.100–02.

42 *Household Words*, IV, p126.

43 *Household Words*, 4 March 1854, IX, p.159.

44 *Household Words*, 4 March 1854, IX, p.163. Emphasis in original.

45 *Household Words*, 6 September 1851, III, pp.565–72.

46 *Household Words*, 23 February 1856, XIII, pp.121–6.

47 *Household Words*, 23 February 1856, XIII, p.122.

48 *Household Words*, 23 February 1856, XIII, p.122.

49 *Household Words*, 23 February 1856, XIII, p.123.

50 'The Asylum for the Houseless' in Henry Mayhew, *London Labour and the London Poor*, 1861–2, New York, 1968, III, pp.428–9.

51 *Household Words*, 23 February 1856, XIII, p.125.

52 *Household Words*, 23 February 1856, XIII, p.124.

53 Edwards, 'Dickens's Young Men', pp.55, 196–7.

54 *Twice Round the Clock*, pp.145–6.

55 'Street the fifth: Drury Lane, London', *Streets of the World* in *The Welcome Guest* IV* (1861) p.676. *III on outer binding, but internal evidence indicates IV.

56 *Household Words*, IV, p.126.

57 'Drury Lane, London', p.677.

58 *Household Words*, 17 January 1852, IV, pp.397–401.

59 *Twice Round the Clock*, p.13.

Index